The Art of Fluid Animation

The Art of Fluid Animation

Jos Stam

CRC Press
Taylor & Francis Group
Boca Raton London New York

CRC Press is an imprint of the
Taylor & Francis Group, an **informa** business

AN A K PETERS BOOK

CRC Press
Taylor & Francis Group
6000 Broken Sound Parkway NW, Suite 300
Boca Raton, FL 33487-2742

First issued in paperback 2017

ISBN-13: 978-1-4987-0020-7 (pbk)
ISBN-13: 978-1-1384-2818-8 (hbk)

Visit the Taylor & Francis Web site at
http://www.taylorandfrancis.com

and the CRC Press Web site at
http://www.crcpress.com

To Pam and Gillian

This is a small replica of the northern portal of the Urnes Stavkyrkje *in Norway. This church was built in 1130, near the end of the Viking domination of Northern Europe. Vikings were highly skilled artists, not just long-haired brutish warriors. I took this photograph at the British Museum in London, England.*

Contents

Preface

What I cannot create, I do not understand.

RICHARD FEYNMAN (FAMOUS AMERICAN PHYSICJST
AND NOBEL LAUREATE)

Lectures which really teach will never be popular; lectures which are popular will never teach.

MICHAEL FARADAY (FAMOUS ENGLISH
EXPERIMENTALIST AND SCIENTIST)

A mathematical theory is not to be considered complete until you have made it so clear that you can explain it to the first man whom you meet on the street.

DAVID HILBERT (FAMOUS GERMAN MATHEMATICIAN)

I have no formal background in fluid dynamics. I am not an engineer nor do I have a specialized degree in the mathematics or physics of fluids. I am fortunate that I did not have to carry that baggage around. On the other hand, I *do* have degrees in pure mathematics and computer science and have an artsy background. More importantly, I have written computer code that animates fluids.[*]

I wrote code. That is the bottom line.

---

[*] Other stuff as well of course. Chess games, Pac-Man rip offs, writing code to make money during summer jobs, ray tracers, particle system simulations, surface modeling, and more recently a unified dynamics solver called *Nucleus*. That is the beauty of writing code. The computer can be taught to do all sorts of things and you can do it anywhere. All you need is a laptop with an Internet connection. Sort of like mathematics. A mathematician is basically a clever mechanism that turns coffee into theorems. Coding and mathematical work can be done anywhere: the Copacabana Beach of Rio Janeiro (Brazil) or a remote cabin in Northern Canada.

I did not just download some code from the Internet and mash it together. Therefore, I think I understand what I am talking about. Of course, it is based on previous work. I did not invent the theories and concepts behind it. Research is a process.

You cannot fool a computer.

You can fool students, colleagues, or friends but not a computer. Why? A computer is like the best pet ever, it is wickedly fast and always obeys. Creating computer code is the ultimate test whether you understand something or not. Teach it to the computer and you will understand it. If you work for a company, you also have to deal with marketing, public relations, sales, and the customer feedback cycle.

Customer feedback is brutally honest. They pay you money for your software and they expect it to work. If it doesn't work, they will let you know. It either works or it doesn't. Postmodern literature debates, on the other hand, are not like that. Everyone is right and everyone is wrong at the same time. But these debates fueled by coffee or wine might be more fun than spending hours fueled by coffee fixing computer code that has to work.

I like writing code. And I like fixing code as long as it is my code.

This book is written by a dilettante of some sorts. However, by writing computer code, I came to understand the dynamics of fluids. This book is not your usual fluid dynamics textbook full of clever equations. I know equations quite well and I love them. They helped me to understand fluids. But to most people, they look like strange hieroglyphs from some other universe.

That is how Chinese characters appear to me.

That is why fancy equations are not very helpful to most people. When I get an e-mail written entirely in Chinese characters, I just ignore it. What? The alternative is that I take a course to learn Chinese characters. That would be cool and help me the next time I travel to China. But that is going to be a lot of work and my time is limited. Besides, it is fun to be a stranger in a strange land.

I want this book to be accessible to people who are not experts in mathematics or physics. I also want to make this a fun book. That is how I do research. I like to have fun even at *work*. Some parts of this book have mathematics. My hope is that the math will be somewhat accessible to most people who are willing to *go along*. This is a common tactic in mathematics when reading a mathematical paper that is not in your area of expertise and trying to understand it. At first, you just try to get the gist of it. Then if it sounds cool, you go through the details. And if you really get excited, then you should try to write some code that implements the content of the paper.

I also provide one-paragraph summaries of the material after each section in this book. I found this to be a good practice when I was learning math and computer science at the university. What did I learn in a nutshell after a lecture? I picked up this practice from a math professor, Pierre de la Harpe, at the University of Geneva who started each lecture with a summary of the material he covered in the previous lectures.

This methodology really helps if you are taking tons of classes. I also tend to understand some material using different tools than what most people are used to. I like to repeat things from different points of view. I like to argue with myself. That way, I can be both right and wrong, just not at the same time. You can learn some interesting stuff from this process. It is also a good tactic before giving a talk. You will be ready to face most questions. No question is stupid, and some can point you in new directions. I am always open to exploring new ideas, and learning. You can never be the smartest or the most creative person in the room.

The main goal of this book is to show how to create computer code that animates the motion of fluids. Computer code will be included in this book. Readers can download the accompanying code and run it on their own computers.

My goal is actually more ambitious. I want programmers to use these codes as a starting point to create their own apps, games, and so on. In fact, some of my code has been available for over 10 years and many people have used it as a starting point to create their own games, fun demos, and apps. Even better would be if programmers rewrite the code in a completely different manner or in a completely different language. That would be so cool. I would like to challenge any reader to write a shorter version of my code in C that is still readable.

I did not want to write a *Fluid Dynamics for Dummies* style of book. This is because I think my readers are smart and creative people who want to know how fluids are simulated on a computer to create nifty animations. In fact, I want smart and creative programmers to read this book and extend the code to create novel applications. Basically, I want this book to inspire people to do their own stuff. To create and not take anything for granted.

Be a rebel.

Not to destroy, but to create.

I love it when I get an e-mail out of the blue from someone far from my home in Toronto, like India, pointing me to a web-based application they created that combines fluids and reaction-diffusion processes. And "wow" the program runs in a web page. And the person thanks me, too. How cool is that. My day is certainly made.

Since there are so many good technical books on fluid dynamics, I want this book to be different and less technical. I want this book to be a bridge between my two favorite fluid dynamics books:

An Album of Fluid Motion (Stanford University, California, 1982), assembled by Milton Van Dyke*

A Mathematical Introduction to Fluid Mechanics (Springer, 2000), written by Alexandre Chorin and Jerrold Marsden

The first book is a collection of photographs of famous fluid experiments. It is the perfect geek coffee table book.

The second book is a brilliant and concise mathematical introduction to fluid dynamics. This book clarified many obscure aspects of fluid dynamics for me through a rigorous mathematical treatment. Consider the following statement: "Pressure is the Lagrange multiplier derived from the divergence free constraint." If this statement makes sense to you, then Chorin and Marsden's book is for you. But please continue reading this book.

This book is also a personal account of how I have dealt with fluid dynamics. Obscure at first, leading to enlightenment followed by writing computer code.

I want to make the narrative of this book somewhat interesting. Research is not just a collection of impersonal facts that seem to come out of nowhere. The science of fluids was created or discovered, whatever, by real people. I think it is important to give homage to them.

---

* I have to tell this story. I ordered this book from Milton Van Dyke's website and did not have to pay for it when I ordered it. Only when I got the book through regular mail, did I see that there was a notice to send a check of some ridiculously low amount of money to a certain Milton Van Dyke living in Palo Alto, California. No one I know would rip off a person who put together such a beautiful book. Of course, I immediately sent the check to the address with "Thanks!" written on the back of the check.

Don't worry.

This book is not going to describe how many wives, husbands, lovers, or kids these scientists had. There are plenty of good books out there documenting their personal lives. I am not an expert in these matters anyway nor am I particularly interested in their extracurricular activities. It is all about their scientific achievements.*

This book is based on many talks I have given over the last 15 years. Which explains the somewhat informal colloquial style of the book. Also, I assume my readers have access to search engines as there is no exhaustive list of references. If you like something in the book and want to know more about it, research it. That is how I work these days. I do miss the days I had to go to libraries, however, that is just nostalgia.

The first time I gave a talk on this subject was at an annual computer graphics conference called SIGGRAPH† in Los Angeles in 1999. The paper I presented was called "Stable Fluids." That was a crazy conference for me. I had other talks on completely different subjects,‡ one in the same afternoon, and I had to lug my hardware, an SGI Octane, using a cab from my hotel room at the Westin Bonaventure up on Figueroa Avenue to the convention center at the bottom of Figueroa.

But it worked out.

This was one of the first times that fluid simulations were shown to react to user input in real time. There was applause. And then there was applause again two years later, again in Los Angeles, when I gave my demonstration of real-time fluids on a Pocket PC.§ I wrote this just for fun. The Pocket PC fits in your pocket (hence the name). Consequently, I was able to show my fluid creations everywhere: at parties, on the subway, or to my family living abroad in Europe.

Only later did people tell me that I disproved some skeptics, that my fast demonstrations two years earlier were only due to using fancy hardware.

---

* But still. Leonhard Euler, one of the heroes of this book, had 13 kids. Legend has it that he did his finest math while holding one of his babies on his lap.

† SIGGRAPH is an acronym for Special Interest Group on GRAPHics and Interactive Techniques. Since 1974, this conference has been held yearly in various places across North America. It is the Mecca for graphics guys. It is the most prestigious place to publish a paper in computer graphics. In 1999, there were over 40,000 attendees.

‡ "Subdivision Surfaces" and "Diffraction Shaders."

§ The Pocket PC was released by Microsoft in 2000 and powered by an operating system called Windows CE. I showed my demo on an iPAQ, which was created by Compaq at the time. In 2007, Apple came out with the iPhone/iPod. I will say more about that later in the book.

When people disagree and challenge your work, that is actually a good sign. If no one cares about your work one way or the other, then why bother doing it.

The skeptics thought my demonstrations were fast because I showed them running on an SGI Octane.* I only needed the Octane because it had three-dimensional hardware texture rendering capabilities. Oh, and also because I got it for free and it was the best workstation at the time. But man, was it ever heavy to carry around.† It wouldn't fit in your pocket. The only reason I wrote apps for a mobile device was because it was a cool thing to do. In the end, it showed that software sometimes overpowers brute-force hardware.

I did this fun stuff when I was living in Seattle, Washington, in the late 1990s. Just after the *grunge scene* left town and moved to Los Angeles.‡ At the same time, our animation software called MAYA was about to take off. We used to have an office in sunny Santa Barbara, California, where everyone is always happy. When I went there on a trip from rainy Seattle and showed them the real-time demos, they immediately wanted to put it into our MAYA software. This was in 2000. After a roller-coaster ride, the fluid solver finally made it into our MAYA 4.5 software in 2002 under the name of "Fluid Effects." This release would have been impossible without the help of many people from the MAYA development team in Toronto, Canada. They did most of the work, getting my research code into a real piece of software and adding their own secret sauces and spices.

Putting research code into a product takes time and a lot of effort. Trust me. But in the end, it made it into MAYA! We shipped it. And people are using it. We didn't waste our time on some vaporware to prove we were busy and hardworking. And more importantly, we had fun doing it. Well, at least I had fun doing it.

In 2008, I wrote a fluid app for the iPhone/iPod. I did this mainly because the iPhone supports OpenGL ES, has an accelerometer, and has a multitouch interface. All the things that I wanted to have in an

---

* At the time, I worked for SGI who actually made the Octane. At the time, it cost over $60,000. Now, you can buy one on eBay for about $200. Oh right: SGI stands for Silicon Graphics Incorporated. It used to be the hottest company in Silicon Valley, California. They are pretty much defunct right now. Google has taken over their old campus in Mountain View.

† An Octane weighs 24.3 kg (54 lb).

‡ There were still a lot of good bands like the "Murder City Devils" and "Rorschach Test," just to name some.

interactive fluid app in 2000. I will say more about this experience later in the book. In 2010, we released Fluid FX, an improved version of the original app.

To summarize: I planted a seed in the area of fluid animation. Others have too. But this is my story.

Jos Stam
Toronto, Ontario, Canada

Acknowledgments

WRITING A BOOK AND DOING RESEARCH IS NOT A LONELY ENDEAVOR. There are many people I want to thank. First, thanks to my wife of 24 years, Pamela, for all her support and love. She is my best friend. To my daughter Gillian because ... because she is my daughter and she is sweet, smart, and beautiful. To my older brother Sim, who introduced me to science and computers. Without him, I would possibly have become a hobo artist in Amsterdam. My parents, Jos and At, and my two sisters, Nel and Go, of course gave me a wonderful kick-start in life. We have short Dutch names in our family. I do not even have a middle name.

I thank CRC Press, especially Rick Adams, for publishing this book. And of course my company Autodesk, which gave me the time to write the book. I especially thank Gordon Kurtenbach, Azam Khan, Francesco Iorio, and the rest of our research group. It is great to be part of such a cool team. Special thanks also to Cory Mogk for creating the cover using MAYA Fluid Effects. Thanks to the Fluid FX team here in Toronto for creating these cool apps, based on my solver after I created my own. I want to single out Dan Pressman and Sergey Buyanov. I also thank the MAYA team we have in Toronto and teams we used to have in Santa Barbara and Seattle. This was a huge team, and if I have to single out one individual, it would be Duncan Brinsmead.

I thank my high school and university friend Marcus Grote for all the stimulating intellectual discussions we used to have. But more related to the current work he pointed me to Chorin and Marsden's book. This book led me out of the confusion and darkness. Since his dad worked at CERN, we got a VIP tour of the future of computing in the early 1980s. Thanks to my final high school year math teacher Nicolas Giovaninni, who taught me the difference between fun math and boring math. All of a sudden, I was getting top grades in math! Thanks to Professor Eugene Fiume for helping me to get accepted at a top North American graduate school: the University of Toronto. Also thanks for always being available and supportive. Professor Fiume was also a good supervisor, letting me work on whatever I wanted and not minding that I showed up at noon and left at five in the afternoon.

Thanks to the cities of Toronto, Paris, Helsinki, and Seattle. That is where I did most of the research described in this book despite all the distractions these cities have to offer. I find it is a good thing to live in different countries. You get rid of any *national pride* and *provincialism* you might have.* That stuff gets in the way of free and creative thinking. Moving around also makes you humble as you have to learn a new language and adapt to a new culture. It also makes you intellectually richer in the end. Just be willing to learn.

I also want to thank the SIGGRAPH Computer Graphics Technical Achievement Award Committee for presenting me with an award in 2005, partly for the work described in this book. Thanks also to the Academy of Motion Picture Arts and Sciences for presenting a Technical Achievement Award for our MAYA implementation of fluids. I am of course leaving out many other people that have influenced me. You know who you are if you are reading this. Thanks to all of you.†

---

* Unless of course Oranje is playing.
† If you feel left out, check out the slide, yes one slide, of my award acceptance speech at the SIGGRAPH Conference in 2005. The link is http://www.autodeskresearch.com/pdf/talks/jos_award05.pdf. If you are still left out, I will put on my Canadian tuck hat and say, "Sorry, buddy, but thanks anyway."

Author

J os Stam was born in the Netherlands and educated in Geneva, where he received dual bachelor degrees in computer science and pure mathematics. In 1989, he moved to Toronto, where he completed his master's and PhD in computer science. After that, he pursued postdoctoral studies as an ERCIM fellow at INRIA in France and at VTT in Finland. In 1997, Dr. Stam joined the Alias Seattle office as a researcher and stayed there until 2003, when he relocated to Alias's main office in Toronto. He now works as a senior research scientist as part of Autodesk's acquisition of Alias in 2006.

Dr. Stam's research spans several areas of computer graphics: natural phenomena, physics-based simulation, rendering, and surface modeling, especially subdivision surfaces. He has published papers in all of these areas in journals and at conferences, most notably at the annual SIGGRAPH conference. In 2005, Dr. Stam was presented with one of the most prestigious awards in computer graphics: the SIGGRAPH Computer Graphics Achievement Award. In addition, he won two Technical Achievement Awards from the Academy of Motion Picture Arts and Sciences: in 2005 for his work on subdivision surfaces and in 2007 for his work on fluid dynamics. Dr. Stam was also featured in a January 2008 *Wired* magazine article.

CHAPTER 1

Introduction

Simple play is also the most beautiful. How often do you see a pass of forty meters when twenty meters is enough? Or a one-two in the penalty area when there are seven people around you and a simple wide pass around the seven would be a solution? The solution that seems the simplest is in fact the most difficult one.

JOHAN CRUIJFF (DUTCH SOCCER LEGEND)

Problems can be complicated. Solutions cannot.

ADVERTISEMENT SPOTTED AT THE COPENHAGEN
AIRPORT AFTER GIVING A TALK ON FLUID DYNAMICS
AT DANSIS

There are times when we're testing an actual explosion, and then there are times when we blow stuff up just because we can.

JAMIE HYNEMAN (CO-HOST OF THE POPULAR SHOW
MYTHBUSTERS)

Visually, fluids are everywhere and nowhere.

That might seem like a weird statement. But let me explain.

Fluids like water, honey, maple syrup, fire, explosions, and oil are everywhere. We can see, smell, and sometimes taste and touch them. On the other hand, air is nowhere to be seen. Air is also a fluid. We usually see the effect of motion of the air on other things like insects, dust, clouds, and the motion of trees. Air is this invisible thing that makes things move. Some fluids are like that. The astonishing fact is that all these fluidlike effects such as liquids and air can be described by a single formal framework called *fluid dynamics.*

We will get to that.

What is a fluid? It really is a technical word that defines a substance that can change its shape in a continuous manner. So, a rock is not really a fluid but when it is heated it becomes one, like lava spurting from a volcano.* It also releases heat that will affect the motion of the fluid that is air. Lava definitely can take many different shapes. In fact that is why fluids are cool. A lava lamp is a good example. The legendary Toronto rock band "Sucker Punch" even has a song called "Cool Like a Lava Lamp." No really, this song rocks.

Since fluids are everywhere and nowhere, why do we want to animate them? There are many reasons actually. First, some fluid effects are hard to recreate, like nuclear explosions, tsunamis, and volcanic eruptions. In these cases, computer-generated fluids can create a multitude of catastrophic effects without anyone being hurt. Except, of course, for the animators who must put in long hours creating these effects, and often end up separating from their significant others. These animations can also create effects that have never been seen before or are impossible to create physically. In the special effects industry, they call actual physical shots with no computer graphics *practical.* I always found this to be an awkward word. Of course, some of these practical shots might be fixed "in post" with computer tools to get the perfect look. Practical means you actually blow stuff up, like they do in the popular television show *MythBusters.* Adam Savage and Jamie Hyneman, the two main hosts of this show, actually used to work for Industrial Light and Magic (ILM), which is a major special effects company based in San Francisco. Think *Star Wars.*

In addition to safety issues, there is another reason to use computers to create fluid animations: artistic control. In movies, people want fluids to behave in specific ways, which can be impossible or near impossible using *practical* methods. How would you get liquid horses coming out of a stream of water like in the *Lords of the Rings* movie using real footage? It might be possible but very improbable to achieve. When you simulate a fluid using computer animation you are playing God. You can vary control parameters

---

* On the other hand, rock formations can be considered in a sense as being very, very, very slow fluids. Think about the drift of continents that cause volcanoes and earthquakes.

to make the fluid do something you have in mind. Of course, this practice of animating fluids has been around since the early days of animation. Think of the classic Disney movies that featured fluids. However, this was a rather tedious method to create a convincing animation of a fluid. Back then every shot had to be hand drawn to create a series of what is called *key-frames*. To get an idea of the motion, artists would use a *flip book* basically flipping rapidly through the pages of a book sequentially. However, in this case, each page has a hand-drawn picture on it created by the artist. By a process of trial and error and intuition, a final fluidlike animation is created. Like that. Some artists were amazing at doing this.

One of the earliest flip books created is shown in Figure 1.1. It was invented in 1868 by John Barnes Linnett, an Englishman from Birmingham. He called it the *kineograph*, a fancy Latin word for *moving picture*. He filed a patent on it too. Why not? In those days there was a tremendous interest in animated pictures. It was not until December 28, 1895,* that the *Frères Lumière* from France showed their first motion

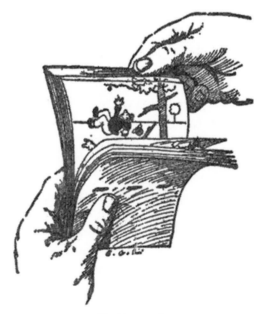

The kineograph

FIGURE 1.1   The first "flip book."

---

* Exactly 70 years to the date before I was born.

FIGURE 1.2 The Lumière brothers.

picture to the public. They are both portrayed in Figure 1.2 and one of the frames of their first movie is shown in Figure 1.3. Legend has it that the audience watching the movie for the first time was frightened. The sight of the train entering the station was so scary that most of the audience ran out of the cinema screaming. This short clip also had a fluid effect in it: the steam emanating from the locomotive. Interestingly, the brothers' last name *Lumière* means *light* in French, yes light, as in bright, not as in not being heavy.

The flip book and the cinema are good metaphors for computer animation. Indeed, the goal of computer animation is to create a sequence of pictures that give the illusion of movement. The bottom line is to fill an array of picture elements called *pixels* on a screen for every snapshot. Traditionally in computer graphics, things are animated in a virtual 3D world and then projected onto a screen. This is called the *rendering pipeline* and is depicted in Figures 1.4 and 1.5. The first figure is an engraving by the *German Leonardo* Albrecht Dürer. This is an early depiction of how perspective projection works and how it is used in art. Figure 1.5 shows the basic methodology of computer graphics. The ball,

FIGURE 1.3   The first movie shown publicly by the Lumière brothers.

FIGURE 1.4   Engraving by Albrecht Dürer.

pyramid, and cylinder shown in Figure 1.5 are all illuminated by a virtual light source and then finally projected onto a plane: a 2D picture. This picture is then digitized into pixels and sent either to a screen or captured by a camera as shown in Figure 1.5. This process is called the rendering pipeline: 3D stuff goes in on one end of the pipe and *ta da* out comes an image. This book is not about the rendering pipeline and how it works. There are many references that explain this process in

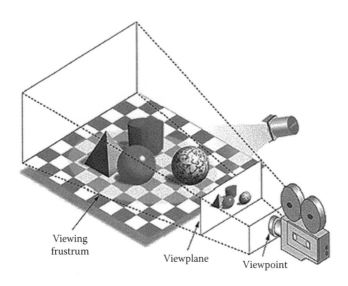

FIGURE 1.5   The rendering pipeline.

great detail.* However, it is important to grasp this basic concept in order to understand the content of this book.

To summarize so far: Our goal is to compute snapshots of a fluid, which are then projected onto a screen to create an animation.

We work in a virtual world that eventually gets projected onto a screen. The screen could also be a standard monitor or a tiny iPhone screen. You name it. But the starting point is a description of a fluid in a space rather than a screen. This brings to mind the famous allegory of "The Cave" by the famous Greek philosopher Plato (424/423–348/347 BCE). In Plato's allegory, slaves are chained and forced to see only the shadows of 3D objects, not the actual objects themselves.† They see only a projection of a reality unbeknownst to them as shown in Figure 1.6, they do not even know about their own *reality*. Plato's point is of course to show that our senses only perceive a projection of some sort of higher ideal reality. In computer graphics, things are modeled in 3D space and then rendered onto a *2D screen*.

Animation adds another dimension: *time*. Things move in three dimensions, so really our space is four dimensional. A fluid that doesn't move

---

* Just type in "rendering pipeline" your favorite search engine.
† Plato, *The Republic*. I do not buy it: life is life. The Dutch have a great saying: "dood is zeker en zeker is dood." Roughly in English: "death is certain and certainty is dead."

FIGURE 1.6   Plato's allegory of the cave.

around is boring. The objects in Figure 1.5 are usually animated, and different snapshots are rendered on a 2D digital canvas. This process results in an animation: a sequence of frames.

The goal in fluid animation is to compute different states of the fluid over time and render these states as flat two-dimensional representations. The artists manipulate and control the fluid's properties in this more complex 4D space. The physics automatically takes care of the motion. The bottom line is: how to get from an artist's conception of a fluid effect to the generation of a set of pixels on a screen. This is what this book is about.

A final thought before we go on. Whether we work in two-, three-, or four (or higher?)-dimensional spaces, the bottom line is that everything gets translated into *bits*. The bits are really all our speedy friend or foe called a computer can ultimately understand.

A bit is a thing that can only be in two states. These are usually called *zero* and *one* or 0 and 1. But it could also be called *false* and *true* or *Pokemon* and *Papa Smurf*. The famous British mathematician George Boole (1815–1864) came up with a formal way to deal with these bits. He used his theories to write a philosophical book entitled *The Laws of Thought*.*

---

* Actually, the real title is *An Investigation of the Laws of Thought on Which Are Founded on the Mathematical Theories of Logic and Probabilities*. He was one of the first people to turn logic into pure arithmetic.

The programming language called *Pascal** even has a *type* named in Boole's honor called Boolean. In another programming language called C++ there is a similar type called *bool*. C++ coders like to type in less characters than Pascal coders. Don't get me started on the *COBOL* programming language.[†]

As an example let's look at the following program written in Pascal computer language.[‡] I know this is an absurd example but that is the whole point.

```
Program PokemonIsNotPapaSmurf;
Var dude    : Boolean;
    dudeName: String;
Begin
  Writeln('Type Pokemon not Papa Smurf');
  Readln(dudeName);
  If dudeName = 'Pokemon' then dude:= True else dude:=
    False;
  If dude then Writeln('Good Job') else
    Writeln('Wrong Dude, Dude');
End.
```

Welcome to the fun world of programming. What this program does is tells the computer to perform a set of precise instructions. The programmer who types in the instructions is the **Master** and the computer is the **Slave**. The **Human** or his **Pet** is the one that uses the program.[§] Why do you think so many good programmers live in their mom's basements or in remote Scandinavian locations? That is actually not true. Programmers like to have fun too. Geez, we even have "brogrammers": Bros who like to party and write code when they are bombed. Do not download their code. More seriously, a lot of programmers are creative types like artists, musicians, builders, mechanics, and so on. Remember you have to **create** code.

---

* We will say a bit more about this programming language below.

[†] **COBOL** stands for **CO**mmon **B**usiness-**O**riented **L**anguage. This is a very verbose language and the brainchild of DARPA.

[‡] The characters in boldface are keywords of the language and the others are just made up by the programmer. No language would have *dude* as a keyword. But who knows? Maybe some brogrammers will come up with such a language.

[§] Sometimes the **Master** has to use his own program. It is called "eating your own dog food" or "dogfooding" in the software industry. Actually, not just for software. I guess people who make dog food were forced to eat their own concoctions themselves, hence the name.

At any rate, the absurd program pretty much works as follows in layman terms:

Master to Slave: My brilliant piece of code is going to be called `PokemonIsNotPapaSmurf`. Got it?

Slave to Master: Yeah whatever.

Master to Slave: I am going to use two locations in your memory. One I am going to call `dude`, and it can only take two values `False` and `True` because it is of type `Boolean`. Pay attention. The next location is called `dudeName` because I say so. This location contains characters and can have any length and so it can take up a lot of your memory. Your job is to fill it up. Got it?

Slave to Master: Yeah I got it. Can we move on a little?

Master to Slave: When **Human** or his **Pet** launches the program, then first print out "Type Pokemon not Papa Smurf" on whatever display device that **Human** or **Pet** is using. You will figure it out.

Slave to Master: Okay, I just did that. They are using a MacBook Pro BTW. You are welcome.

Master to Slave: Read whatever the **Human** or **Pet** types in through whatever input device, I don't care, and return it to me as soon as possible in a location in your memory called `dudeName`.

Slave to Master: Not even a please huh? **Human** or **Pet** have arrived and are typing in characters. I will store them at a location starting at `0x0000ab345f1d5ecf`* in my memory and I will label it `dude-Name` because you said so. Okay, here you go. Have fun.

Master: Alright, I got the information I wanted. Thanks, you piece of dumb hardware. At least you didn't hang or crash on me this time.

Master: Now let's check it out. Option 1: Our **Human** or **Pet** typed in `Pokemon`. Good job. I will ask that piece of hardware to write out `Good Job`. Option "anything else really" and I will ask that same piece of hardware to write out `Wrong Dude, Dude`. Yes, even in the case if the **Human** or his **Pet** typed in `Eyjafjallajökull` as long as it is not `Pokemon`.

---

* Assuming that **Slave** is using a 64-bit architecture.

Human or Pet: Whoa? What is the point of this dumb piece of software that I downloaded for free?

Slave to Human or Pet: Don't blame me. Intermediate slave named **Compiler** translated all of **Master's** nonsense into the following string of bits: 00001010101010010101010100000001111101010101010 10011010101010101010101010101010101010101100101010101010101010100 00000001011111111000000000111111111101010101010101010101010010 10101010011111111111111000000000011100101010101010101010101010100 00001111111110000000010111100001110010101000111111110010110 101011000001101011010100101010101010100101.

Slave to Himself: That is all I understand. I know I am mildly autistic just like my **Master**.

To summarize: Fluid animations are created with the help of computers. They generate a sequence of frames that result in an animation: a sequence of pictures. A computer is a speedy, dumb piece of hardware. But it makes for a good pet.

CHAPTER 2

Observations, Equations, and Numbers

Someone told me that each equation I included in the book [*A Brief History of Time*] would halve its sales.

STEPHEN HAWKINS (FAMOUS ENGLISH PHYSICIST)

2.1 BEAVERS, CAVE PERSONS, AND FIRE

80,000 years ago, man's survival in a vast uncharted land depended on the possession of fire. For those early humans, fire was an object of great mystery, since no one had mastered its creation. Fire had to be stolen from Nature; it had to be kept alive–sheltered from wind and rain, guarded from rival tribes. Fire was a symbol of power and a means of survival. The tribe who possessed fire, possessed life.

J.H. ROSNY FROM THEIR BOOK *QUEST FOR FIRE*

Since fluids are everywhere, humans have always been fascinated by them and also feared them. Not only humans by the way. Think of beavers and their dam-building capabilities. No wonder they have a beaver on the logo of the University of Toronto where I got my PhD degree in computer science (see Figure 2.1).

FIGURE 2.1   The official logo of the University of Toronto.

Humans, just like beavers, learned how to deal with fluids early on. Probably the first biggest achievement on the human side was the taming of fire. This is well documented in the epic movie *Quest for Fire* by Jean-Jacques Annaud based on the book by the author "J.H. Rosny."*

Humans back when they lived in caves found many ingenuous ways to create and preserve fire. Fire is a fluid too. There are of course many other caveman (I mean caveperson) stories involving other fluids like water, sweat, mud, blood, and so on.

Dealing with the effects of fluids in practice is one thing but how do you describe them precisely and control them?

To summarize: Humans and animals had to deal with fluids very early on. They did not rely on equations however.

---

* I always wondered about the "J.H." part of the name: could it be Jean-Henri or Jaques-Hubert perhaps? Who knows? It turns out it is a pseudonym made up by two brothers named Joseph Henri Honoré Boex (1856–1940) and Séraphin Justin François Boex (1859–1948). Basically, the "Boex Bros." They both lived in the city of Brussels in Belgium. They also wrote books together. They wrote a lot of early science fiction books. At some time, there was a rift between the two brothers and the elder one wrote the Fire book under his new pseudonym *J.H. Rosny, aîné*. The last word means "the elder one" in French.

2.2 FROM CAVES TO GREEKS: ARCHIMEDES, GOLD, AND MEDALS

Eureka!

ARCHIMEDES (LEGENDARY GREEK MATHEMATICIAN)

Let us fast forward from cave land to ancient Greece. Archimedes (circa 287–circa 212 BCE) is probably the first person to come up with a principled approach to fluids.

According to legend, this is his story.

A golden crown had been made for King Hierio II. The king was suspicious, however, that some silver had been substituted for the gold by a dishonest blacksmith, but how could he prove it? The king turned to his favorite mathematician, Archimedes.

Let him figure it out.

While bathing one day, Archimedes noticed that the level of water went up as he entered the tub. *Eureka!* Legend again has it that he ran down the streets of Athens naked after his discovery. Back then it was alright to walk or run around naked. Why not? It is hot in Greece. If Archimedes made his discovery in Northern Canada during the winter, he would be running around in the snow in a bear-made fur coat yelling "Awesome dude!"

"Geez Louise I guess crazy Archie next door came up with another discovery, eh?"

To prove that the King had been ripped off and since the crown couldn't be smelted, Archimedes came up with this clever solution. He asked for a piece of pure gold (guaranteed by a trustworthy source) that had the same weight as the King's crown. He then submerged the crown first and then the sample of gold in his bathtub. Since water is highly incompressible, the amount of displaced water determines the volume of the submerged object exactly. Therefore, once you know the volume you know the density. The density of pure gold is known.* So, given that the masses of the crown and the sample are fixed and assuming that they are both pure gold, they should displace the same amount of water. This turned out not to be the case. The crown's gold had been laced with silver, a material cheaper and less dense than gold. The crown displaced more water than the sample made of pure gold. Hence, the crown had more volume than the sample and therefore the crown was less dense than pure gold.

---

* To be precise: 19.30 g/cm³.

This is logical and mathematical reasoning at its best. The difference was slight however. The blacksmith was a smart man. No one knows what happened to the clever blacksmith after the Eureka moment of Archimedes.

Just to hammer in this argument, imagine a huge ball of Styrofoam having the same weight as a small lead marble. It is pretty obvious that they are not made of the same material. No need to immerse them in your bathtub.

The reason I mention this story is that Archimedes discovered an essential fact about fluids. A fluid is highly incompressible. This is not only true for water but it is also true for air. Yes, even air can be considered incompressible in most practical cases; more about that follows later. If you do not believe this fact, clap your hands and ask yourself where the air went between your hands.

Archimedes was a genius and made many early contributions to mathematics. This is why his is the figure on the *Fields Medal* shown in Figure 2.2. In this depiction, he doesn't look like someone who would readily run naked through the streets of Athens. Why do they make him look so serious? Mathematicians I know are fun people who do fun stuff.

FIGURE 2.2 The Fields Medal has a depiction of Archimedes on it.

The medal is named after the Canadian mathematician, John Charles Fields (1863–1932). The medal is awarded every four years to a few mathematicians who did some outstanding work. One caveat: they have to be under the age of 40. No Fields Medals for old geezers.

The awards ceremony is held at the "International Congress of Mathematics." A gathering of the brightest minds in mathematics: a mathematical Mecca. Fields organized the congress in Toronto in 1924 and lobbied for an award at the meeting. The Fields Medal was eventually first awarded at the 1936 Congress in Oslo, Norway, four years after Fields had died.

The Fields Medal is the equivalent of a Nobel Prize for mathematics. Legend has it that Nobel didn't like mathematics because his wife had an affair with a mathematician. Knowing mathematicians personally this seems very unlikely. Most likely, Nobel was more like the infamous Barbie Doll from the early 1990s that said, "math is hard."

Another one of Archimedes contributions related to fluids, is the idea of *buoyancy*.* It is rightly called *Archimedes' principle*. It goes as follows:

> Any object, wholly or partially immersed in a fluid, is buoyed up
> by a force equal to the weight of the fluid displaced by the object.

This is pretty obvious right. A heavy marble will sink and a rubber ducky will float. The genius element here is that he found a practical principle or law that can predict the exact upward force on the immersed object. It is exactly related to the weight of the fluid that was displaced. It predicts exactly why an object floats or sinks. It explains why a human who cannot swim will die when thrown in a lake. Gravity in this case wins over buoyancy. A hypothetical human made of something less dense than water will survive on the other hand. Actually, it is a bit more complicated. If you are thrown into highly salted water you might float without any effort. People float in the Dead Sea in Israel. This is because the weight of displaced salty water is higher than pure water. Also, people with a lot of body fat have a net density close to water and they might easily float in the ocean. Muscle is denser than fat. So, if you cannot swim it is better to be fat than muscular.

---

* It is derived from the word *buoy* which is derived from the Dutch word *boei*. You know, the things you see floating in harbors.

To summarize: Some ancient Greeks like Archimedes liked to run down the street naked. Make sure your kids learn how to swim from an early age. Bathtubs are a good place to relax and do science.

2.3 LONG, CURLY HAIRED MATHEMATICIANS, THE ABYSS AND THE AIRBRUSH

> Before you know it, the Renaissance will be here and we'll all be painting.
>
> WOODY ALLEN'S CHARACTER PLAYING THE FOOL
> IN HIS MOVIE *EVERYTHING YOU ALWAYS WANTED TO
> KNOW ABOUT SEX BUT WERE AFRAID TO ASK* (1972)

> The Dutch customs once thought my pictures were photos. Where on earth did they think I could have photographed my subjects? In Hell, perhaps?
>
> HANS RUDOLF GIGER (LEGENDARY SWISS
> AIRBRUSH ARTIST)

> After exponential quantities the circular functions, sine and cosine, should be considered because they arise when imaginary quantities are involved in the exponential.
>
> LEONHARD EULER (FAMOUS SWISS MATHEMATICIAN)

We move from ancient Greece to Renaissance France. Blaise Pascal* (1623–1662) is another genius who studied fluids. Not only that but he was one of the first people to build a computing machine. A computer language created by Niklaus Wirth† called *Pascal* is named in his honor. Since I grew up in Geneva, Switzerland, this was one of the first computer languages I had to code in. It is a somewhat overly formal language. I still remember how one of my teachers spent a lot of time explaining what a *pointer* is. In another language called *C* it is completely obvious, just the location of something in the physical memory of a computer. That's it. A company called Borland founded by the Frenchman Philippe Kahn,

---

* I always joke that he should be from Texas. Pascal is a popular first name in French. In Texas there are many people with last names like "Joe," "Paul," "Randy," etc.
† He is a professor at the *Eidgenössische Technische Hochschule Zürich*. Gesundheit: the short version we use is ETHZ.

created a wickedly cool compiler released in the 1980s called *Turbo Pascal*. It was cheap, fast, and user friendly. I loved it. It was fast because everything was kept in slave's memory when it was translated to 0 and 1, not on those dinky floppy drives. Of course, this was all cool until your computer crashed. In that case, oh well. Rewrite your code. At any rate, Version 2.0 usually ends up being cleaner.*

Now, back to the real Pascal and his work on fluids.

One of Pascal's more memorable experiments is his *crève-tonneau*, which literally means "barrel buster" in French. It sounds like something out of a Renaissance *MythBuster* episode. Figure 2.3 shows a portrait of Blaise Pascal (he looks like a dude you want to chill out with) and Figure 2.4

FIGURE 2.3   Blaise Pascal.

---

* Geek story. When I coded at VTT in Espoo, Finland, I lost one month worth of writing code because I was using the "vi" editor. I hit the ":wq" keys and my computer was low on disk storage. It couldn't do the "w" operation but then executed the "q" anyway. I lost everything. Lessons learned: (1) break up your code into smaller files, (2) type in ":w" first and then type in ":q," and stay away from ":q!", and (3) do not use "vi" unless you are a hipster buying vinyl. My version 2 of the code was actually better. I was careless and should have known better.

Fig. 45.—Hydrostatic paradox. Pascal's experiment.

FIGURE 2.4 The crève-tonneau experiment.

shows his famous *tonneau* experiment. So, why would anyone climb up a 10-m ladder to make a barrel burst? Of course because it makes science look cool. Science is fun *Messieurs, Dames et Mademoiselles*. Pascal was making a point. It confirmed his principle.

> Pressure applied to an enclosed fluid is transmitted undiminished to every part of the fluid, as well as to the walls of the container.

This is directly related to the fact that a fluid is highly incompressible. This is how it works. Pascal connected a vertical 10-m pipe to a barrel already filled with water. Then he climbed the ladder and poured water into the pipe. This raises the overall pressure in the barrel. And since the barrel was poorly made, it burst: *crevé*. The burst factor depends both on the strength of the barrel and on the height of the pipe. More concretely, the necessary height of the pipe to burst the barrel is proportional to the strength of the barrel.

No wonder the unit of pressure is named after Pascal. It is equal to the amount of force exerted per area. This is the reason why it is a bad idea to walk in stiletto heels on Copacabana Beach. Too much force on a tiny area. On the other hand, it is a good idea to wear snowshoes also known as *racket shoes* when walking on soft snow in Northern Canada. The rackets make your feet bigger and redistribute the force caused by your weight to create a lower pressure.

The pressure of the atmosphere at sea level is 101,325 Pa. That is huge: a lot of curly, long-haired French philosophers. Consequently, if the inside of your body were a vacuum, you would shrink to a freaky mess. The pressure at the bottom of oceans is even higher. Humans wouldn't survive there but many fish and other creatures whose body density is almost the same as water are doing just fine.

The deepest known location in the world's oceans is the so-called *Mariana Trench* near the island of Guam in the western part of the Pacific Ocean. It is about 11 km below sea level and the pressure there is a thousand times higher than the atmospheric pressure. It is deeper than how tall the Mount Everest is: 11 versus 8 km. Humans first reached the bottom of the trench using a specially built *bathyscaphe* called the *Trieste* in 1960 (see Figure 2.5). This is sort of an Everest climb in reverse. Figure 2.6 shows some of the bizarre creatures you might encounter at those depths.* This layer is known as the *abyss*. Marine biologists are slowly discovering the life in this fascinating world below us. National Geographic even claims that 86% of all life on earth is still unknown to humankind.† Looking at the creatures in Figure 2.6, one can only imagine what else is down there.

Thus far we have dealt only with static fluids: fluids that do not move. Until Pascal's barrel burst that is. Let's look at an example that involves moving fluids. Let's introduce the airbrush.

---

* For more pictures see Claire Nouvian's book, *The Deep: The Extraordinary Creatures of the Abyss.* Of course it is always easier to Google it. These creatures can resist the high pressure because their tissues are composed of essentially a nondeformable liquid that is also gelatinous; this allows these creatures to balance the external pressure with internal pressure.

† http://news.nationalgeographic.com/news/2011/08/110824-earths-species-8-7-million-biology-planet-animals-science/

FIGURE 2.5 The bathyscaphe called the *Trieste* that made it to the bottom of the Mariana Trench. (Courtesy of the U.S. Naval Historical Center, Washington, DC.)

FIGURE 2.6 Some of the creatures you might encounter in the abyss. This is for real. These are not computer generated.

I spent most of my teenage years painting with the airbrush until I realized computers could create pictures as well. The airbrush enables you to create wicked pictures but first you need to master the technology in order to create them. The airbrush is basically a spray can with controls over the outflow and the color of the paint. I usually liked acrylics and watercolors over oil paints. Acrylics are cool but they dry really fast so you have to make sure to clean everything really rapidly. Watercolors are user friendly but they are not as vivid as acrylics. Oil paints are the ultimate paint when using a traditional brush. They take forever to dry however. I remember painting outside in the summer and bugs would get stuck on the oil paint. My experience with oils and the airbrush were not very good: big mess. Turpentine to the rescue! I am always amazed what *graffiti artists* can produce with their clunky spray cans. They are highly skilled badass artists.

Let's see how the airbrush really works since it involves fluid *kinematics*. Kinematics is a fancy word for fluids that actually move and this is related to fluid animation. We will get to the *dynamics* of fluids below, which describes how the kinematic properties of a fluid, like velocities, evolve over time.

Figure 2.7 is a photograph of my old Paasche airbrush and Figure 2.8 shows a schematic depiction of the hardware involved in using an airbrush. It is not as easy as going to the local art store and purchasing paints, brushes, and canvases or paper. First, you need a supply of compressed air. Air can be compressed when trapped in a container such as a cylinder.* Usually, airbrush artists prefer a *compressor*: a device that is also useful to pump bicycle and car tires. It fills up a tank of compressed air now and then when the pressure is below a certain threshold. Some industrial

FIGURE 2.7 My Paasche airbrush.

---

* My mom drove me to an industrial part of Geneva where they rented these cylinders. You only pay for the air inside the cylinder and you rent the cylinder. The guys at the warehouse were puzzled why a tall, gangly teenager and his mom would want to rent one of them. They had never heard of airbrush art. The cylinder was cool but it ran out of gas even before I finished my second painting. That is when I convinced my parents to buy me a compressor. After that I convinced my dad to buy me a Sinclair QL computer and an Amiga computer.

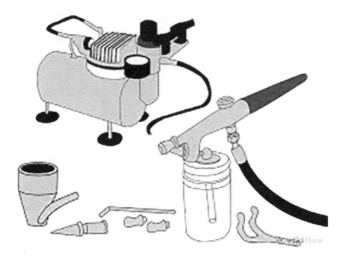

FIGURE 2.8   A cartoon of an airbrush setup.

compressors can be very noisy, but the ones built for artists typically emit only a small hum. They are however more expensive and smaller.* The compressor is connected via a hose to the airbrush, usually at the bottom. That is the input of air. The input of paint comes via a container attached to the airbrush. Where the fluid kinematics comes in is when both air and paint are mixed and ejected out of the nozzle. Sort of like colored water coming out of a garden hose set on *spray* or *mist* but not on *soak*. Anyone who has a backyard will know what I mean.

The basic mechanism of how an airbrush works goes back to the work by the Swiss mathematician Daniel Bernoulli. Figure 2.9 shows him and the cover of his famous book on fluid dynamics. Back then it was okay for mathematicians to wear a curly wig. He comes from a famous family of mathematicians. There are Bernoulli numbers, Bernoulli distributions, Bernoulli principles, and so on.

One member of the Bernoulli family even proved that the following sum does not have a finite value:

$$H = 1 + \frac{1}{2} + \frac{1}{3} + \cdots$$

---

* I once used an industrial compressor and it almost gave my friend's cat a heart attack when the cat was awakened from a deep sleep because the compressor automatically turned itself on. We got away with some nasty scratches.

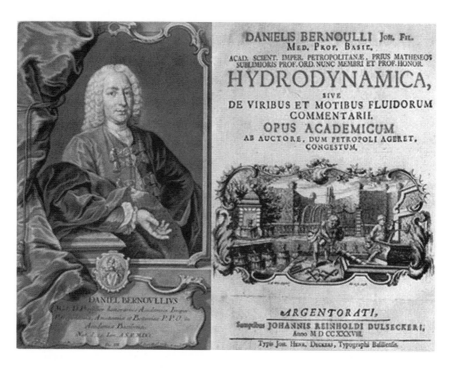

FIGURE 2.9   Daniel Bernoulli (left) and the cover of his treatise of fluids (right).

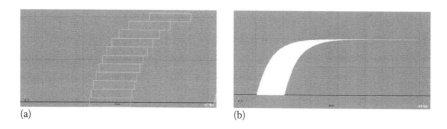

(a)   (b)

FIGURE 2.10   How to stack 10 books (a) and 10,000 books (b).

It is infinite. The "…" of course means that the sum involves an infinite number of terms. The next one is 1/4, then comes 1/5, and so on. It would take an infinite amount of paper to write down the entire sum. This sum is called *harmonic*. It crawls toward infinity very slowly however.

One fun practical way to visualize this phenomenon is through the *book stacking problem*. Here is the problem: given identically sized books how would one stack them up in order to reach the furthest distance possible? Figure 2.10 shows how to stack 10 books and 10,000 books.* In principle,

---

* I created these figures in our MAYA animation software using an MEL script.

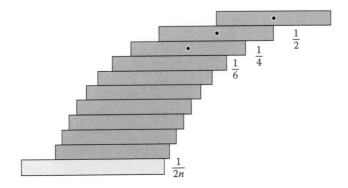

FIGURE 2.11 Optimal *classic* solution of the book-stacking problem.

you could reach any distance given enough books, there is an optimal manner of doing this.

Do try this at home.

The optimal stacking formula is shown in Figure 2.11. It shows that the distance between the adjacent books is in a decreasing series:

$$\frac{1}{2}, \frac{1}{4}, \frac{1}{6}, \cdots$$

The total distance from the table is therefore equal to the sum of the terms of the series:

$$\text{Overhang Distance} = \frac{1}{2} + \frac{1}{4} + \frac{1}{6} + \cdots$$

This sum also goes to infinity. This means that any distance can be reached given enough books. Again, try this at home.

Actually, a stack of playing cards will do a better job. You would have to go to your local "Dollar Store" and be ready to spend about a thousand dollars or more and have a lot of time on your hands to stack them properly. Also, make sure you close all windows and have your pet locked up in another room. This will get you the stacking shown in Figure 2.10b.

Not all infinite sums have infinite values even if you need an infinite amount of paper to write them down. For example, check out the following series:

$$1 = \frac{1}{2} + \frac{1}{4} + \frac{1}{8} + \frac{1}{16} + \frac{1}{32} + \cdots$$

This is the sum of the inverses of all the powers of two and it is equal to one. That is why Zeno's turtle or rabbit can cross a road. "Zeno's Paradox"* roughly states that the turtle will never reach the other side of the road because there is always another halfway to go. Actually, in the original story it is that the rabbit can never catch up to the turtle once he arrogantly took a nap.

Zeno's Paradox is only paradoxical if you do not accept infinities. And if you do, *no problemo amigo*.

Welcome to the world of infinities.

The sum of an infinity number of halves and halves of themselves eventually converges to a finite number. So no problem; our turtle is able to cross the road, unless it is run over by a car. Many interesting results like this came from the Bernoulli family.

Infinite series are wicked. Consider this astonishing result:

$$1+2+3+4+5+6+\cdots = -\frac{1}{12}.$$

This is crazy right? Nevertheless, it is used in Bosonic String Theory[†] and implies that space time has to have 26 dimensions. Look it up.

Let's get back down to earth and Daniel Bernoulli's work on fluids. His principle roughly states that.

When airspeed increases, pressure decreases.

This explains how an airbrush works. The paint gets sucked up from the container through the pipe and gets mixed with the air and eventually leaves the nozzle of the airbrush to create a cool painting.

Daniel Bernoulli actually contributed a lot more to science than this principle; he gave us an equation.

Equations are mathematical objects which help to think clearly about problems. Equations also help to communicate results in a universal language: Mathematics. As an example, let's look at one of the most beautiful equation in mathematics:

---

* The paradox is named after the Greek philosopher Zeno of Elea (–490 | –430). He is not to be confused with Zeno of Citium of course. A fun paradox is: "This sentence is false." A geekier version is due to the British philosopher Bertrand Russell that states: "Let *A* be the set of all sets that do not contain themselves. Is *A* an element of *A*?" This statement destroyed Gottlob Frege's theory of Logic that he had worked on for many years.

† The term *Bosonic* has no relation to *Bozo the Clown*. It is named after the famous Indian physicist Satyendra Nath Bose (1894–1974).

$$e^{i\pi} + 1 = 0.$$

This equation combines five fundamental constants of mathematics into one equation. Any mathematician will acknowledge its beauty regardless of his or her cultural background or mother tongue.* It is a universal truth and it is elegant. This equation was discovered or created, whatever, by another famous Swiss mathematician named Leonhard Euler. We will discuss his fundamental contributions to fluids as follows.

The equation states that Napier's constant e raised to the power of the complex number i times π plus one is equal to zero. These five numbers show up all over the place in mathematics and Euler combined them all in one equation.

This is pure genius.

What it really says in plain language is: "if you rotate a vector counterclockwise in the plane by 180° it will point in the opposite direction. And if you take the sum of the original vector and the rotated one it will be zero." That seems pretty obvious. Euler's genius was to concoct an equation from this obvious fact that involves very different mathematical constants. They show up all over the place in different mathematical fields but here they are all united by Euler's formula. I think any high school math course should mention this wonderful equation. It will teach students about awesome numbers, more about these following numbers.

Of course, any book that mentions equations has to state Einstein's famous equation stating that energy is related to mass via the speed of light squared. Here you go:

$$E = mc^2.$$

I just lost one-quarter of the readers at this point according to Hawking's quote at the beginning of this chapter. No worries. We do not need these equations to animate fluids. But there will be more equations to come. Too bad that equations scare people as in most cases they actually make understanding things simpler, not more complicated. Some people abuse equations; however, they are called math snobs. It makes them look clever

---

* This is kind of like *soccer, voetbal, futebol,* … In almost any country I have traveled to, you just have to mention a team's name or a soccer legend to have an instant bond in the foreign land. When I was in South Korea I mentioned that I was born in Holland and most people immediately responded *Guus Hiddink!*

but they are understood only by a few mortals. I went to many math talks and usually everyone is lost after the first two or three slides. Then some expert in the audience wakes up at the front of the audience and asks a really clever question at the end of the talk. In my experience, older mathematicians give clearer presentations. The famous mathematician, Stephen Smale, comes to mind: he proved the Poincaré Conjecture for dimensions larger than four on the beach of Rio and got a Fields Medal for it. His talks, at least the ones which I had the privilege to attend, were crystal clear. Look it up.

There is, however, one difference I want to point out between these two equations. Euler's equation is a *truth* which has a widely accepted proof: a series of logical arguments that starts with known facts and then ends with the equation in the final step.* You could say mathematics is a beautiful and clever solitary game. When I say solitary I do not mean that it is not competitive. Everyone wins when a result is proven. That is progress. Of course there is some competition between mathematicians about who will find the first proof or the most elegant one. But in the end it's all good. They all go to the pub to celebrate a new *truth*.†

Einstein's equation is different and much more ambitious as it tells us something about the way nature works. It is based on physical principles which are then condensed into an equation. The speed of light denoted by *c* is different from a mathematical constant like π. The speed of light has to be measured while the constant π can be defined exactly as, are you ready, "half the length of the perimeter of an (ideal) circle having a radius equal to one." Or, and this is pure mathematical magic, you could define it as the number π that makes Euler's equation true. From that you can then derive the perimeter of a circle: magic. Mathematics is all about starting with some facts and then deriving other facts from them from different angles of attack. Most often, the simplest argument is preferred. This principle goes by the name of *Occam's razor*. When there are alternate theories to explain a phenomenon, just pick the simplest one.

Now back to Einstein's equation. In 1983, the speed of light became a constant through a clever trick. The unit of length (the meter) was redefined so that its value was fixed once and for all. The meter used to be defined as the length of a bar of metal called *l'étalon* held in some safe

---

* Mathematicians usually put *QED* at the end of their proofs. **QED** is an acronym for **Quod Erat Demonstrandum**. This is Latin for "which had to be demonstrated."
† David Hilbert famously wrote that: "Mathematics is a game played according to certain simple rules with meaningless marks on paper."

location in Paris, France (not in Texas). After many measurements, the international community decided that length *au contraire* should be defined by the speed of light and not the other way around. So, they came up with the following definition: "a meter is the distance traveled by light in vacuum during a time interval of $1/c$ seconds." The speed of light is a rather ugly looking constant determined by experiments:

$$c = 299{,}792.458 \text{ km/s.}$$

This approach seems to do the job so far.

You cannot prove a physical theory, you can only disprove it.

In a nutshell that is the difference to me between mathematics and physics. Of course, this is oversimplifying the dichotomy. Anyone can always disprove a mathematical result. But you do not need an experiment just a counter-mathematical argument.

Speaking of physical equations and elegance, I cannot stop myself from mentioning the *Lagrangian of the Standard Model* used in particle physics. It is depicted in all its full glory in Figure 2.12. It makes for great wallpaper. Seriously, it does work, apparently. One of the terms captures the recently discovered *God particle* also known as the *Higgs Boson*.* Try to spot the Higgs term. Mathematicians call these equations not elegant, inelegant, ugly, a disgrace, garbage, and "that is why I am not doing physics." Too bad the elegant equations do not always work. Einstein and Newton's equations are exceptions rather than the rules.

Let's get back to fluids.

Daniel Bernoulli's equation precisely relates the speed (velocity) of the flow and the pressure. From his principle, we know they are inversely related. However, we have to keep in mind that this result is valid only for simple fluids. What that means is that we ignore dynamics and things like turbulence. The cool stuff we will deal with later in this book. But it works in many cases where it is a good approximation.

To establish a quantitative relation between the velocity and pressure, we will use a somewhat unconventional derivation called *dimensional analysis*. The following is going to be a bit geeky but please bear with me. I promise it will not involve any calculus, even though I love calculus.

---

* A *Boson* is named after the same Satyendra Nath Bose mentioned earlier. Peter Ware Higgs (1929) is a British physicist who was awarded the Nobel Prize in 2013.

$$-\tfrac{1}{2}\partial_\nu g^a_\mu \partial_\nu g^a_\mu - g_s f^{abc}\partial_\mu g^a_\nu g^b_\mu g^c_\nu - \tfrac{1}{4}g_s^2 f^{abc}f^{ade}g^b_\mu g^c_\nu g^d_\mu g^e_\nu +$$
$$\tfrac{1}{2}ig_s^2(\bar{q}^i_\sigma \gamma^\mu q^j_\sigma)g^a_\mu + \bar{G}^a \partial^2 G^a + g_s f^{abc}\partial_\mu \bar{G}^a G^b g^c_\mu - \partial_\nu W^+_\mu \partial_\nu W^-_\mu -$$
$$M^2 W^+_\mu W^-_\mu - \tfrac{1}{2}\partial_\nu Z^0_\mu \partial_\nu Z^0_\mu - \tfrac{1}{2c_w^2}M^2 Z^0_\mu Z^0_\mu - \tfrac{1}{2}\partial_\mu A_\nu \partial_\mu A_\nu - \tfrac{1}{2}\partial_\mu H \partial_\mu H -$$
$$\tfrac{1}{2}m_h^2 H^2 - \partial_\mu \phi^+ \partial_\mu \phi^- - M^2 \phi^+ \phi^- - \tfrac{1}{2}\partial_\mu \phi^0 \partial_\mu \phi^0 - \tfrac{1}{2c_w^2}M\phi^0 \phi^0 - \beta_h[\tfrac{2M^2}{g^2} +$$
$$\tfrac{2M}{g}H + \tfrac{1}{2}(H^2 + \phi^0 \phi^0 + 2\phi^+ \phi^-)] + \tfrac{2M^4}{g^2}\alpha_h - igc_w[\partial_\nu Z^0_\mu (W^+_\mu W^-_\nu -$$
$$W^+_\nu W^-_\mu) - Z^0_\nu (W^+_\mu \partial_\nu W^-_\mu - W^-_\mu \partial_\nu W^+_\mu) + Z^0_\mu (W^+_\nu \partial_\nu W^-_\mu -$$
$$W^-_\nu \partial_\nu W^+_\mu)] - igs_w[\partial_\nu A_\mu (W^+_\mu W^-_\nu - W^+_\nu W^-_\mu) -$$
$$A_\nu (W^+_\mu \partial_\nu W^-_\mu - W^-_\mu \partial_\nu W^+_\mu) + A_\mu (W^+_\nu \partial_\nu W^-_\mu - W^-_\nu \partial_\nu W^+_\mu)] - \tfrac{1}{2}g^2 W^+_\mu W^-_\mu W^+_\nu W^-_\nu +$$
$$\tfrac{1}{2}g^2 W^+_\mu W^-_\nu W^+_\mu W^-_\nu + g^2 c_w^2(Z^0_\mu W^+_\mu Z^0_\nu W^-_\nu - Z^0_\mu Z^0_\mu W^+_\nu W^-_\nu) +$$
$$g^2 s_w^2(A_\mu W^+_\mu A_\nu W^-_\nu - A_\mu A_\mu W^+_\nu W^-_\nu) + g^2 s_w c_w[A_\mu Z^0_\nu(W^+_\mu W^-_\nu -$$
$$W^+_\nu W^-_\mu) - 2A_\mu Z^0_\mu W^+_\nu W^-_\nu] - g\alpha[H^3 + H\phi^0 \phi^0 + 2H\phi^+ \phi^-] -$$
$$\tfrac{1}{8}g^2 \alpha_h[H^4 + (\phi^0)^4 + 4(\phi^+ \phi^-)^2 + 4(\phi^0)^2 \phi^+ \phi^- + 4H^2 \phi^+ \phi^- + 2(\phi^0)^2 H^2] -$$
$$gMW^+_\mu W^-_\mu H - \tfrac{1}{2}g\tfrac{M}{c_w^2}Z^0_\mu Z^0_\mu H - \tfrac{1}{2}ig[W^+_\mu(\phi^0 \partial_\mu \phi^- - \phi^- \partial_\mu \phi^0) -$$
$$W^-_\mu(\phi^0 \partial_\mu \phi^+ - \phi^+ \partial_\mu \phi^0)] + \tfrac{1}{2}g[W^+_\mu(H\partial_\mu \phi^- - \phi^- \partial_\mu H) - W^-_\mu(H\partial_\mu \phi^+ -$$
$$\phi^+ \partial_\mu H)] + \tfrac{1}{2}g\tfrac{1}{c_w}(Z^0_\mu(H\partial_\mu \phi^0 - \phi^0 \partial_\mu H) - ig\tfrac{s_w^2}{c_w}MZ^0_\mu(W^+_\mu \phi^- - W^-_\mu \phi^+) +$$
$$igs_w MA_\mu(W^+_\mu \phi^- - W^-_\mu \phi^+) - ig\tfrac{1-2c_w^2}{2c_w}Z^0_\mu(\phi^+ \partial_\mu \phi^- - \phi^- \partial_\mu \phi^+) +$$
$$igs_w A_\mu(\phi^+ \partial_\mu \phi^- - \phi^- \partial_\mu \phi^+) - \tfrac{1}{4}g^2 W^+_\mu W^-_\mu[H^2 + (\phi^0)^2 + 2\phi^+ \phi^-] -$$
$$\tfrac{1}{4}g^2\tfrac{1}{c_w^2}Z^0_\mu Z^0_\mu[H^2 + (\phi^0)^2 + 2(2s_w^2 - 1)^2\phi^+ \phi^-] - \tfrac{1}{2}g^2\tfrac{s_w^2}{c_w}Z^0_\mu \phi^0(W^+_\mu \phi^- +$$
$$W^-_\mu \phi^+) - \tfrac{1}{2}ig^2\tfrac{s_w^2}{c_w}Z^0_\mu H(W^+_\mu \phi^- - W^-_\mu \phi^+) + \tfrac{1}{2}g^2 s_w A_\mu \phi^0(W^+_\mu \phi^- +$$
$$W^-_\mu \phi^+) + \tfrac{1}{2}ig^2 s_w A_\mu H(W^+_\mu \phi^- - W^-_\mu \phi^+) - g^2\tfrac{s_w}{c_w}(2c_w^2 - 1)Z^0_\mu A_\mu \phi^+ \phi^- -$$
$$g^1 s_w^2 A_\mu A_\mu \phi^+ \phi^- - \bar{e}^\lambda(\gamma \partial + m_e^\lambda)e^\lambda - \bar{\nu}^\lambda \gamma \partial \nu^\lambda - \bar{u}^\lambda_j(\gamma \partial + m_u^\lambda)u^\lambda_j - \bar{d}^\lambda_j(\gamma \partial +$$
$$m_d^\lambda)d^\lambda_j + igs_w A_\mu[-(\bar{e}^\lambda \gamma^\mu e^\lambda) + \tfrac{2}{3}(\bar{u}^\lambda_j \gamma^\mu u^\lambda_j) - \tfrac{1}{3}(\bar{d}^\lambda_j \gamma^\mu d^\lambda_j)] + \tfrac{ig}{4c_w}Z^0_\mu[(\bar{\nu}^\lambda \gamma^\mu(1 +$$
$$\gamma^5)\nu^\lambda) + (\bar{e}^\lambda \gamma^\mu(4s_w^2 - 1 - \gamma^5)e^\lambda) + (\bar{u}^\lambda_j \gamma^\mu(\tfrac{4}{3}s_w^2 - 1 - \gamma^5)u^\lambda_j) +$$
$$(\bar{d}^\lambda_j \gamma^\mu(1 - \tfrac{8}{3}s_w^2 - \gamma^5)d^\lambda_j)] + \tfrac{ig}{2\sqrt{2}}W^+_\mu[(\bar{\nu}^\lambda \gamma^\mu(1 + \gamma^5)e^\lambda) + (\bar{u}^\lambda_j \gamma^\mu(1 +$$
$$\gamma^5)C_{\lambda\kappa}d^\kappa_j)] + \tfrac{ig}{2\sqrt{2}}W^-_\mu[(\bar{e}^\lambda \gamma^\mu(1 + \gamma^5)\nu^\lambda) + (\bar{d}^\kappa_j C^\dagger_{\lambda\kappa}\gamma^\mu(1 + \gamma^5)u^\lambda_j)] +$$
$$\tfrac{ig}{2\sqrt{2}}\tfrac{m^\lambda_e}{M}[-\phi^+(\bar{\nu}^\lambda(1 - \gamma^5)e^\lambda) + \phi^-(\bar{e}^\lambda(1 + \gamma^5)\nu^\lambda)] - \tfrac{g}{2}\tfrac{m^\lambda_e}{M}[H(\bar{e}^\lambda e^\lambda) +$$
$$i\phi^0(\bar{e}^\lambda \gamma^5 e^\lambda)] + \tfrac{ig}{2M\sqrt{2}}\phi^+[-m^\kappa_d(\bar{u}^\lambda_j C_{\lambda\kappa}(1 - \gamma^5)d^\kappa_j) + m^\lambda_u(\bar{u}^\lambda_j C_{\lambda\kappa}(1 +$$
$$\gamma^5)d^\kappa_j] + \tfrac{ig}{2M\sqrt{2}}\phi^-[m^\lambda_d(\bar{d}^\lambda_j C^\dagger_{\lambda\kappa}(1 + \gamma^5)u^\kappa_j) - m^\kappa_u(\bar{d}^\lambda_j C^\dagger_{\lambda\kappa}(1 - \gamma^5)u^\kappa_j] -$$
$$\tfrac{g}{2}\tfrac{m^\lambda_u}{M}H(\bar{u}^\lambda_j u^\lambda_j) - \tfrac{g}{2}\tfrac{m^\lambda_d}{M}H(\bar{d}^\lambda_j d^\lambda_j) + \tfrac{ig}{2}\tfrac{m^\lambda_u}{M}\phi^0(\bar{u}^\lambda_j \gamma^5 u^\lambda_j) - \tfrac{ig}{2}\tfrac{m^\lambda_d}{M}\phi^0(\bar{d}^\lambda_j \gamma^5 d^\lambda_j) +$$
$$\bar{X}^+(\partial^2 - M^2)X^+ + \bar{X}^-(\partial^2 - M^2)X^- + \bar{X}^0(\partial^2 - \tfrac{M^2}{c_w^2})X^0 + \bar{Y}\partial^2 Y +$$
$$igc_w W^+_\mu(\partial_\mu \bar{X}^0 X^- - \partial_\mu \bar{X}^+ X^0) + igs_w W^+_\mu(\partial_\mu \bar{Y}X^- - \partial_\mu \bar{X}^+ Y) +$$
$$igc_w W^-_\mu(\partial_\mu \bar{X}^- X^0 - \partial_\mu \bar{X}^0 X^+) + igs_w W^-_\mu(\partial_\mu \bar{X}^- Y - \partial_\mu \bar{Y}X^+) +$$
$$igc_w Z^0_\mu(\partial_\mu \bar{X}^+ X^+ - \partial_\mu \bar{X}^- X^-) + igs_w A_\mu(\partial_\mu \bar{X}^+ X^+ - \partial_\mu \bar{X}^- X^-) -$$
$$\tfrac{1}{2}gM[\bar{X}^+ X^+ H + \bar{X}^- X^- H + \tfrac{1}{c_w^2}\bar{X}^0 X^0 H] + \tfrac{1-2c_w^2}{2c_w}igM[\bar{X}^+ X^0 \phi^+ -$$
$$\bar{X}^- X^0 \phi^-] + \tfrac{1}{2c_w}igM[\bar{X}^0 X^- \phi^+ - \bar{X}^0 X^+ \phi^-] + igMs_w[\bar{X}^0 X^- \phi^+ -$$
$$\bar{X}^0 X^+ \phi^-] + \tfrac{1}{2}igM[\bar{X}^+ X^+ \phi^0 - \bar{X}^- X^- \phi^0]$$

FIGURE 2.12 The Lagrangian of the Standard Model of particle physics. (Courtesy of Thomas D. Gutierrez.)

Physical quantities have units. There are three fundamental units: length (L), time (T), and mass (M). Their actual values in this derivation do not matter since they depend on convention. Most people use the metric system: meters for length, seconds for time, and kilograms for mass. The United States, on the other hand, uses inches for length, seconds for time, and pounds for mass. This doesn't matter as we can convert from one to the other. For example, 1 in. equals 0.0254 m. In Canada where I live, height is usually measured in feet and inches even though they adopted the metric system in the 1970s. But in the end, it doesn't matter as we have these conversion factors. No one but the insane or a mathematician will say: "Hey, I ordered a foot-long veggie hot dog and you gave me a 0.3048 one."*

Velocity (V) has the units of length divided by time: $[V] = [L/T]$. The latter is not really a strict equation but relates the units of a quantity to the fundamental units, hence the brackets. For example, $[A] = [-A]$ makes sense for any physical quantity A. Usually in math, $A = -A$ implies $A = 0$.† Not the case with the brackets. Pressure (P) has units of mass divided by length and also divided by the time squared: $[P] = [M/L/T^2]$.‡ This follows from the fact that pressure is equal to the force divided by area. As most of you know: "force is equal to em times ah." The units of "em" are mass $[M]$ and the units of "ah" are that of an acceleration $[L/T^2]$. So, the units of force are $[F] = [M L/T^2]$. Therefore, the units of pressure are $[P] = [M L/T^2]/[L^2] = [M/L/T^2]$.

This was a bit involved and technical. But the bottom line is that:

> The units of pressure are equal to mass divided by length and divided by time squared.

Given these relations, we want to derive an equation that captures exactly the principle that says "velocity is inversely proportional to pressure." We can try: $V = -P$. Well that does not work since the units of $[V]$ are not equal to the units of $[P]$. Next, we could try $V^2 = -P$. In this case, the units of the velocity squared $[L^2/T^2]$ are still not equal to the units of pressure $[M/L/T^2]$. But we are getting there.

Enter the density of the fluid. What is a density of a fluid? The units of density (D) are the amount of mass per volume: $[D] = [M/L^3]$. Air is less dense than water, for example. In fact, the ratio between these two densities is one to one thousand. Water is a thousand times denser than air. Imagine two bins of equal volume. One bin contains air and the other bin contains water. Guess which one is heavier? The one containing water of course because it is denser. Now, let's try the following equation: $D V^2 = -P$. Bingo. The units now match: $[D] [V] = [M/L^3] [L^2/T^2] = [M/L/T^2] = [P]$.

Dimensional analysis is a powerful tool to find equations. It is also a good tool to verify if equations are correct. If the units do not match on

---

* When people ask me how tall I am here in Canada, I usually respond "six eight." A European would have absolutely no clue.
† Good luck trying to find another number that has that property. Unless "numbers" live in a "field" with only two elements. Let's call them "0" and "1." In that case we have that: $0 + 0 = 0$, $0 + 1 = 1$, $1 + 1 = 0$, $0 \times 0 = 0$, $0 \times 1 = 0$, and $1 \times 1 = 1$. Mathematicians denote this field by $\mathbb{F}_1$. The French call it $\mathbb{F}_{un}$. This is a bad pun.
‡ T^2 stands for T multiplied by itself: $T^2 = T \times T$ and L^3 stands for $L \times L \times L$.

both sides of the equal sign of an equation, then you know there is something fishy going on. It is then time to go back to the black or whiteboard.

We can now write Bernoulli's equation in fancy math symbols.*

$$\rho \frac{1}{2} v^2 + p = 0.$$

You might ask about that one-half factor in front of the velocity squared. This doesn't follow from our dimensional analysis. One way to determine this constant could be through experimentation. There are of course more conventional derivations which use kinetic and potential energy to get at this exact result. This is what you find in most standard textbooks. To take into account effects due to gravity, Bernoulli's equation has to be slightly changed to

$$\rho \frac{1}{2} v^2 + \rho\, g\, h + p_0 = \text{constant}.$$

It takes into account the effects of gravity through the number g which at sea level and in standard units is approximately equal to

$$g = 9.81 \text{ m/time squared.}$$

Bernoulli's equation also includes the effect of height denoted by h on the total pressure. The constant pressure denoted by p_0 is usually equal to the atmospheric pressure. The constant on the right-hand side is not really important as the equation is often used to relate pressures and velocities at different points in the flow so the constant is canceled out.

We can use these results to make some predictions about fluids. That is what science is all about. If the practical measures do not agree with the predictions of your theory, then too bad, your theory is *wrong* and useless.

The following is a textbook example that shows how to get concrete predictions out of Bernoulli's equation. It is normally known as *Bernoulli's tank*. Figure 2.13 shows the setup (with Bernoulli's original drawing on the right). We have an arbitrarily shaped tank filled up with some liquid,

---

* The symbol ρ is Greek for "r" and is pronounced "rho" and is often used to denote density, do not ask me why.

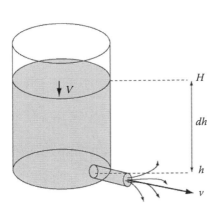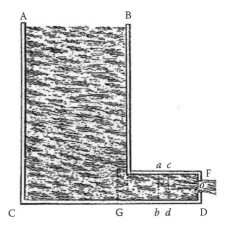

FIGURE 2.13   Bernoulli's tank.

let's say water. At the bottom, there is an opening that lets the water exit from the tank. As expected, the level of water will drop and eventually exit the tank. The question is: "at a given level of water what is the velocity of the water flowing out of the hole at the bottom?" We can answer it by using Bernoulli's equation. We have to make some simplifying assumptions, however. Both at the top of the liquid and at the bottom where the water flows out, Bernoulli's equation holds and therefore:

$$\rho \frac{1}{2} V^2 + \rho\, g\, H + p_0 = \rho \frac{1}{2} v^2 + \rho\, g\, h + p_0.$$

We get a simple equation by assuming that the velocity of the flow at the top is much slower than the bottom. It follows that we can assume (approximately) that $V = 0$. Let the difference between the heights be denoted by $dh = H - h$. Then we have that

$$g\, dh = \frac{1}{2} v^2 \text{ and consequently } v = \sqrt{2\, g\, dh}.$$

Notice that we canceled equal terms from both sides of the equation like atmospheric pressure which is the same at the bottom and the top of the tank. The similar is true for the density which is also the same at both ends. The velocity at the outflow decreases with the height of the liquid.

This is a common experience when one is relieving oneself in a urinal. This might happen after *shotgunning* a can of beer. I had never done a shotgunning beer contest until 2003 after giving a keynote talk at a conference in Northern Sweden. I have heard that this practice is popular at North American colleges. Here is the experiment: you hold the beer can horizontally and punch a hole near the bottom of the can facing you. Then you slowly tilt the can with your mouth on the hole. When the can is vertically positioned, crack the can open and there you go. Amazingly, I was able to take it all in. In Sweden, they do this with half-liter beer cans. Some contestants were not so lucky.

Thanks to Bernoulli, you will know exactly what the velocity of the beer flowing out of the can is. It is wickedly fast! Kids do not try this at home.

More seriously, the velocity at the bottom hole is equal to the velocity of an object dropped from the same height (neglecting forces like drag).

To summarize: The Bernoulli family did rock. They did so much cool math and came up with a lot of cool equations. Kids do not try the shotgunning experiment until after you give a keynote presentation at some remote location in Northern Europe.

CHAPTER 3

Euler–Newton Equations or Navier–Stokes Equations

W<small>HAT AN AMOUNT OF</small> famous name-dropping in a single title. All these math stars are depicted in Figure 3.1. The reason for naming them in the title is that collectively, they gave us a principled description of how fluids evolve over time. How cool is that?

But first.

3.1 LEONARDO DA VINCI

The merit of painting lies in the exactness of reproduction. Painting is a science and all sciences are based on mathematics. No human inquiry can be a science unless it pursues its path through mathematical exposition and demonstration.

LEONARDO DA VINCI (ITALIAN RENAISSANCE MAN)

Of course, one has to mention the quintessential *Renaissance man*, Leonardo Da Vinci (1452–1519), who painted the famous portrait of Mona Lisa on display at the Louvre museum in Paris, France. It is almost a *cliché* really to mention him in an artsy science book. He studied the motion of fluids and derived the first version of the *equation of continuity*, which is depicted in Figure 3.2 alongside his magnificent drawing of a turbulent flow. Visually, he understood that *incompressibility* leads to turbulent

FIGURE 3.1 From left to right, Newton, Euler, Navier, and Stokes.

(a)

(b)

FIGURE 3.2 Leonardo Da Vinci (a) and his epic drawing depicting turbulence in fluids (b).

swirling looking fluids. Actually, he understood that *continuity* leads to swirling flows, which is the same thing, and will be explained later in this book. This is a key visual feature of any fluid.

Da Vinci was a hypercreative smart person. I feel bad only spending one paragraph on his achievements related to fluids.

To summarize: Da Vinci was a true Renaissance man and understood both the beauty and the fundamental principles of fluids. He could not animate them. But he could draw them beautifully and explain some of their key properties.

3.2 EULER AND CONTINUITY

Il cessa de calculer et de vivre.*

MARQUIS DE CONDORCET (FRENCH MATHEMATICIAN)
ABOUT EULER'S DEATH

---

* "He ceased to calculate and to live."

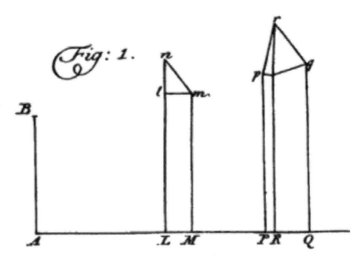

FIGURE 3.3   Euler's derivation of the continuity equation. (From pleasemakenote. blogspot.com.)

As mentioned earlier, Euler and his amazing equations combine five fundamental mathematical constants. Personally, I felt that Euler should get most of the credit for finding the basic equations of fluid dynamics. It is no wonder why I chose his picture in Figure 3.1, looking away from the other three geniuses who are more somber looking. His contributions are a big piece of the puzzle. Euler's first insight was to derive an equation for the velocity of fluid at any point in space, assuming that the fluid is incompressible. A hand-drawn figure of Euler's original derivation is depicted in Figure 3.3.

What led Euler to formalize the motion of fluids into equations? First, he formulated an equation for the continuity or equivalently the incompressibility of the fluid. As he was primarily a mathematician, he first considered an *ideal fluid*, that is, a fluid that does not dissipate. If a fluid is set in motion, it will move forever, like the elusive perpetual motion machines. Figure 3.4 shows three examples of the so-called *perpetual motion machines*. Of course, all of them would eventually grind to a halt due to wear and tear and the effects of friction and damping. Even solar-powered devices will halt before the sun runs out of energy. And if not, they will halt at some point, when the sun eventually runs out of energy.

The beauty of mathematics is that we can just assume that such ideal fluids exist. What does continuity or incompressibility mean? At an intuitive level, it is possible to change the shape of liquid, but this does not mean that its volume changes, that is, a liquid takes the shape of its container but

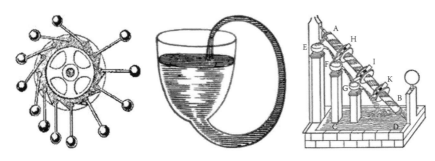

FIGURE 3.4 Three examples of perpetual motion machines that have been proposed.

its volume does not change. Since it is easier to depict flat figures, consider a 2D fluid. Assume that a soapy foam residue floats on the surface of water in the bathtub. It is a good approximation of a 2D fluid. From the studies of Archimedes, it was observed that problem-solving methods were carried out in bathtubs. Figure 3.5 shows two shapes. If the fluid is ideal, then the area of the shape on the right has to be equal to the area of the shape on the left.*

The property of preserving the area is *global*. It involves both the entire shape and the entire fluid. Euler on the other hand came up with a *local* property which guarantees that the area is preserved for small pieces of the fluid. Piecing together these local conditions results in a global condition in practice. More details about this connection will be given later.

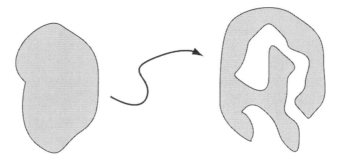

FIGURE 3.5 The area of two shapes is preserved exactly over time in an ideal continuous fluid.

---

* I tried my best in Adobe Illustrator to make the two shapes have an equal area. But hopefully you get the idea.

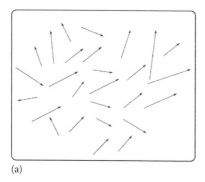
(a)

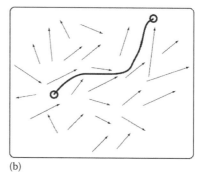
(b)

FIGURE 3.6   A 2D vector field (a) and a path of a particle through it (b).

At this point, we will introduce the key concept of a *velocity field*. Mathematicians call it a *vector field*. It can be observed initially from this book that visually some fluids such as air are nowhere to be seen. We cannot view the velocity of a fluid, but can only see or feel its effect on things. The way that mathematicians deal with this is to assign a fluid's velocity to every point in space. Imagine an arrow sitting at every point in space. Its direction indicates the direction of the flow and its magnitude indicates the speed of the flow. Figure 3.6a shows a vector field for a 2D fluid. Of course, the figure only shows a subset of all the vectors of the flow. Drawing all of the vectors would just result in a black mess. A complete black picture is not very helpful.

Imagine a tiny particle dropped in the fluid. The particle will then follow a path in time guided by the velocity field as shown in Figure 3.6b. Mathematicians would say "the path of the particle is tangential to each vector." The velocity of the particle on its path depends on the magnitude of the vectors. You can imagine a cyclist that has to follow signs saying "go here," "go there," "slow down," and "go faster." But not "stop now." It would have to be a fit cyclist, cycling forever.

Figure 3.7 shows a collage of photographs that I took in Venice, Italy. I felt like a *particella* trying to navigate myself using vectors in order to find the famous Rialto Bridge and the famous Piazza San Marco (or St. Mark's Square in English). I found both of them. Notice that the arrow in the center picture guiding me to San Marco is not very helpful. In this case, the flow is divergent and not incompressible. But I got to the square anyway! They should have a convergent arrow when you actually get to the square. These arrows were very helpful since it is extremely easy to get lost in Venice. I wish they had arrows guiding me to my hotel. This is when

FIGURE 3.7 Venetians have a vector field to send you to both the Piazza San Marco and the Rialto Bridge.

human communication comes in handy. Yes, I know that I could have used my smart phone, but data roaming rates are expensive when you do not live in Italy. Besides, you get to meet friendly people eager to help. No one sent me off in the wrong direction. I got to my hotel: *grazie!*

We all know what an arrow is. But how do you describe it exactly? A 2D vector is decomposed into two components, namely a sideway one and an upward one. These are both numbers that can be positive and negative. In three dimensions, there would also be an additional third number.

Figure 3.8 shows some examples of vectors in two dimensions. Each vector is defined by their sideway and upward direction. That is two numbers, arrow = (side, up). This is called a *tuple*. Just a fancy name for two numbers separated by a comma and squeezed in between two parentheses. *Side* and *up* are called the *coordinates* of the arrow. They are sometimes called Cartesian coordinates, named after the French philosopher, René Descartes (1596–1650). He also famously wrote *"Cogito ergo sum"*: "I think, therefore I am."* Reality is an illusion fabricated by my mind. He was a solipsist of some sorts.

---

* I am. I am, I exist, I think, therefore I am; I am because I think, why do I think? I don't want to think any more, I am because I think that I don't want to be, I think that I... because... ugh!" Excerpt from the French existentialist philosopher Jean-Paul Sartre's (1905–1980) novel called *Nausea.*

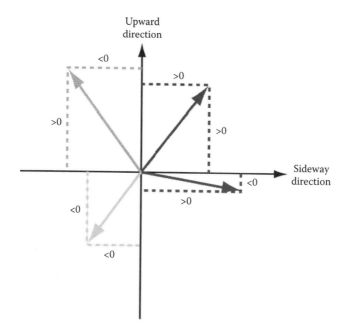

FIGURE 3.8   Four vectors in a 2D plane and their coordinates.

The numbers *side* and *up* can have any value both positive and negative. Consider again Figure 3.8. If *side* is positive, the arrow point to the right (the red arrow and the purple arrow). If *side* is negative, the vector points to the left (the green arrow and the yellow one). If *up* is positive, the vector points upward (the green one and the purple one). If *up* is negative, it points downward (yellow guy and the red guy).

The length of a vector is given by a result first stated by Pythagoras*:

> The length of the arrow squared equals the length of its coordinate *side* squared plus its coordinate *up* squared.

Because we are taking squares, even if either *side* or *up* is negative, their squares will add up to a positive number: the length squared. Therefore, we can always use the square root to get the length. No need for awesome numbers yet.

In Figure 3.8, it is pretty easy to spot which colored vector is the largest. I think it is the green one. Someone else might say "No, no, no it is the red one." Oh really? Since we have the coordinates and we can compute the

---

* Pythagoras of Samos (−570 | −495) is another Greek philosopher and mathematician. His theorem is surely known to anyone who has finished high school. In math speak: $a^2 + b^2 = c^2$.

length of both of these vectors using Pythagoras' result, the argument can be settled once and for all. I was right this time. Just as easily, I could have been wrong this time. But through math, the question is settled once and for all.

By the way, vectors can live in higher dimensions than two and three.

In a perfect fluid as shown in Figure 3.5, the area is preserved. What Euler showed is that it is equivalent to saying: "What flows in a tiny piece of the fluid has to flow out." What goes in has to come out. No sinks or sources are allowed in an ideal fluid for now. This is illustrated in Figure 3.9a for an arbitrary piece of fluid. To get an equation, we consider a *tiny* square piece of fluid as shown in Figure 3.9b. In this case, we only consider the flow through the horizontal and the vertical sides of the square. Vectors that point in a sideway direction are positive, so do the vectors that point in the upward direction. In Figure 3.9b there are four vectors and the continuity condition states that they have to sum up to zero:

$$a - b + d - c = 0.$$

Euler generalized this result. If u denotes the sideway velocity and v denotes the upward velocity, then this equation can also be written as follows:

$$u_{right} - u_{left} + v_{top} - v_{bottom} = 0.$$

In the case of Figure 3.9b, we have that: $u_{left} = a$, $u_{right} = -b$, $v_{top} = d$, and $v_{bottom} = -c$.[*]

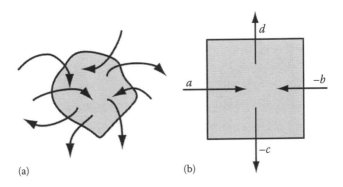

(a) (b)

FIGURE 3.9 An arbitrary piece of fluid (a) and an axis-aligned square piece of fluid (b).

---

[*] If the reader got to this point she might have substituted the variables and noticed it is a different equation from the previous one, but it still holds for Figure 3.9b!

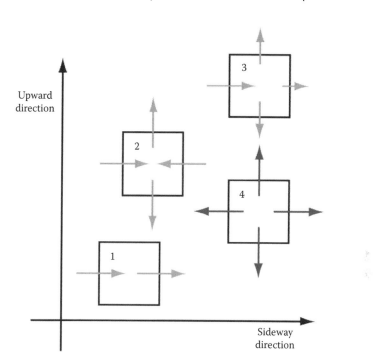

FIGURE 3.10 Euler's local continuity condition in various parts of the fluid.

For an incompressible flow, this relation has to hold for every square piece of a fluid. Figure 3.10 depicts four square pieces of the flow denoted as "1," "2," "3," and "4." Pieces "1," "2," and "3" satisfy the continuity condition while piece "4" does not. Piece "4" has all vectors pointing out of the square, and therefore, the square acts like a source of flow. This means that the flow expands, and therefore, it is not incompressible.

What about a 1D flow that is incompressible? In this case, the *squares* are line segments, as shown in Figure 3.11. In this case, the flow has to be constant. This is obvious because there is nowhere for the flow to go but in one direction. What comes in on one side of the segment has to exit on the

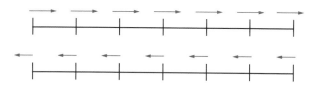

FIGURE 3.11 One-dimensional incompressible fluids are *trivial*: they must have a constant velocity everywhere.

other end of the segment. The flow is stuck in one dimension. Specifying the velocity at any point determines the flow everywhere and it is equal to that velocity. Mathematicians call these cases trivial, obvious, banal, easy, or of no interest.*

That was Euler's first contribution: what goes in has to come out. This result leads to trivial flows in one dimension but leads to highly complex flows in two and three dimensions as shown in Leonardo Da Vinci's drawing.

To summarize: Euler is one of the key players in animating fluids. We discussed continuity of a fluid and vector flow fields. These fields tell us where things should move and we want to preserve their mass. Euler gave us a condition on the vector flow field that guarantees mass preservation. It is very simple: what flows into a piece of the fluid has to come out. Beware though, it is a local condition not a global one.

Now, we will give a more geometrical interpretation of the continuity condition using what is called the *Helmholtz–Hodge decomposition* of a vector field.

3.3 INCOMPRESSIBILITY, CONTINUITY, HELMHOLTZ, AND HODGE THEORY

> Ski racing, especially downhill, is a dangerous activity and there are many accidents. It would be really too bad to lose everything because of a crash.
>
> HERMANN "THE HERMINATOR" MAIER (LEGENDARY AUSTRIAN DOWNHILL SKIER)

The Helmholtz–Hodge theory of vector fields is a monumental result that sheds light on the solution of the incompressibility problem of fluids.

This theory is the brainchild of two geniuses: the German scientist Hermann von Helmholtz (1821–1894) and the Scottish mathematician William Vallance Douglas Hodge (1903–1975). They are both depicted in Figure 3.12.†

I like Helmholtz's work. He has also done some fundamental research in explaining visual perception as well. This is very relevant to computer

---

* Russian mathematicians call many results *trivial* even though it takes other mathematicians many pages to prove the result.
† At some point, mathematicians stopped wearing long, curly haired wigs.

FIGURE 3.12   Helmholtz (a) and Hodge (b).

graphics. Our perception is not like a camera, it is more subtle. But I digress. He also worked in many other areas.

Hodge's name shows up in one of the problems that are part of the 10 Millennium Clay Prizes that we will mention later. The conjecture goes as follows:

> The Hodge conjecture asserts that for particularly nice types of spaces called projective algebraic varieties, the pieces called Hodge cycles are actually (rational linear) combinations of geometric pieces called algebraic cycles.

I am not going to explain what this means because I do not know what it means exactly. Well sort of but not well enough. But if you solve this problem, you get a million bucks and fame. Good luck. Some people who call themselves mathematicians actually care about this stuff.

We will present the Helmholtz–Hodge decomposition in two dimensions. Remember that we want the flow that enters a piece of fluid to be equal to the fluid that comes out.

The problem simply stated is how do we turn an arbitrary vector field into an incompressible one?

The Helmholtz–Hodge decomposition solves this problem.

The result loosely states that:

> Any vector field is the sum of an incompressible field and a gradient field.

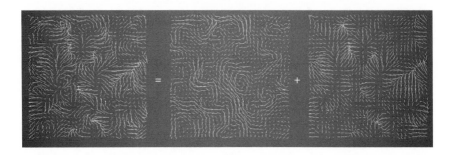

FIGURE 3.13   Any vector field is the sum of an incompressible field and a gradient field.

This is illustrated in Figure 3.13. The vector flow in the center is what we are striving for. It could be noted that it has nice whorls and vortices just like in Da Vinci's wonderful depiction of a flow in Figure 3.2b. The gradient vector field on the right-hand side of Figure 3.13 has exactly the opposite property: the flow is convergent and divergent at pretty much any point.

Bad flow! But still, have a treat, because we need you.

The strategy is to remove the bad part of the vector field to get a nice looking incompressible flow.

The procedure in order to get the nice flow is shown in Figure 3.14: original flow minus bad boy flow equals cool dude flow. The key ingredient in this decomposition is to figure out how to compute the (bad) *gradient field* from the original vector field.

How do we achieve that?

What is a gradient field anyway?

Consider the height field depicted in Figure 3.15. A height field is like a landscape. The height is just the height of that landscape measured from

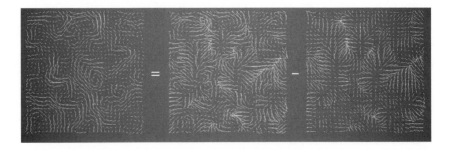

FIGURE 3.14   The incompressible field is obtained by subtracting the gradient field from the arbitrary vector field.

FIGURE 3.15   A height field. It is also periodic by the way.

some arbitrary chosen fixed elevation, for example, sea level. It does not matter because it is all about the change of height not the absolute values of height. There are peaks and valleys. If you wander in this landscape, there is always a pair of directions that will be the most efficient for you to move upward or downward. Hikers and skiers (if there is snow) usually do not choose those directions unless they are crazy and are into fast down-hill skiing or extreme mountain climbing.

The gradient field is handy for the crazies who are trying to achieve the biggest thrill of their lives in the least amount of time. I am not of one of them anymore. In Chamonix, France, they have a semilegit epic slope called *Le Couloir Poubelle.** There is even a gondola that takes you there. You make one mistake and you are going to be injured for sure. Not for the faint at heart. But if you get to the bottom alive and in one piece you definitely have *ski-cred.* Wear a headcam to prove you did it. I have gone down crazy slopes but not that crazy. I did not usually follow the gradient: the direction of steepest descent.

The gradient field is the opposite of the incompressible field. At most points, the flow is divergent or convergent as shown in Figure 3.13 (right).

Epic ski antics aside, the crucial problem now becomes: how does one compute the bad gradient field from the flow field we started with? The answer is that we have to find the height field first. Then, it is easy that we just choose the direction of steepest descent or steepest ascent. Some

---

* *Poubelle* means garbage can in French. They used to drop garbage from the top lodge down this particular *couloir. Couloir* basically means passageway in French. It was the fastest way to get gar-bage down the hill. You have to climb over a fence to get to the poubelle. Look it up on YouTube.

crazy people do both and they climb up a mountain slope along the shortest path with their skis on their back first and then go down skiing along the steepest path.

The height field turns out to be the pressure of the fluid flow.

What?

Remember pressure is a single number not a vector. If we can compute the pressure, then its gradient is the bad as field we are looking for.

The true role of pressure in computing incompressible fluid flows was an epiphany for me: pressure is not an independent quantity for *incompressible* flows. That's it.

Pressure is just an intermediate quantity to enforce incompressibility in a fluid. For an incompressible flow, it is always possible to extract the pressure from the flow vector field if you like. Pressure of course is real. But from a computational point of view, it is just an aid to animate incompressible flows. That is how I understand it. When I give talks I always leave pressure out of equations. This sometimes makes for animated conversations afterward with some computational fluid dynamics experts wearing their backpacks.

"You are using the wrong equations, you missed the pressure term!"

"No, I did not since it is just a Lagrange multiplier to enforce the divergence free condition."

"That is heresy!"

"But the animations looked pretty cool, no?"

"Yeah, but you are still wrong!"

"Whatever dude. Have a nice day."

To summarize: Helmholtz and Hodge showed us how to get an incompressible field from an arbitrary field by computing the pressure of the velocity field. This is followed by a step correcting the velocity field by subtracting the gradient field of the pressure from it. We will see below how to compute this pressure field using a *fish equation*.*

---

* This is bad humor. It is actually named after the French mathematician called Poisson. *Poisson* means fish in French. Coders in the early 1980s were onto this and called their libraries written in **FORTRAN77** "**FISHPACK**" to solve "elliptic partial differential equations." The Poisson equation is a special case of these types of equations.

3.4 EULER AND THE MOTION OF FLUIDS

Strange fascination, fascinating me/Changes are taking the pace I'm going through.

LYRICS FROM THE SONG "CHANGES" BY DAVID BOWIE
(FAMOUS BRITISH GLAM ROCK STAR)

Plus ça change, plus c'est la même chose.

FRENCH PROVERB

The velocity of a fluid tells us how things like points immersed in the fluid move over time. Now, we need an equation for the change of velocity over time. Welcome to fluid *dynamics*. The quantity that describes how the velocity changes over time is called the *acceleration* of fluid. It determines the change of what causes the change of the motion of a point in the fluid. Got that? Imagine the arrows in Figure 3.6 moving over time. Good thing that does not happen in Venice. Then, obviously, the point will take a different path over time than the one shown in Figure 3.6. The motion of the arrows over time is determined by the acceleration.

We now turn to Euler's second contribution to fluids: an equation of how the velocity of an ideal fluid evolves over time. An essential property of this description is that it is *nonlinear*.* Usually, pretty much everything that happens around us is nonlinear. Linearity, to be linear, is actually the exception. But scientists like linear problems because they are easy to solve. Very often a nonlinear problem is locally cast into a linear one and *voilà!* The problem is solved approximately. But things can go horribly wrong, because by making a nonlinear problem linear you are essentially solving another problem.

What does it mean to be linear versus being nonlinear? Figure 3.16 illustrates the difference. The curves on the left and on the right cross the horizontal line. The left one is straight, and it is easy to figure out where it will cross the line. For this line, the problem is linear: *easy peasy.* Determining the line crossings for the curve depicted on the right-hand side of Figure 3.16 is more complicated. That curve even crosses the horizontal line multiple times. The curve is nonlinear. It is much harder to

---

* The term *nonlinear* has always annoyed me since nonlinearity is actually the norm; as in *non-not-normal*, double negative. Linearity should be called *not-normal* and *nonlinearity* should be called *normal*.

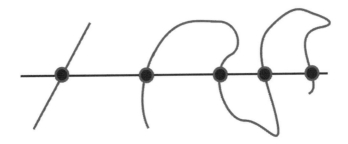

FIGURE 3.16   A linear curve (left) compared to an instance of a nonlinear curve (right).

figure out where it crosses the horizontal line than the linear case. Visually of course it is as easy. I was able to place the dots of intersection quite easily by visual inspection.

But computing their locations in a precise manner is much more difficult. There is no standard mathematical recipe that will work for all nonlinear cases. Choosing a method of solution is akin to a form of art. In many cases, one has to invent new techniques specific to a particular nonlinear problem. If you are lucky, these techniques will turn out to be useful for other nonlinear problems as well.

Personally, I like to explore very simple instances of a problem at first. I think and work like *a freak* apparently.* This is a good time to cite one of the most famous quotes from Albert Einstein. Drumroll.

> Everything should be made as simple as possible, but no simpler.

There you have it. Einstein was a *freak*.

Euler's equations for the fluid's change in velocity over time are nonlinear.† Therefore, they are notoriously hard to deal with. The basic idea is to consider how things change under the influence of a vector field.

Euler's equations are all about change.

There are two ways to describe a change of something immersed in a fluid.

To illustrate this, let us start with a simple experiment involving a bathtub‡ and temperature. Everyone who has taken a hot bath knows that it takes awhile for the hot water coming out of the faucet to reach the other

---

* Reference to the recent book by Steven D. Levitt and Stephen J. Dubner entitled *Think Like a Freak*.
† I will stick to the usual nomenclature and refrain from using the word *normal* instead of *nonlinear*.
‡ Again! This time we will leave Archimedes out of the bath. No naked Greeks running down the street.

side of the tub. Before jumping in the tub you put your hand at the other side, doing so you can sense a change in temperature. *Bravo!* You just measured the change in temperature in an *Eulerian** framework. Why? You did not move your hand. You measured something like temperature in a fixed location.

Now let's imagine that you move your hand toward the input of hot water from the faucet. Obviously, the temperature will rise as you move your hand. *Bravo!* You just measured the change of temperature along a path in the bathtub in a *Lagrangian†* framework. Actually, this is a bit of a lie. In fact, Joseph Lagrange *only* allows you to move your hand along the flow of the water. So, a better analogy is that you measure the temperature of the water with your rubber ducky floating in the bathtub. But it is not as appealing as immersing your hand in hot water. I guess that we could attach a thermometer to the ducky and check out the reading by connecting the thermometer using Bluetooth to your iPhone as it bobs around in the bathtub. That is kind of geeky but it is Lagrangian.

In the first case, it took awhile for your hand to warm up, and in the second case, your hand got warmer way faster. This example shows that describing the change of something in a fluid is not so simple. Either you stay put or you move with the flow. But in both cases, you were measuring the change of something concrete over time: temperature. Just in a different way.

Mathematicians like to generalize stuff like that. There are other properties than temperature that can change in a fluid over time. For example, oil spills, the density of fish, the amount of foam, plankton, garbage, and so on. The motion of all these quantities changes over time while immersed in a fluid. Let us denote any of these quantities by the letter *s*. That is, the beauty of mathematical abstraction: *s* can stand for any of these things and much more. It can stand for pretty much anything that lives in a fluid really. This can even include the density of all the readers of this book.

In serious science, *s* has to be something you can measure, though. It cannot stand for the density of "three-headed and four-legged angels," for example. On the other hand, if you are doing computer animation like we do you can pretty much immerse anything into a fluid including a "six-headed troll with one foot."

---

* Named after Euler.
† Named after Joseph-Louis Lagrange (1736–1813). He was a genius French mathematician. Actually, he was born in Sardinia (now part of Italy) under the name Giuseppe Lodovico Lagrangia.

Let's get down to business, serious and geeky again.

We denote the Eulerian measure of change of some quantity labeled s by

$$Euler(s).$$

It measures the change of a quantity s at a single location in the fluid over time. Similarly, let us denote the Langrangian measure of change by

$$Lagrange(v, s).$$

Here, v denotes the velocity of the fluid. The quantity s can be the temperature or the density of some dye injected into the fluid. I know that I said this before, but it is good to repeat it again.

And here comes the *coup de génie** of Euler.

No really.

Euler went one step further and considered s to be the velocity itself. This is when the nonlinearity business kicks in: the change of velocity depends on the velocity itself. He found an equation for

$$Lagrange(v, v).$$

The reason that this change is nonlinear is that the velocity shows up twice in the expression. The change is affecting the change. Sounds weird no? Nonlinearity is weird, and linearity is also weird because it is the exception. Therefore, nature is weird, but geniuses have found tools to harness some parts of nature's weird behavior.

Let's first consider the evolution of some dye of paint in an ideal fluid. Recall that ideal fluids do not dissipate, they roam forever, and thus, they preserve the area of anything dropped into them. Well, Euler formalized this by an equation that I will paraphrase as:

The density of paint will not change when following the flow of an ideal fluid.

And the math version is the *Lagrangian measure of change of the paint density flowing along the velocity is equal to zero.*

$$Lagrange(v, \text{paint density}) = 0.$$

---

* In English: *Stroke of genius.* It just sounds better in French.

The equation is more concise and saves us from typing in long complicated phrases.

Remember that Euler dealt with ideal fluids and also only dealt with an initial amount of paint. Consequently, the initial paint gets moved around mindlessly through the fluid without losing its initial density.

This is the ideal case with no external forces, sources of density, and sinks.

A good way to introduce external factors influencing fluids is through an artistic process called *paper marbling*. This is a technique that uses a liquid and various paints to create funky patterns. Figure 3.17 shows how they are created. And Figure 3.18 shows three examples. These *fluid textures* are usually created to decorate the first pages of some serious old

Marbreur de Papier.

FIGURE 3.17   The process of creating marbling art.

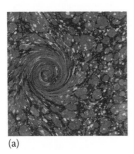 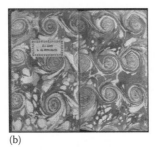 

(a)　　　　　　　　　　(b)　　　　　　　　　　(c)

FIGURE 3.18 Three examples of marbling art. Marbled endpaper from a book bound in France around (a) 1880 and (b) 1735 (detail). (c) Album cover "L'invitation au suicide" (1984 From New Rose Records, Paris, France).

books as shown in Figure 3.18a,b or the cover of the Punk/Goth French band from the 1980s called *Jad Wio* (Figure 3.18c). Alternatively, marbling can be practiced just for *art for art's sake*.

Very briefly, this is how the marbling technique works.

A shallow tray is first filled with water as shown in Figure 3.17. Then, paints of different colors are injected into the fluid, normally with a brush. In many cases, chemicals are added to make sure the paints do not dissolve too fast. So things are closer to *ideal*. Patterns are then created by either blowing on the paint or using a fine filament like a swine's hair to stir the fluid. The pattern is then transferred to a piece of paper or cloth.

The equation for the fluid's motion in this case is like this:

$$\text{Lagrange}(v, v) = \text{blowing and stirring with a swine's hair}$$

It says:

Blow on and stir the fluid with a swine's hair and the fluid's velocity will evolve in a manner that we can predict.

Consequently, the distribution of the density of paints immersed in the fluid will be affected and create funky fluid patterns. Science meets art. Da Vinci would be thrilled.

More generally, Euler's equation states that the change of velocity in an ideal fluid is caused by *external forces* like blowing, stirring with a swine's hair, smashing, throwing stuff, spitting, cannonballing, and so on. All of these external effects are forces that we can add up and denote by a single vector field f. Therefore, Euler's second equation can be written more generally as:

$$\text{Lagrange}(v, v) = f.$$

That is it for ideal fluids. This is not how Euler's second equation is usually written in mathematics, engineering, and physics books. It is my version. But this description is sufficient to explain how to write code that creates cool animations of fluids. I like to do things differently.

I cannot believe I haven't written a single partial differential so far in this book. It is so tempting.* We will show the usual notations when we go to the beach in Puerto Vallarta, Mexico below.

To summarize: Euler found the fundamental equation for the evolution of an ideal fluid over time. It involves a nonlinear process of velocities affecting velocities and being affected by external forces. Combined with his incompressibility condition, we have an exact description for an ideal incompressible fluid.

3.5 NEWTON AND VISCOSITY

> I can calculate the motion of heavenly bodies, but not the madness of people.
>
> SIR ISAAC NEWTON (FAMOUS ENGLISH
> MATHEMATICIAN AND PHYSICIST)

Sir Isaac Newton (1642–1727) is of course famous for his three laws of motion and his invention of calculus. He made many more contributions in many other fields of mathematics and physics; most famously, his theory of gravity can predict the motion of planets and other bodies. Everyone knows the probably apocryphal story that he understood gravity when an apple fell on his head one day. This was another Eureka moment that changed science forever.

His contribution to the fluid puzzle is the introduction of the concept of *viscosity*: one of the things that make fluids nonideal. If you stir a fluid with a swine's hair, it will eventually come to a rest state. It depends on the fluid. It will take longer for water than honey. The difference is that water has a lower viscosity than honey. The less viscous a fluid is, the livelier its motion is. The more viscous a fluid is, the slower its motion is. Slam dancing is less viscous than line dancing. That is why I used to like slam dancing over line dancing.

---

* I feel like the French writer Georges Perec who wrote a novel called *La Disparition* that does not contain a single instance of the most popular letter "e" in the French language. It is actually a good read. This book has been cleverly translated into English under the title *A Void*. This footnote by the way used the letter "e" 39 times.

To describe viscosity, it is easier to start with a similar effect that involves simpler quantities like temperature or a density moving in a liquid.

And bugs!

Consider this simple experiment: drop a spot of ink in a glass of water. The dot of ink will slowly get fuzzier over time. Assuming that the spot of ink is red, then eventually the water in your glass will look sort of pink-ish. The process of going from a concentrated dot of red paint that results in a pink mixture is called *diffusion*. This is a process, meaning that it describes something that evolves over time.

Sounds familiar right?

Diffusion is everywhere. Let us say you heat up a metal bar on one end. Then, eventually, the heat will diffuse to the other end and the bar will reach a uniform temperature. Smell is like that too. If a person with a strong perfume odor walks by you, it takes a certain amount of time before you can smell it.* It has to diffuse through the air. The closer you are to the person, the stronger the smell and the more immediate is that sensation.

The important point here is that perfume loses its potency when traveling through the air. In an ideal fluid, as we have seen earlier, it would just mix with the air but its potency would be unaffected.

Remember that the equation for some substance injected into an ideal fluid is

$$\text{Lagrange}(v, \text{perfume}) = 0.$$

This does not hold in the real world. We have to change that "0" to something else to account for diffusion.

How does one describe the process of diffusion?

Let's look at the motion of a single pesky bug crawling around your floor as depicted in Figure 3.19.† The bug just aimlessly crawls around in a seemingly erratic manner. Next, consider the case of many bugs all starting at a bounded location and set free to crawl as they wish. Their motions are erratic and independent of each other. These bugs are not ants, alright, with their complicated emergent behaviors. Our bugs are dumb, even collectively.

---

* Other examples include bad breath, the smell of grass after a rainstorm, or the scent of a fine Bordeaux wine when you sniff it.
† The usual example is that of a drunken mathematician attempting to get home from a bar.

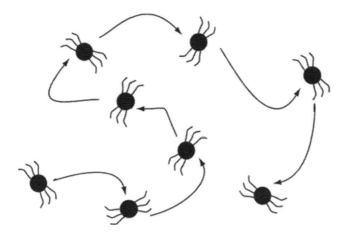

FIGURE 3.19   A bug crawling around in an incoherent pattern.

Mathematicians call the motion of these bugs as being *random.** They all perform a selfish *random walk* on their own: "Sorry excuse me, sorry excuse me, coming through. Thank you. I will just crawl over you."

Now enters the concept of a *density of bugs.*

> Where there are a lot of bugs the density is high, and where there are a few bugs the density is low.

Figure 3.20 shows the evolution of many bugs being initially dropped in a tiny location. Notice how the bugs disperse over time. For each snapshot of their random crawl, we show the circle that bounds all the bugs. No bug is outside of the circle. This is not some boundary from which they cannot escape. I did not say: "no bug is *allowed* outside of the circle." It is just a measure of their spread. It is not a rubbery Petri dish. What one can observe is that the circle in general grows in size.

Consequently, since the number of bugs is constant, the density of bugs within the circle decreases. Yes, the *density* of bugs not the *number* of bugs. We are not killing any of them (yet). The bugs are just spread over a larger area.

More specifically, the number of bugs divided by the area of the bounding circle tends to decrease.

---

* According to the *Online Etymology Dictionary*: "having no definite aim or purpose," 1650s, from at random (1560s), "at great speed" (thus, "carelessly, haphazardly"), alteration of Middle English noun random "impetuosity, speed" (c. 1300), from Old French *randon* "rush, disorder, force, impetuosity," from *randir* "to run fast," from Frankish **rant* "a running" or some other Germanic source, from Proto-Germanic **randa* (cognates: Old High German rennen "to run," Old English rinnan "to flow, to run"; see run [v.]).

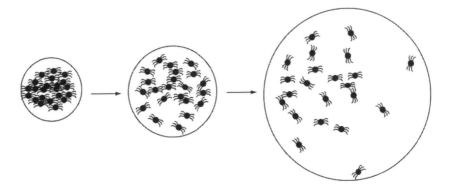

FIGURE 3.20   Many bugs crawling around over time.

That is diffusion in a nutshell.

Of course, we could have chosen drunkards, perfume particles, crack-heads, or dust particles instead of bugs, anything really that wanders about in a seemingly random manner.

There actually is a relation between the crawling of the bugs and the radius of the bug-bounding circle over time. What could affect the size of the radius? Obviously, a major factor is the speed of these pesky bugs that crawl around. If these bugs were all asleep nothing would happen. In that case, the circle would remain unchanged. Once the bugs wake up and start crawling around, the radius of the circle will start to expand at a rate related to their average velocity of crawling. Here is the actual relationship*:

$$R^2 = 4D_{thing}t.$$

where
    R denotes the radius
    D_{thing} characterizes the rate of diffusion of a *thing*
    t denotes time, of course

It is instructive to find out what the units of D_{thing} are. From the equation, it follows that in terms of units $[L^2] = [D]\,[T]$. Therefore, the units of the rate of diffusion are $[D] = [L^2]/[T]$. Hence, D_{thing} characterizes how many *thingy*

---

* I am just stating this equation "as is." Einstein derived it in 1905 in his paper where he made a good case for the existence of particles via *Brownian motion*. For 3D diffusion it is $R^2 = 6D_{thing}\,t$. In general, for a n-dimensional space the formula is $R^2 = 2nD_{thing}\,t$. This equation is probabilistic. It actually states that the **average** radius behaves in this way.

dinghies flow through an area over time. In this book, we will assume that it is a constant for a given phenomenon and it is the same for the entire population. It assumes that every bug behaves in the same manner.* This is less likely so for the hordes of drunken mathematicians being kicked out of the same bar after last call.† But one can always take an average of their behaviors and come up with a single diffusion rate. My guess is that

$$D_{bugs} > D_{drunken\ mathematicians}$$

Crawling bugs is the *microscopic* point of view of diffusion.

The *macroscopic* point of view on the other hand, only deals with densities and diffusion rates: of bugs, drunken mathematicians, or perfume particles and what not. This approach is typical in science: go from something *fundamental* and then move onto something more manageable by averaging or using some other form of approximation. This procedure sometimes goes by the fancy name of *homogenization*. Small-scale details, such as bugs crawling, are homogenized into a time-evolving density. Bye individual bugs and welcome to a bug milkshake.‡

At the macroscopic level, we do not care about the individual paths. We only care about the rate of diffusion *D* that characterizes the collective behavior of the individuals. When looking at clouds we do not see individual water droplets, rather we see white fluffy things floating and evolving in the sky.

The process of diffusion of a density over time is very akin to the condition of incompressibility that we mentioned earlier in this book. Remember incompressibility means: what flows in has to come out. The difference is that incompressibility is instantaneous. Diffusion at the macroscopic level is different. It is a process that evolves over time just like an ideal fluid.

As shown in Figure 3.21, each piece of space exchanges densities with its neighbors. It is a two-way process. The first piece is called *thing one*. It will give some density to another piece called *thing two* and *thing two* will give

---

* It doesn't have to be a constant. The diffusion rate can vary over time and spatial locations. Scientists can deal with it. But I want to focus on the essentials in this book without unnecessary complications.

† This bar would have to be in the middle of nowhere. Since sidewalks, buildings, cars, buses, trams, police officers, monuments, and garbage cans, for example, would get in the way of a truly drunken mathematically rigorous random walk.

‡ Politics is like that too. Politicians don't care about a single individual. But they care about a large collection of the individuals who will vote for them.

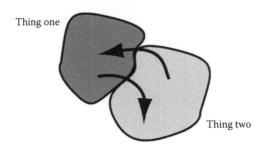

Thing one

Thing two

FIGURE 3.21 The densities of thing one and thing two exchange densities through diffusion.

some density to *thing one*. These exchanges go on over time, and eventually, every piece will have the same density. From then on, no exchanges will take place. That's it. The final state of the density is called the *steady state* and it is completely determined by the initial densities and the diffusion rate.

Calling these pieces *thing one* and *thing two* is of course a reference to the legendary book that was both written and illustrated by Dr. Seuss: *The Cat in the Hat Comes Back*. It is a perfect illustration of how pink liquid stuff does not lose mass but spreads all over the place. It diffuses in a playful manner throughout the story. It is one of the best introductions to diffusion that I can think of. It made a lasting impression on me ever since I read it as a kid.*

In between thing one and thing two, we can define a *flux* of density through their common boundary. Obviously, the flux depends on the diffusion rate and the difference in density between the pieces:

The flux of density equals the diffusion rate times the difference in density between the pieces.

This is actually known as *Ficks's law*. It is named after the German physiologist, Adolf Eugen Fick (1829–1901). In the following equation:

$$\text{Flux}_{12} = D \times (\rho_1 - \rho_2).$$

Consider two simple cases: if the density of thing two is zero and the density of thing one is nonzero, then the flux is in the direction of thing one to thing two. On the other hand, if the density of thing one is zero and the density of thing two is nonzero, then the flux is in the opposite direction. In general, the flux is a combination of these two cases. Consequently, there will be an exchange of densities between the two things.

---

* It also taught me basic English at a young age.

It is pretty intuitive what flux stands for. The name is aptly chosen. But then again what are the units of flux? Let us do the math: $[F] = [D][R] = [L^2/T] \, [M/L^3] = [M/T/L]$. In other words, flux stands for the rate of transfer of the mass of bugs per unit length. So far so good. We have a description for the flux. What about the change in density caused by diffusion? That is, what we are looking for after all.

It is assumed that no density is lost, just exchanges of densities between things occur. The overall sum of densities remains the same. Remember that we do not kill our pesky bugs living in the microscopic world quite yet.

The flux determines what goes into and out of thing one. The same is happening for thing two. The loss or gain of thing one's density is determined by the flux.

> Over some interval of time the density after equals the density before plus the flux between the pieces.

This is Fick's Second Law.

Naively, we can try this relationship:

$$\rho_1^{after} = \rho_1^{before} - \text{Flux}_{12}.$$

But this is not correct since flux does not have the units of density: $[M/L^3]$ does not equal $[M/T/L]$. It works out if we divide the flux by the area of the boundary A_{12} and multiply it by the time interval Δt between *before* and *after*. In that case, we get

$$\rho_1^{after} = \rho_1^{before} - \frac{\Delta t \times \text{Flux}_{12}}{A_{12}}.$$

This equation makes sense. The units now work out: $[M/L^3] = [T][M/T/L]/[L^2] = [M/L^3]$. The change of density depends on the previous density, the time interval, the area, and the flux.

And similarly, for thing two we have that

$$\rho_2^{after} = \rho_2^{before} + \frac{\Delta t \times \text{Flux}_{12}}{A_{12}}.$$

If we combine the two equations it is easy to notice that the total density is conserved:

$$\rho_1^{after} + \rho_2^{after} = \rho_1^{before} + \rho_2^{before}.$$

It is a fair game. This is true for all the other things that are adjacent to things one. It all adds up. That is the diffusion equation. Mass is conserved but it is redistributed between the many parts.

We can now introduce a diffusion function for thing one. It is a function of all the fluxes from all its neighboring things. Not just thing two. Let us say that thing one has n neighboring things. We are really interested in the change of density. A good way to measure change is to take the difference of the densities before and after of thing one over a time step.

$$\frac{\rho_1^{after} - \rho_1^{before}}{\Delta t} = -\text{Flux}_{12} - \text{Flux}_{13} - \cdots - \text{Flux}_{1(n+1)} = D \times \text{Diffuse}(\rho_1).$$

Where we defined

$$\text{Diffuse}(\rho_1) = \frac{1}{A_{12}} \times \rho_2 + \frac{1}{A_{13}} \times \rho_3 + \cdots + \frac{1}{A_{1(n+1)}} \times \rho_{(n+1)} - A \times \rho_1.$$

And

$$A = \frac{1}{A_{12}} + \frac{1}{A_{13}} \cdots + \frac{1}{A_{1(n+1)}}.$$

This was a kind of heavy going in order to describe diffusion mathematically. Intuitive phenomena are not always straightforward to describe precisely. Dr. Seuss did a much more fun job with his cat and the pink stain on the mother's dress.

These relations are for an arbitrary number of pieces exchanging densities. Let us specialize this to the particular situation shown in Figure 3.22. There the pieces are squares and have four neighbors they can exchange densities with. In this special case, $n = 4$. Concretely, the expression for the diffusion in this situation is as follows:

$$\text{Diffuse}(\rho_1) = \frac{1}{h^2} \times (\rho_2 + \rho_3 + \rho_4 + \rho_5 - 4 \times \rho_1).$$

This is a particular case. One can derive diffusion operators for many other configurations of things in a similar manner: 2D space divided into triangles, 3D cubical cells, 3D tetrahedra, 4D hypercubes, and so on.

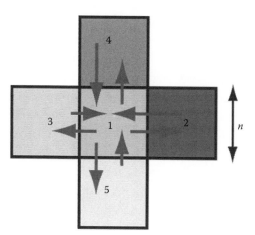

FIGURE 3.22 Diffusion between square pieces in two dimensions.

Combining the diffusion operator with the equation for the change of perfume in an ideal fluid we get

$$\text{Lagrange}(v, \text{perfume}) = D_{perfume} \times \text{Diffuse}(\text{perfume}).$$

So, perfume propagates both because it is carried along with the fluidlike air and because it diffuses. Both factors influence how we experience the smell of a person walking past us with a particular body odor. We replaced the "0" in our previous equation with the diffusion operator. This accounts for the decrease of potency of the odor.

Phew! We finally have something mathematicians call an *advection/ diffusion* equation. Advection is another fancy word for measuring the change of something along the fluid's velocity.

These equations describe the diffusion of quantities modeled by a single value over time and space. This is the macroscopic description of diffusion. No bugs.

What about viscosity that affects the velocity of a fluid? The difference with what we described earlier is that the velocity is a vector quantity. There are two components in two dimensions and three components in three dimensions.

Here is how Newton defined viscosity in his classic *Principia* from 1687:

> The resistance which arises from the lack of slipperiness of the parts of the liquid, other things being equal, is proportional to the velocity with which the parts of the liquid are separated from one another.

The way I see it is that viscosity is simply the diffusion of each component of the velocity's field. Heresy! One can interpret the viscosity usually denoted by v as the rate of diffusion of each component of the velocity.* Of course, this is a simple case. The viscosity might change over time or vary spatially. But again in the spirit of this book we want to keep things simple. In fact, our code uses the same method to animate diffusion for densities and to animate the fluid's velocity with viscosity.

It is the same thing really. Diffusion for temperatures and perfume particles tend to redistribute their properties over time. It is the same with the fluid's velocity. Any fluid that is stirred with a swine's hair will come to a perfect rest state.

So, without further ado here is what I call the *Euler/Newton equation*:

$$\text{Lagrange}(v, v) = v \times \text{Diffuse}(v) + f.$$

This equation pretty much describes most of fluid dynamics: the way fluids evolve over time. Of course, the condition of incompressibility has to be added to it. Remember: what flows in has to come out.†

To summarize: Euler came up with the equations for an ideal fluid and Newton added viscosity. Euler the mathematician and his perfect mathematical fluid model was complemented by the practical approach of Newton. Newton brought us back down to earth where things diffuse and dissipate.

3.6 NAVIER AND STOKES AND THEIR EQUATIONS

Science is a differential equation. Religion is a boundary condition.

ALAN TURING (BRITISH GENIUS MATHEMATICIAN
WHO LAID THE FOUNDATIONS OF COMPUTER SCIENCE)

So, what did Navier and Stokes contribute that Euler and Newton hadn't already done? The equation mentioned previously is usually called the *Navier–Stokes equations*. It is in the plural this time, because when they are written with fancy partial differentials there is a whole bunch of them. Three equal signs in this case for a 3D fluid. These equations are shown in Figure 3.23. They are the standard scriptures of fluid dynamics. They look

---

* This is another Greek symbol. This time it stands for *nu* basically the Greek version of n. Again do not ask me why they chose this symbol.
† At this point, some experts carrying their fluid mechanics luggage will ask: what happened to our dear pressure? If you want the pressure for an incompressible fluid, I can give it to you at any time. See below.

$$\rho\left(\frac{\partial u}{\partial t}+u\frac{\partial u}{\partial x}+v\frac{\partial u}{\partial y}+w\frac{\partial u}{\partial z}\right)=$$

$$\rho g_x-\frac{\partial p}{\partial x}+\frac{\partial}{\partial x}\left[2\mu\frac{\partial u}{\partial x}+\lambda\nabla\cdot V\right]+\frac{\partial}{\partial y}\left[\mu\left(\frac{\partial u}{\partial y}+\frac{\partial v}{\partial x}\right)\right]+\frac{\partial}{\partial z}\left[\mu\left(\frac{\partial w}{\partial x}+\frac{\partial u}{\partial z}\right)\right]$$

$$\rho\left(\frac{\partial v}{\partial t}+u\frac{\partial v}{\partial x}+v\frac{\partial v}{\partial y}+w\frac{\partial v}{\partial z}\right)=$$

$$\rho g_y-\frac{\partial p}{\partial y}+\frac{\partial}{\partial y}\left[2\mu\frac{\partial v}{\partial y}+\lambda\nabla\cdot V\right]+\frac{\partial}{\partial z}\left[\mu\left(\frac{\partial v}{\partial z}+\frac{\partial w}{\partial y}\right)\right]+\frac{\partial}{\partial x}\left[\mu\left(\frac{\partial u}{\partial y}+\frac{\partial v}{\partial x}\right)\right]$$

$$\rho\left(\frac{\partial w}{\partial t}+u\frac{\partial w}{\partial x}+v\frac{\partial w}{\partial y}+w\frac{\partial w}{\partial z}\right)=$$

$$\rho g_z-\frac{\partial p}{\partial z}+\frac{\partial}{\partial z}\left[2\mu\frac{\partial w}{\partial z}+\lambda\nabla\cdot V\right]+\frac{\partial}{\partial x}\left[\mu\left(\frac{\partial w}{\partial x}+\frac{\partial u}{\partial z}\right)\right]+\frac{\partial}{\partial y}\left[\mu\left(\frac{\partial v}{\partial z}+\frac{\partial w}{\partial y}\right)\right]$$

FIGURE 3.23   The usual form of the Navier–Stokes equations in Cartesian coordinates.

pretty complicated right? Still they are simple compared to the *Lagrangian of the Standard Model* in particle physics. Remember Figure 2.12.

The Navier–Stokes equations are even scarier looking when the velocity of the fluid is described in *spherical coordinates*: each point is now described by two angles and a radius. The two angles determine a point on a sphere of radius one and the radius models by how much the point is removed from the center of the sphere. These equations are shown in Figure 3.24.

There is a more compact version however. I was able to write down the Navier–Stokes equations in the sand while on vacation on one of my many trips to the beach of Puerto Vallarta in Mexico as shown in Figure 3.25. I used part of a wooden stick I found to write a more elegant version of the Holy Scriptures. This is of course not my invention. Just a standard

$$r:\rho\left(\frac{\partial u_r}{\partial t}+u_r\frac{\partial u_r}{\partial r}+\frac{u_\phi}{r\sin(\theta)}\frac{\partial u_r}{\partial\phi}+\frac{u_\theta}{r}\frac{\partial u_r}{\partial\theta}-\frac{u_\phi^2+u_\theta^2}{r}\right)=-\frac{\partial p}{\partial r}+\rho g_r+$$

$$\mu\left[\frac{1}{r^2}\frac{\partial}{\partial r}\left(r^2\frac{\partial u_r}{\partial r}\right)+\frac{1}{r^2\sin(\theta)^2}\frac{\partial^2 u_r}{\partial\phi^2}+\frac{1}{r^2\sin(\theta)}\frac{\partial}{\partial\theta}\left(\sin(\theta)\frac{\partial u_r}{\partial\theta}\right)-2\frac{u_r+\frac{\partial u_\theta}{\partial\theta}+u_\theta\cot(\theta)}{r^2}-\frac{2}{r^2\sin(\theta)}\frac{\partial u_\phi}{\partial\phi}\right]$$

$$\phi:\rho\left(\frac{\partial u_\phi}{\partial t}+u_r\frac{\partial u_\phi}{\partial r}+\frac{u_\phi}{r\sin(\theta)}\frac{\partial u_\phi}{\partial\phi}+\frac{u_\theta}{r}\frac{\partial u_\phi}{\partial\theta}+\frac{u_r u_\phi+u_\phi u_\theta\cot(\theta)}{r}\right)=-\frac{1}{r\sin(\theta)}\frac{\partial p}{\partial\phi}+\rho g_\phi+$$

$$\mu\left[\frac{1}{r^2}\frac{\partial}{\partial r}\left(r^2\frac{\partial u_\phi}{\partial r}\right)+\frac{1}{r^2\sin(\theta)^2}\frac{\partial^2 u_\phi}{\partial\phi^2}+\frac{1}{r^2\sin(\theta)}\frac{\partial}{\partial\theta}\left(\sin(\theta)\frac{\partial u_\phi}{\partial\theta}\right)+\frac{2\sin(\theta)\frac{\partial u_r}{\partial\phi}+2\cos(\theta)\frac{\partial u_\theta}{\partial\phi}-u_\phi}{r^2\sin(\theta)^2}\right]$$

$$\theta:\rho\left(\frac{\partial u_\theta}{\partial t}+u_r\frac{\partial u_\theta}{\partial r}+\frac{u_\phi}{r\sin(\theta)}\frac{\partial u_\theta}{\partial\phi}+\frac{u_\theta}{r}\frac{\partial u_\theta}{\partial\theta}+\frac{u_r u_\theta-u_\phi^2\cot(\theta)}{r}\right)=-\frac{1}{r}\frac{\partial p}{\partial\theta}+\rho g_\theta+$$

$$\mu\left[\frac{1}{r^2}\frac{\partial}{\partial r}\left(r^2\frac{\partial u_\theta}{\partial r}\right)+\frac{1}{r^2\sin(\theta)^2}\frac{\partial^2 u_\theta}{\partial\phi^2}+\frac{1}{r^2\sin(\theta)}\frac{\partial}{\partial\theta}\left(\sin(\theta)\frac{\partial u_\theta}{\partial\theta}\right)+\frac{2}{r^2}\frac{\partial u_r}{\partial\theta}-\frac{u_\theta+2\cos(\theta)\frac{\partial u_\phi}{\partial\phi}}{r^2\sin(\theta)^2}\right].$$

FIGURE 3.24   The Navier–Stokes equations in spherical coordinates.

FIGURE 3.25   The Navier–Stokes equations written on the beach in Mexico.

condensed version. But it was fun to write these equations down on the beach of Puerto Vallarta.

Why did Navier and Stokes get all the credit and not Euler and Newton?

Claude-Louis Navier (1785–1836) was a French engineer who studied at the *École des Ponts et Chaussées*.* He went onto become a mathematician, however, and he was the first person to combine Euler and Newton's work to formulate the equations shown in Figure 3.23.

Independently, in Cambridge, England,† Sir George Gabriel Stokes (1819–1903) found the same equations but using more conventional techniques. His derivation is what you can find in standard textbooks unlike the *voodoo* derivations in this book that you are reading now.

There you go. That is the reason why the Holy Scriptures of fluid dynamics are called the *Navier–Stokes equations*. It is a perfect compromise between Continental French and Island British mathematical rivalry.

Just for fun I created a *bitstrips*‡ cartoon depicted in Figure 3.26. This is a web-based cartoon creation tool that my daughter introduced me to. My daughter Gillian is featured in the cartoon alongside Lenny, Izzy, Claude, and George.

---

* In English: "School of Bridges and Pavements." This is important stuff to study in order to help people move around in France: lots of rivers, mountains, lakes, monuments, and aggressive drivers.
† Stokes was born in Ireland, however.
‡ http://www.bitstrips.com.

FIGURE 3.26   A brief history of the Navier–Stokes equations.

The Navier–Stokes equations can also make you rich and famous. In 2000, the *Clay Mathematics Institute* (*CMI*) proposed eight outstanding problems: the so-called millennium problems. Anyone who solves one of these problems will receive a million dollars.

Only one millennium problem has been solved thus far. This exploit is due to the eccentric Russian mathematician Grigori Perelman. He solved the so-called *Poincaré conjecture* which very roughly states that any 3D shape with no holes can be transformed continuously into a 3D sphere. This problem was previously solved for all other dimensions. Surprisingly, the Poincaré conjecture was easier to prove for higher dimensions. Higher dimensions provide more space and freedom apparently. There is more space to move stuff around.

Perelman did not care for the money and refused to accept the million dollars. Not only that but he also refused to accept the Fields Medal (remember the gold medal with the stern-looking Archimedes on it). Therefore, he did not get rich but definitely became famous. He is a humble man. As far as I can tell, his point is that he only closed some gaps in proofs that were based on a huge amount of previous work. Therefore, Perelman concluded that he should not get the prize. This is tricky. Research is never done in complete isolation. Apparently, Perelman now lives with his mom in a tiny apartment in St. Petersburg, Russia.

Another one of the millennium prizes concerns the Navier–Stokes equations. The problem on the official CMI web site* is stated as follows:

> Prove or give a counter-example of the following statement.
> In three space dimensions and time, given an initial velocity field, there exists a vector velocity and a scalar pressure field, which are both smooth and globally defined, that solve the Navier–Stokes equations.

In two dimensions, this problem was proven by the Russian mathematician, Olga Ladyzhenskaya, in 1969. Three-dimensional flows are inherently more difficult than 2D ones. Just as in the case of the Poincaré *spheres*.

The Navier–Stokes problem in three dimensions is still wide open. Recently, a mathematician from Kazakhstan named Mukhtarbay Otelbaev proposed a proof, but it is only available in Russian. Then, Terence Tao, a famous Australian mathematician who works at UCLA, proposed an

---

* http://www.claymath.org/millennium-problems.

argument that this problem could not be settled. Terrence Tao accepted the Fields Medal in 2006 for some other breakthroughs he worked on. The saga continues as of the writing of this book.

To summarize: Navier and Stokes put all the pieces together provided by Newton and Euler. If you can prove that these equations are well behaved, you might even reap a million bucks and be famous even if you are over 40 years old.

We now have to deal with the Achilles Heel of Fluid Dynamics: *boundary conditions*.

Boundary conditions are the hardest part of coding fluids simulations and getting it right. At least that is my experience.

In some of my other research, it is even trickier. The interaction of light between surfaces is all about boundaries: reflection, refraction, scattering, absorption, and so on. Those boundary conditions are much harder than the ones encountered in fluid animation. But that is not the topic of this book.

3.7 BOUNDARIES, BOUNDARIES, BOUNDARIES, BOUNDARIES, AND BOUNDARIES

I like pushing boundaries.

LADY GAGA (AMERICAN POP STAR)

It is interesting that viscosity, usually a damping mechanism, is here responsible for the generation of a geometrical progression of eddies.

KEITH MOFFATT (FAMOUS SCOTTISH FLUID
DYNAMICS EXPERT)

Thus far, we have described fluids without boundaries. We assumed that our bugs could crawl endlessly without bounds. Well guess what? The bugs can crawl all they want but they are confined to a room bounded by walls, humans, a dog, or a bed. This limits their ability to crawl. What follows is about what happens when the bugs hit the wall.

It turns out that there are many different boundary conditions for fluids. Let us list them straight ahead, and later, we will provide examples.

These are the five exclusive (XOR)* commandments for bugs at a specific boundary:

1. Thou shalt not cross this boundary.

2. Thou shalt not cross this boundary and be at rest when hitting this boundary.

3. Thou shalt be thrown into a fluid with a specific velocity through this boundary.

4. Thou shalt be free to escape the boundary.

5. Thou shalt be transported from this boundary to the opposite boundary.

In fluid dynamics speak, it is more like this:

1. SLIP

2. NOSLIP

3. INFLOW

4. OUTFLOW

5. PERIODIC

Alternatively, the different boundary conditions are illustrated in Figure 3.27 using pesky bugs.

In computer animation, the *slip* boundary condition rules. It just says that nothing can leave or enter a boundary. When you are pouring a liquid in a container you do not want the liquid to leak out of it. Unless of course you deliberately poke a hole in the container so that water will pour out on purpose. Remember Bernoulli's tank? Technically, when a bug encounters a wall it is only allowed to move sideways from the wall not through the wall.

---

* XOR stands for **exclusive or.** The way the word "or" is usually used is as an inclusive "or." As in "Joe had a banana for breakfast" or "Joe had a latté." Both can be true at the same time. Not so for the exclusive "or" denoted by XOR. For example: "Joe had a banana at exactly 10 a.m." XOR "Joe had a pear at exactly 10 a.m." Joe, like most people, cannot stuff a banana and a pear in his face at exactly the same time, especially at precisely 10 a.m.

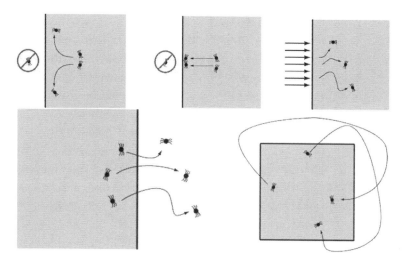

FIGURE 3.27 Boundary conditions for bugs. Slip, no slip, inflow, outflow, and periodic.

The *no slip* boundary condition means that the bugs will get stuck if they reach the wall. This is actually what happens in real fluids. Consider a ceiling fan. Check out the top of the blades. I can bet that there is dust on them. There is on mine. Even though the blades have been flapping around keeping you cool on those hot summer nights, they accumulate dust on their surface. When no slip rules, the dust particles like the bugs get stuck at the boundary. The velocity of the air at the boundary is zero. Hence, there is no escape. Until you dust the fan blades of course.

The no slip condition is the right physical thing to enforce. How come we do not use it in computer animation? The short answer is as follows: because it slows down the flow near boundaries. We do not like that. We want *lively* flows. In engineering and other *serious* applications, it is important however to enforce the no slip boundary condition.*

The *inflow* boundary condition means that at the boundary a certain velocity flows in. Think of a wind tunnel. It is a constant flow of air coming in from the boundary. Consequently, our bugs are blown all over the place as shown in Figure 3.27.

---

* Another fun story: the fluid feature of our MAYA software has a no slip boundary option. Almost 10 years after we released Fluid Effects, we did a test with no slip and it crashed the software. As far as I know, none of our customers had reported a crash in this situation. That is because no one went to the *Church of no slip.*

The *outflow* condition means that the bugs are allowed to leave the domain. Yes! We are free. However, little is known about their fate when they cross the boundary. Maybe their fate is like those poor lemmings that ran off a cliff. For incompressible flows with an inflow boundary condition, you need to have an outflow condition somewhere else. If not you will be in trouble, like when Pascal's barrel burst. But viscosity can come to the rescue.

The case of *periodic* boundary condition is interesting. It is a nonphysical condition, but it is useful in practice. In fact, I will describe a solver that entirely relies on this condition and that uses some very cool math later. In Figure 3.27 (bottom right), it seems that the bugs travel in outer space to reach the opposite boundary. This is not actually the case. All you have to do is to glue opposite sides of the square and now the bugs are free to crawl from one side to the other in a seamless manner. This situation is illustrated in Figure 3.28.

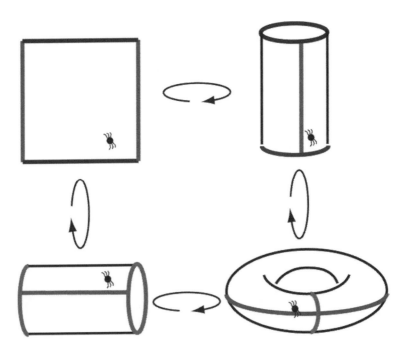

FIGURE 3.28 Periodic boundary conditions can be visualized by gluing together opposite boundaries. By first gluing two opposite boundaries, we get a cylinder (top right and bottom left). When gluing all opposite boundaries, we get a donut. The bug can wander freely.

Think of a donut with bugs crawling on it. Yikes. Mathematicians call a donut a *torus*. Any shape really with only one hole is a torus to a particular type of mathematician called a *topologist*.*

A torus and a donut are the same to a mathematician because they only have one hole.

There are other boundary conditions, of course, but these are the ones I have dealt with and turned into computer code.

The no slip condition is really the most realistic one. But it is not the one we use very often in computer animation. However, I want to spend some time describing one example that deals with a combination of boundary conditions called the *lid-driven cavity flow*. The setting is depicted in Figure 3.29.

This is an imaginary fluid made up by mathematicians. First, it is two dimensional. The velocity is denoted by the tuple (u,v). Remember that it is a vector field described by two numbers. The left, right, and bottom boundaries have a no slip condition. And the top boundary has an inflow boundary condition. This is a bit of a misnomer, because in this case the flow is sideways. There is no outflow. But viscosity takes care of that. Viscosity will redistribute any inflow. In fact, it turns out that

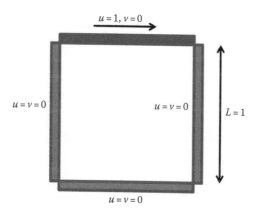

FIGURE 3.29 The setup of the lid-driven cavity problem.

---

* A popular albeit somewhat crude joke that mathematicians like to tell goes as follows. "A topologist is someone who can't tell the difference between his ass and **one** hole in the ground, but who can tell the difference between his ass and **two** holes in the ground." A respectable engineer at a math conference I attended started his keynote talk with this joke. LMFAO.

the flow reaches a *steady state*. After awhile, the flow settles into a stable pattern like we observed with diffusion. This pattern is a function of the viscosity of the fluid.

Ahem, not quite. We have to introduce a fundamental quantity that characterizes the behavior of a fluid first.

Sir George Gabriel Stokes (the Stokes in Navier–Stokes) introduced a *dimensionless* quantity called the *Reynolds number* named after Osborne Reynolds (1842–1912) who popularized the concept. Dimensionless, "that which has no units," means no meters, no kilograms, and no seconds. It is just a *pure* number. Here is the definition:

$$\text{Reynolds number} = \frac{\text{typical velocity} \times \text{typical length}}{\text{viscosity}}.$$

Let's verify that it really has no units. Velocity has units of [L/T], length has units of [L], and viscosity has units of [L²/T] (remember it is a diffusion rate). So if we put it all together, we get that [Reynolds number] = [L/T][L]/[L²/T] = 1. So, yes indeed the Reynolds number has no units. Why do we care about the Reynolds number? The reason is that this number allows us to compare different flows with the same Reynolds number. If they have the same Reynolds number, they sort of behave in the same manner.

To illustrate this concept, let us fill up a bathtub and let the water settle.* Now imagine filling up a gigantic pool the size of Switzerland with water. The viscosity of the bathtub and the pool are the same since they both contain water (no soap this time). This situation is shown in Figure 3.30, and on the right-hand side, there is an outline of the country of Switzerland and below it is a gigantic pool. Of course the bathtub and the pool are not drawn to scale. The bathtub is 2 m in length (I wish I had one of these) and the Swiss pool is approximately 200,000 m wide. So, 100,000 bathtubs lined up can cross Switzerland without accounting for the Alps of course. We assume that Switzerland is as flat as Holland in this case.

Everyone agrees that it would be quite a challenge to build a pool the size of Switzerland.† The beauty is that we do not have to. We can do experiments in our bathtub that can be applied to the gigantic Swiss pool as well.

---

* This time it will involve a Swiss person not a Greek.
† It might be possible in Saudi Arabia but not in Switzerland.

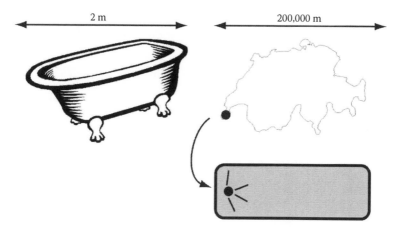

FIGURE 3.30   A bathtub and a pool the size of Switzerland.

How?

We just have to make sure that the Reynolds number of the bathtub is the same as the Reynolds number of the Swiss pool. Since the viscosities are the same and the lengths are given, we are left with the following condition on the velocities by equating their Reynolds numbers:

Velocity of the bathtub × 2 = velocity of the pool × 200,000.

Let's say you wanted to measure the effect of a *Genevois** cannonballing on the left side of the Swiss pool and calculate the effect that it causes. Let us additionally assume that the velocity created by the impact is 1 m/second in the gigantic Swiss pool. Thanks to Reynolds, we can reproduce this experiment in the bathtub. However, it is going to get messy. In order to get the same Reynolds number in the bathtub, the velocity caused by the impact would have to be

$$\text{Velocity of the bathtub} = 1 \times \frac{200,000}{2} = 100,000 \text{ m/second.}$$

That is wickedly fast and probably impossible to accomplish. Compare this velocity with the speed of sound which is approximately

---

* A Genevois is someone from the city of Geneva, which is located all the way to the left of Switzerland. The size of the Genevois is not drawn to scale. In the picture it seems like we are throwing the entire town of Geneva in the Swiss pool.

340 m/second.* Flows that are faster than the speed of sound are called *supersonic*.† Bullets (fired, not thrown) are supersonic, for example. I will not deal with such flows which are quite complicated. I like to keep things simple. There are a few depictions of supersonic fluid flows in Milton Van Dyke's book.

Another way to replicate the giant Swiss pool experiment is to fill the bath with a liquid that has a lower viscosity than water. Hence, in this case, the velocities and the lengths are fixed but we have to search for a fluid that has a much lower viscosity than water. How much lower? We can use the expression of the Reynolds number again. In this case, assuming that we stir both the gigantic pool and the bathtub with a swine's hair at 1 m/second, we get that

$$\frac{2}{\text{viscosity of the fluid in the bathtub}} = \frac{200,000}{\text{viscosity of water}}.$$

Therefore, the viscosity of this imaginary fluid that we will pour in the bathtub would have to be 100,000 times smaller than the viscosity of water. We could try air since it is a fluid but it is only a thousand times less viscous than water.

In conclusion, I do not think the bathtub will do the job to replicate the gigantic Swiss pool experiment.

What about an Olympic-sized pool which is 50 m in length? Now, we need to move the water in the bathtub to a velocity of 25 m/second. This is more manageable but still it is quite fast. Do not try this at your local community center.

To summarize: The Reynolds number characterizes one aspect of the behavior of a fluid. It helps to realize fluids with different scales and viscosities. But it is not always feasible in practice.

Now, let us get back to our lid-driven cavity experiment. Remember that the flow is two dimensional and has to be zero on three boundaries

---

* It is fast, but not as fast as the speed of light. Assuming your cell phone connection is speedy. Then it will take less time for your voice to travel to someone else's phone across the street than to yell at the same person directly.
† Here is another dimensionless number for you: the *Mach number*. It is the ratio between some speed and the speed of sound. Supersonic means that the Mach number is bigger than one. This is also known as the *sound barrier*. Chuck Yeager was the first pilot to go past the sound barrier by flying a custom made Bell X-1 in 1947. His Mach number was 1.06.

and it is stirred sideways at the top, a mathematician's concoction. This is a famous benchmark for fluid codes. It means that you spend weeks writing fluid code and now you want to know whether you are doing it the right way. You enter the lid-driven cavity boundary conditions in your program and then run it and check out the results. Next, it is important to check whether your results agree with the existing literature. These papers have been scrutinized and judged by other experts and eventually end up being published in journals.* The results in these papers are usually created using computer code. Some papers include actual physical experiments and these are approximations since 2D fluids, strictly speaking, do not exist in nature.

Figure 3.31 shows the results for the lid-driven cavity flow for different values of the Reynolds number from a respectable source—starting from a Reynolds number equal to zero (top left) to a Reynolds number equal to 10,000 (bottom right).

The lines in the pictures in this figure are *streamlines*: paths traced out by bugs or rubber duckies trapped in the liquid. They are *portraits* of the flow for different values of the Reynolds number. This is one of the many ways one can visualize a fluid. One thing we can notice is that more vortexes appear as the Reynolds number is increased. This phenomenon is called a *Hopf Bifurcation*† by mathematicians.

Actually, for every value of the Reynolds number, the portraits in Figure 3.31 have an infinite amount of vortexes. They just get exaggerated when the Reynolds number is increased.

Figure 3.32 shows a cartoon of the lid-driven cavity flow. Because of the discontinuity at the two lower corners, a cascade of vortices spinning in opposite directions is created. The vortices diminish in strength as well and there are an infinite number of them. In the right of Figure 3.32, we show a blowup of the right bottom. And this can be repeated *ad infinitum*. As with Bernoulli's infinite sums, this goes on and on. Of course in actual experiments, the smaller vortices eventually get blurred due to the effect of turbulence. Mathematically, they all still exist.

---

* This is the *peer reviewing* process. Publish or perish. These are not journals you can buy in your usual corner store. At any rate, these days everything is online. They are expensive though: about $20 for an article. But if you are a student at some university or an adjunct professor as I am, it is free. So kids, stay in school!

† These bifurcations are named after the great German mathematician Heinz Hopf (1894–1971).

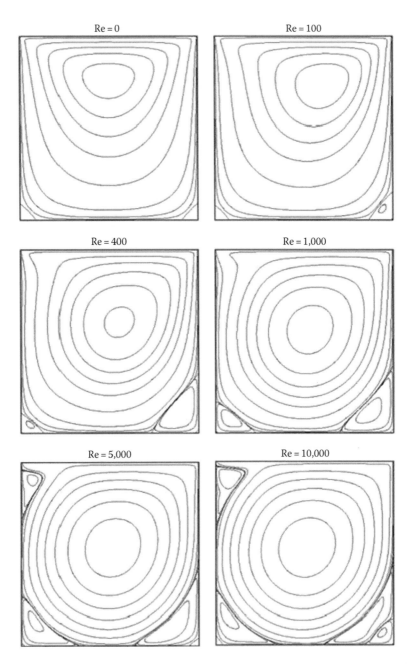

FIGURE 3.31 Lid-driven cavity solution for different values of the Reynolds number. (From Samin, M. and Owens, R.G., *Int. J. Numer. Methods Fluids*, 42, 66, 2003. With permission.)

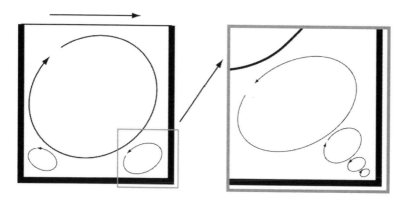

FIGURE 3.32 The lid-driven cavity flow generates an infinite number of counter-rotating vortices.

It is hoped that this example shows that boundaries are tricky and can give rise to exotic behaviors. Do not underestimate the role that boundaries play in trying to write fluid animation code. It is the hardest part.

To summarize: Boundary conditions are tricky. Do not underestimate them. They are only lower-dimensional boundaries but they affect the motion of the larger fluid contained in them in a crucial manner. In fact, they are in charge. The little guys control the bigger guys.

CHAPTER 4

The Early Days of Computational Fluid Dynamics

Young man, in mathematics you don't understand things. You just get used to them.

JOHN VON NEUMANN (HUNGARIAN-AMERICAN
GENIUS MATHEMATICIAN)

Richardson was a very interesting and original character who seldom thought on the same lines as his contemporaries and often was not understood by them.

SIR GEOFFREY INGRAM TAYLOR (ENGLISH
MATHEMATICIAN AND PHYSICIST AND AN EXPERT IN
FLUID DYNAMICS)

Can com'uters be able to mult'ply: 9999999999999999999999999999
99999999999 point 999999999999999999999999999999999999
99 by undredundredundredundredundredundredundred point 8889999
99991212121214141414...

Yes! (A scientist intervenes)

Yo! Yo! I am not done. ...Undredundred and 9! Can we move
on a little? When does techmology goes horribly wrong?

ALI G. PLAYED BY SACHA BARON COHEN
"INTERVIEWING" SCIENTISTS (ENGLISH ACTOR BEST
KNOWN FOR PLAYING BORAT)

Typically, *Computational Fluid Dynamics* goes by the acronym of *CFD*. It stands for the process of creating the motion of a fluid on a computer. It involves computation. There are usually two components:

1. A representation of the fluid that our computer can understand.

2. A process to update this representation over time for each snapshot of the fluid.

The representation has to be *discrete*, unlike the mathematical models which are *continuous*. This means that the representation has to be described by a finite number of numbers. There are a lot of choices but the ones we will deal with here are either *grid based* or *particle based*. Either you keep your hand steady in the bathtub or you follow your rubber ducky floating along.

Once the representation is chosen, we need a discrete representation in time of the dynamical laws stated earlier to update the representation. I hope this clarifies the distinction between the continuous and discrete representations of fluids.

Where do we start with a brief account of computational fluid dynamics? Computing machines have been around since the time of Pascal and Leibniz. Did they compute the motion of fluids? As far as I can tell they didn't. Their early computer creations predated the Navier–Stokes equations.

FIGURE 4.1   Lewis Fry Richardson.

The true pioneer in this area, I believe, is Lewis Fry Richardson (1881–1953),* he is portrayed in Figure 4.1. He was an English mathematician, a physicist, and a pacifist. But more importantly, he tried to put his talents into predicting the weather. This is easy in Britain: rain, rain, and more rain. In California it is sunshine, sunshine, and more sunshine. This is not strictly always true: sometimes there is sunshine in Britain and sometimes it rains in California.

Richardson wrote a treatise in 1922 called the *Weather Prediction by Numerical Process*. He was decades ahead of his time since computers as we know them today did not exist back then. No supercomputers, PCs, fancy laptops, iPads, or cloud-based computing.

A *computer* at the time was a person who would type in instructions in a calculator and report the results to another computer or themselves.

---

* There was however previous work published in 1904 by the Norwegian scientist Vilhelm Bjerknes (1862–1951) and the work by the Austrian scientist Felix Exner (1876–1930) in 1908. Their predictions were even worse than Richardson's. But they were all true pioneers.

FIGURE 4.2   A "computer" at work in 1922.

They were mostly women.* One of those *computers* is depicted in Figure 4.2. They were supposed to work in harmony. They would compute something and then pass it to another *computer*. This process would go back and forth. Obviously, this was quite a tedious and time-consuming task. A computer as we call it today is basically a dumb piece of hardware that does the same task, just way faster. But back then a computer was an aggregate of smart hardworking women cooperating together.

Richardson invented a representation of the fluid flow for Europe that is depicted in Figure 4.3. It is a coarse grid where every square is supposed to represent the velocity and pressure of the fluid. This is essentially a grid-based approach. Each cell corresponds to a woman-computer sitting in a square and passing notes to her four neighbors after doing a computation. This process would go on and on: iteratively. The prediction of this computation concerning weather prediction, by the way, was completely wrong.

This is what Richardson had to say about his first computation when he tried it in his office without the help of computers. Talk about dedication:

> It took me the best part of six weeks to draw up the computing forms and to work out the new distribution in two vertical

---

* I know calling a woman a computer is degrading. Computers as we know them today are dumb, while women clearly are not. This terminology is wrong but that is what these smart women were called back then.

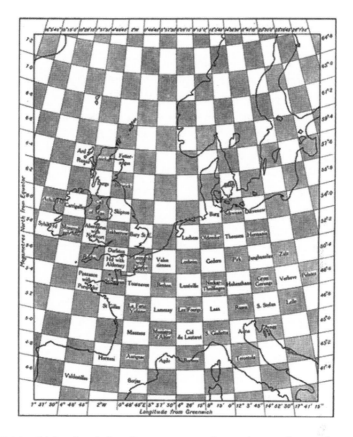

FIGURE 4.3 Richardson's first discretization of a weather prediction for Western Europe.

columns for the first time. My office was a heap of hay in a cold rest billet. With practice the work of an average computer might go perhaps ten times faster. If the time-step were 3 hours, then 32 individuals could just compute two points so as to keep pace with the weather.

Richardson was actually even more ambitious than that. He wanted to model the fluid circulation of the entire earth. Just like what global weather scientists are trying to do today. This is how he described his *fantasy*. The quote is a bit long but well worth reading in my opinion. Remember that this was in the 1920s, way before electronic computers existed. Richardson was a true visionary.

After so much hard reasoning, may one play with a fantasy? Imagine a large hall like a theatre, except that the circles and galleries go right round through the space usually occupied by the stage. The walls of this chamber are painted to form a map of the globe.

The ceiling represents the north Polar Regions; England is in the gallery, the tropics in the upper circle, Australia on the dress circle, and the Antarctic in the pit.

A myriad of computers are at work upon the weather of the part of the map where each sits, but each computer attends only to one equation or part of an equation. The work of each region is coordinated by an official of higher rank. Numerous little *night signs* display the instantaneous values so that neighboring computers can read them. Each number is thus displayed in three adjacent zones so as to maintain communication to the North and South on the map.

From the floor of the pit a tall pillar rises to half the height of the hall. It carries a large pulpit on its top. In this sits the man in charge of the whole theatre; he is surrounded by several assistants and messengers. One of his duties is to maintain a uniform speed of progress in all parts of the globe. In this respect he is like the conductor of an orchestra in which the instruments are slide-rules and calculating machines. But instead of waving a baton he turns a beam of rosy light upon any region that is running ahead of the rest, and a beam of blue light upon those who are behindhand.

Four senior clerks in the central pulpit are collecting the future weather as fast as it is being computed, and dispatching it by pneumatic carrier to a quiet room. There it will be coded and telephoned to the radio transmitting station. Messengers carry piles of used computing forms down to a storehouse in the cellar.

In a neighboring building there is a research department, where they invent improvements.

But there is much experimenting on a small scale before any change is made in the complex routine of the computing theatre. In a basement an enthusiast is observing eddies in the liquid lining of a huge spinning bowl, but so far the arithmetic proves the better way. In another building are all the usual financial, correspondence and administrative offices. Outside are playing fields, houses, mountains, and lakes, for it was thought that those who compute the weather should breathe of it freely.

(a)   (b)

FIGURE 4.4 Richardson's fantasy. (a: From author's own image. b: From Tripnvisit.blogspot.com.)

Figure 4.4 shows the setup. It is basically a discrete cylindrical representation of the earth as depicted on Figure 4.4a. To implement Richardson's fantasy, one could use the venue of *La Scala* in Milan, Italy, depicted on Figure 4.4b. Usually, it is a venue for concerts and operas. But Richardson could have rented it out, placed a person-computer in each booth and had them compute. They would exchange their computations with the computers in the booths above, below, left, and right. La Scala is a fancy place really but it is just one-half of a cylinder. Oops. But through a clever mechanism one could in principle carry out these computations for the entire cylinder world. Two computers could be working side by side in each booth, for example. Or one computer could multitask.

Another option for Richardson would have been to rent the legendary *Wembley Stadium* in London, England, shown in Figure 4.5.* The stadium was inaugurated in 1923 and could seat 127,000 people. Of course it wouldn't be as classy and comfortable as La Scala. There would also be the challenge for Richardson to find 127,000 person-computers to do the task. Doing fluid computations in Wembley Stadium would roughly result in a 1270 by 100 2D cylindrical grid. Not bad actually even by current standards. If only enough computer-persons would show up to achieve this task.

Richardson is also the man who invented a technique to accelerate the convergence of series in a very clever way. It is a technique to get a computation from previous computations in a much faster manner. Not surprisingly,

---

* In 1996, I was lucky enough to see a soccer game live at Wembley Stadium (the new one) between England and Switzerland in the European Championship. It turned out to be a tie: 1–1. It was also the opening game of the tournament. Germany ended up winning the final. I happened to be in Hamburg on my way to Finland from Paris when the Germans won. Lots of beer and fireworks!

FIGURE 4.5   The old Wembley Stadium that opened in 1923.

it is called the *Richardson extrapolation*. We do not use this technique in our code so we won't elaborate on it. But it is worth looking up.

Then there was World War II. This catastrophic and tragic event, however, accelerated many technological advances in many areas such as aviation, explosives, and atom bombs but also computing. Examples include Konrad Zuse in Germany, Hewlett and Packard in the United States, the *Bomb* based on the work of Alan Turing,* the *Harvard Mark 1* created by Howard Aiken, and many more. This was a fertile time for the development of machines that compute instead of people- computers. Secret codes had to be cracked and ballistic trajectories had to be predicted in order to win the war. Computers were an essential part of the solution.

John Von Neumann was I think one of the biggest pioneers in computer theory and practice. He laid out the architecture of all computers we use today: the *Von Neumann machine*. A machine that can read in programs and is not hardwired for a specific problem. Turing of course envisioned this before. But in 1945, Von Neumann was involved in a project to build a better *ENIAC* computer, which stands for *Electrical Numerical Integrator And Calculation*. In Figure 4.6, John Von Neumann is shown next to the ENIAC computer. Many of the first programmers were women who were probably happy not to be called computers anymore. In Figure 4.7, we show two new programmers.

The ENIAC was one of the first computers to perform computational fluid dynamics, and it was based on Richardson's work from the 1920s.

---

* For a good account of Turing's contributions during the war and his other achievements read *Alan Turing: The Enigma* by Andrew Hodges. Sadly, Turing committed suicide because his homosexuality was viewed as a crime in Britain at the time. Such a waste. Here is a genius mathematician and a war "hero" who made major contributions to win a ridiculous war.

FIGURE 4.6   John Von Neumann (left) and part of the ENIAC computer (right).

FIGURE 4.7   Computers became programmers programming a computer.

This time the computations were faster but still extremely slow compared to our computers today. The ENIAC could roughly perform 100,000 operations per second. That was huge back then and required a lot of power. The ENIAC was located in Philadelphia and legend has it that when the ENIAC was powered on all the lights in the city slightly dimmed. Nowadays, any average personal computer can operate roughly 1,000,000,000 instructions per second and if you boot up your PC no one will notice. Not even your neighbor.

Apart from his fundamental contributions to computer science, Von Neumann was a genius with a photographic memory. He advanced many fields including the mathematical foundations of *Quantum Mechanics*.

Most people know the town of Los Alamos in New Mexico. That is where the foremost scientists in the United States during World War II developed the Atom bomb.

FIGURE 4.8   Frank Harlow.

After the war, Los Alamos Laboratories was a hotbed for research using mechanical computers to simulate fluids. One of the main characters involved in this research was Francis (Frank) Harley Harlow. Figure 4.8 shows a picture of him.* He devised, with the help of colleagues, many clever techniques to simulate fluids on a computer. Those were the *glory days* of computational fluid dynamics. He picked a lot of low hanging fruits. His creations are essential to how we model fluids numerically today.

After this period, there were of course tremendous improvements in computer power and software to improve the simulation of fluids. We will not delve into those improvements since they are well documented elsewhere.

To summarize: Richardson was a true pioneer in weather prediction, even though his predictions were way off. But he laid the foundations for computational fluid dynamics. Women had a crucial role in the early days of weather prediction: first as computers then as programmers of computers.

Let us briefly mention the topic of *turbulence*. This is a somewhat vague and controversial topic. That is what makes it interesting and cool.

---

* Sadly, I couldn't find a better picture of Harlow. This one I found on Google images extracted from a YouTube video.

CHAPTER 5

Kolmogorov and Turbulence

... the smallest eddies are almost numberless, and large things are rotated only by large eddies and not by small ones, and small things are turned by small eddies and large.

LEONARDO DA VINCI (ITALIAN RENAISSANCE MAN)

Big whorls have little whorls,
which feed on their velocity;
And little whorls have lesser whorls,
And so on to viscosity.

LEWIS FRY RICHARDSON (ENGLISH MATHEMATICIAN,
PHYSICIST, AND PACIFIST)

When I meet God, I am going to ask him two questions: Why relativity? And why turbulence? I really believe he will have an answer for the first.

WERNER HEISENBERG (FAMOUS NOBEL LAUREATE,
GERMAN PHYSICIST)

NOT THE DUDE FROM *BREAKING BAD*

What is turbulence? No one really knows. It is a mess. But it involves fluids. For most people turbulence is often associated with air travel, fastening seat belts, being shaken around unpleasantly, and having coffee spilled all over your pants.

There are plenty of models of turbulence for fluids.

If you are in this turbulence business, you will be in this business for a long time. That is as long as no experiment proves that your business is wrong. But then you will just change your business model. And you are back in business.

Really, there is no proper understanding of turbulence as of yet. We already mentioned earlier that the dynamics of fluids are nonlinear. That means that large-scale features influence small-scale features. But also the other way around: smaller scales influence larger scales.

The so-called Arab Spring event is a good analogy of this nonlinear turbulence behavior.

Totalitarian regimes (large scale) controlled the masses (small scale) but then a small tragic event in Tunisia (small scale) ripples through the Arab world and challenges these totalitarian regimes (small scales influence large scales). The totalitarian regimes (large scale) step down because of revolts (small scales becoming large scales) and subsequently elections (an aggregate of small scales) bring in a new party (large scale), which is then brought down by the military (medium scales influencing large scales). This is an ongoing saga as of the writing of this book: large scale versus small scale and small scale versus large scale.

Bottom line: turbulence is a mix or a battle between scales.

My description of the Arab Spring is just an analogy of course and an oversimplification of the real situation.

We still haven't precisely defined what turbulence is.

One pathetic attempt at a definition could be "turbulence is the small stuff we cannot model at large scales." It is the complicated stuff that happens at the smaller scales of fluids. On the other hand, these smaller scales influence the larger scales. That is why turbulence is a hard nut to crack.

One of the most famous models of turbulence was created by the great Russian mathematician Andrey Kolmogorov (1903–1987). Figure 5.1 shows a picture of Kolmogorov in action explaining some fundamental concepts using sketches and pictures. Recall the quote mentioned above in the Preface of this book. To humbly paraphrase: well understood mathematics is best explained with no fancy mathematics at all.

FIGURE 5.1   Kolmogorov in action. Cool, just diagrams.

His work on turbulence is called the *K41 Theory*. This is because he published three influential papers on turbulence in 1941 and the "K" stands for Kolmogorov of course. By far, this work is not his only contribution to science and mathematics.

For example, he defined complexity as follows. The complexity of a problem is equal to the number of bits of the smallest program that encodes the solution to the problem. Got it? The smaller the program that solves the problem is, the less complex the problem is. I love it because it makes it so concrete.

A program that prints the number *1* a trillion times is less complex than printing a trillion digits of the number π.*

Compare the size of a program that prints:

1111111111111111111111111111111111111111111111111111111111111111111 1111111111…

---

* The record for memorizing π was achieved by Akira Haraguchi who recited π from memory to 100,000 decimal places in 16 hours on October 3, 2006. Each digit requires about 4 bits. So, the total amount of bits is $4 \times 67,890 = 271,560$. The length of his program is what he memorized. That is a lot of bits. For most people π is 3.14. Indiana House Bill #246 introduced on January 18, 1897 claimed that $\pi = 3.2$. A small complexity declared by fiat. Of course computer programs that compute the digits of π do not do it from something stored in memory. There are many clever ways of generating these digits. As of the writing of this book, the record is held by a program called "y-cruncher." In 2013, it computed 12,100,000,000,050 digits of π in 94 days.

To a program that prints:
3.14159265358979323846264338327950288419716939937510582097494
4592307816406286…

A truly random sequence cannot be computed by a program smaller than itself.

What was Kolmogorov's contribution to turbulence?

The starting point of Kolmogorov's theory of turbulence is Richardson's poem quoted at the beginning of this chapter. Kolmogorov assumed that there is a cascade of energy transfer from large structures to smaller structures and that energy is eventually dissipated at the smallest scale because of viscosity. This setup assumes no boundary conditions at all. Figure 5.2 is a cartoon depiction of this scenario. The circles indicate the size of a *structure*. Think of these structures as vortices or any discernible pattern in the flow. This is somewhat sketchy but there is really no precise definition of turbulence. Structures of different sizes are clearly visible in Da Vinci's drawing (see Figure 3.2b). The wiggly line in our cartoon figure is the scale where the features "pop" and disappear because of viscous dissipation.

This picture and the theory is really an approximation of what really goes on. But abstracting complex problems like this can lead to useful results and insights. Kolmogorov's theory assumes that the energy of the fluid is transferred from large scales to smaller scales. As we mentioned earlier, this is not realistic because energy also gets transferred from small scales to large scales: a fluid is nonlinear after all.

In Figure 5.2 we show two arrows: one on the left and one on the right. Why? The right one is obvious and shows that as you go upward the circles

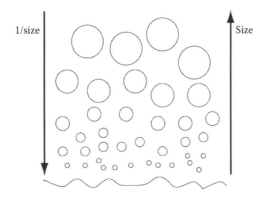

FIGURE 5.2   A cartoon of Kolmogorov's cascade. These are not bubbles!

get bigger. Their size increases. Kolmogorov uses the left-hand arrow. This arrow goes in the opposite direction and shows the increases of what is called the *wave number* of a structure.* We will see more about these wave numbers when we discuss about the Fourier transform, but really in our figure it just stands for "one divided by the length." Small structures have larger wave numbers than larger structures which have smaller wave numbers. Confusing? A big number is big, but if you divide a small number like 1 by a big number then the result is tiny. Compare 1,000,000 with $1/1,000,000 = 0.000001$.

Kolmogorov first assumes that the fluid has constant density, and therefore we can ignore mass. This means that energy has units of $[L^2/T^2]$. Kolmogorov derived an equation of how the energy depends on the size of these whimsical structures.

Actually, Kolmogorov derived an equation not for the energy but for the *energy per wave number*. This is the energy for each structure in the flow and we denote it by E. You can think of E as a density of the total energy for each structure of a specific size. The wave number is usually denoted by k and it is related to 1/size.

Kolmogorov postulated that the energy density E should only depend on some nondimensional constant C,[†] the rate of flow of energy which we call *flow*, and on the wave number k. This density of energy per wave number has units of $[L^3/T^2]$. Kolmogorov used dimensional analysis to come up with his formula. We mentioned this technique above to derive Bernoulli's law. The *flow* variable is energy per unit time. Therefore *flow* has units of $[L^2/T^3]$. A first attempt at a law could be

$$E(k) = C \times \text{flow} \times k.$$

What about the units? Do they match? Let's try it out: $[E] = [C] \times [\text{flow}] \times [k]$. Thus $[L^3/T^2]$ has to be equal to $[L/T^3]$. That unfortunately doesn't work.

Here enters the *coup de génie* of Kolmogorov.

He introduced two exponents a and b to be determined such that

$$E(k) = C \times \text{flow}^a \times k^b.$$

---

* Hopefully, I will make it clear why they are called wave numbers instead of *reciprocal sizes* or *one over size* later in this book.

† This constant can be determined through experiments. It is just a number that depends on the fluid.

Now we have an equation for the exponents a and b using dimensional analysis. $[L^3/T^2] = [L^{2a}/T^{3a}] \times [L^{-b}]$. This gives us two equations for a and b since the exponents have to match on both sides: $3 = 2a - b$ and also $2 = 3a$. And the only solution is that a must be 2/3 and that b must be −5/3.* And *ta da!* From this follows Kolmogorov's law:

$$E(k) = C \times \text{flow}^{2/3} \times k^{-(5/3)}.$$

This is also known as Kolmogorov's "5/3 Law." Given the assumptions stated earlier to this argument holds for any fluid.

That is the beauty of it.

Of course this is a far cry from settling the problem of turbulence. The reason I mention this particular result of Kolmogorov's is that this formula and its derivation are relatively simple. No need for any fancy mathematics.

More importantly, we use this expression when we introduce numerical models for turbulence in computer animation.

To summarize: Turbulence is far from being understood. But Kolmogorov gave us a simple formula that characterizes the cascade of energy from large scales to small scales. It is a power law. Like *fractals*!

---

* For those of you not familiar with exponents we have the following facts. Let X be any number then we have that: $1/X^a = X^{-a}$ and $X^a \times X^b = X^{a+b}$. For example: $X^2 \times X^3 = X \times X \times X \times X \times X = X^5$. That is why exponents are awesome: they turn multiplication into addition. Unless you are a prodigy, I think most people would rather add numbers than multiply them in their head.

CHAPTER 6

Introduction to Fluid Animation

If it sounds good, it is good.

DUKE ELLINGTON (FAMOUS AMERICAN JAZZ
MUSICIAN)

We now focus on the problem of animating fluids. This is a research area of its own that of course relies heavily on all the previous fluid work described earlier.

Research is a process that constantly evolves.

Generally in computer animation the motto is:

If it looks good, it is good.*

That is the bottom line. It might seem simplistic and unscientific at first glance.

Anything goes really, but not really. It is hard to make things look good. In that sense it is unscientific. But that doesn't make it less interesting. Making things that look good with computers involves using both principled models and using artistic intuition.

---

* I only heard of Duke Ellington's quote from a fellow researcher in a restaurant in Fukuoka, Japan in 2012.

My approach in fluid animation research has always been to use any technique that creates good-looking fluids. I am a model agnostic. Whatever model gets the job done is a friend of mine. Quite often I meet people who equate models to reality (without ironic quotation marks). To them any model for fluids *has* to use the Navier–Stokes equations. Everything else is garbage, whatever. But with this kind of attitude you are going to miss out on a lot of fun and cool stuff.

Besides, computer animation is not about *reproducing* reality but about the *creation* of an imaginary and controllable virtual reality *inspired* in part by conventional physical models of *reality*. I do not own an apology to anyone. I do what I do.

Computational fluid dynamics (CFD) is of course a great tool. It has derivations that are principled, it has fancy equations, and it has a lot of successes that are backed up by rigorous experiments. I love CFD, and I am using some of their concoctions. Mathematical models, once you understand them and tried them, can be highly addictive. But we should not be carried away by their allure.

In fluid animation we can augment and take liberties to improve the visual quality of the fluids. Just taking existing respectable fluid codes and visualizing their results doesn't always do the trick in fluid animations. In fact a lot of CFD papers do not depict fluids at all. In some cases, they are just 2D plots of some quantity. Da Vinci would not be pleased.

To summarize: Enough said. Let's turn to the business of writing code that simulates fluids for computer animation.

6.1 DISCRETIZE! BUGS, GRIDS, AND BUGS MOVING THROUGH GRIDS

It is better to destroy one's own errors than those of others.

DEMOCRITUS (GREEK PHILOSOPHER KNOWN FOR HIS THEORY OF DISCRETE MATTER)

Before we write code we have to decide how to turn our perfect continuous fluids into a discrete representation that our computers can handle. Remember everything has to be crammed into a finite number of bits that the computer can process. The continuous models are just fictions made up by mathematicians. But, and this is a big but, these models are extremely useful to writing code. How cynical is that?

6.1.1 Bugs

> There are, as is known, insects that die in the moment of fertilization. So it is with all joy: life's highest, most splendid moment of enjoyment is accompanied by death.
>
> SOREN KIERKEGAARD (DANISH PHILOSOPHER AND
> THEOLOGIAN)

One model is to use bugs running around. However, this time they just cannot crawl around just as they please. They have to cooperate: no climbing over each other. They are more social than our diffusion bugs mentioned earlier. Ideally, they have to remain at a certain distance from each other. This distance is usually fixed by the programmer.* If they get too close, a *spring* is attached to them temporarily so they don't bang into each other. The density of the bugs doing their wild dance is then approximately constant. And their velocities are approximately incompressible. Remember: flow in equals flow out. Figure 6.1 shows this situation. On the left the bugs are free to move but on the right they are connected with springs to keep them apart. These springs come and go.

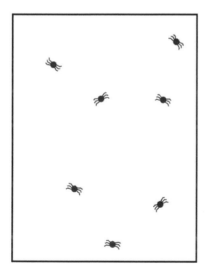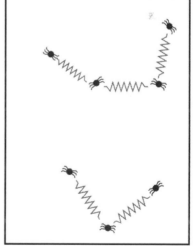

FIGURE 6.1   Free bugs (left) and constrained bugs with *springs* attached (right).

---

* In the case of humans, this distance varies from culture to culture and from country to country. In my experience, in most of Europe that distance is smaller than in North America.

This is not what these methods are normally called. They often go by many names like *griddles, particle based, smoothed particle hydrodynamics*, and so on. A bug is usually called a particle in these models. There are various models for the *springs*.

A famous model for the *spring* is the so-called *Lennard-Jones force* between particles. I use the word particles because this force was originally designed for atoms and molecules, not bugs. Figure 6.2 shows the strength of the Lennard-Jones force as a function of the distance between particles. For small distances the force is highly repulsive. Actually, the force is equal to infinity when the two particles share the same location. This is problematic when you try to code this model. Computers do not like infinities. Remember they can only handle a finite number of bits. The force is zero for a certain given distance r_0. This is the *comfort zone*. For distances larger than r_0 the force is attractive but much weaker than the repulsive force.

Another popular model is the *hard sphere model* for fluids. In this case, each bug is put into a sphere that protects them from other bugs. Their spheres collide when they get too close. So, it is like a wild game of billiards with a bug in each ball. This situation is depicted in Figure 6.3. One can also replace the bugs with hamsters. Anyone who owned a hamster knows that you can buy those transparent balls that allow them to roam through your house. Do this on the first floor. You do not want your hamster

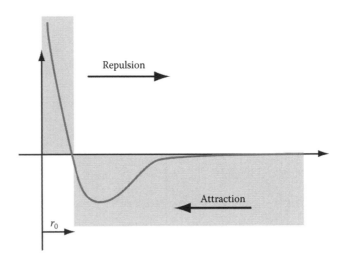

FIGURE 6.2 The Lennard-Jones force between two particles as a function of distance.

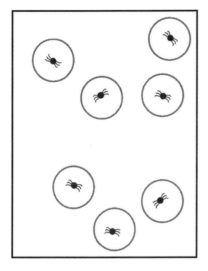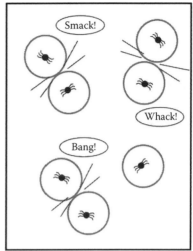

FIGURE 6.3   The hard sphere model of a fluid.

tumbling down the stairs. Now, imagine 1,000,000,000,000,000 hamsters in their mighty spheres all banging into each other. That would be kind of a realistic implementation of a hard sphere fluid model.

Alternatively, there is a model called *SPH*, which stands for *smoothed particle hydrodynamics*. It is quite popular these days in computer animation and was originally developed to model the dynamics of galaxies. These models try to explain how galaxies form, collapse, merge, or disappear in a black hole. This means the model is perfect for fluids that compress and diverge.

Briefly, the way SPH works is as follows:

Unlike our hamsters, each bug now has an *aura* around them that determines the interactions with other bugs. This is depicted in Figure 6.4. The poor bugs are now in the dark driven only by their aura. Once the auras of the bugs overlap they interact. That is the smoothed part in SPH. Bugs are not trapped in hard spheres but have this glowing aura around them. Kind of like a new age energy thing. In computer graphics, the official nomenclature is that every bug is surrounded by a *blob*.* The blob is strongest at the bug and then it drops off to zero after a fixed distance. If you add up the blobs then you get a fuzzy function everywhere: a global aura of energy. The velocity of each bug is determined by its own velocity

---

* Or if you are in Japan, *blobs* are called *meta-balls*. Sometimes they have been misspelled in papers as *meat-balls*.

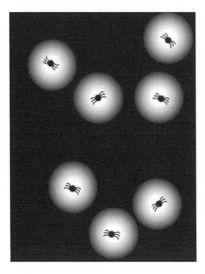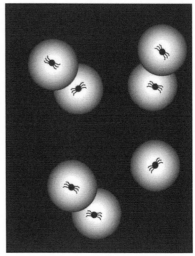

FIGURE 6.4   In the SPH method each bug is surrounded by a blob. Interactions occur when blobs overlap.

and the velocities of the neighboring new age bugs whose auras overlap. Once you have the velocity of the bug it now knows where to move next: It is the same for the other new-ager bugs. Through their interactions, an emergent fluidlike behavior emerges.

That is SPH in a nutshell.

What about incompressibility?

That is the *Achilles heel* of SPH.

However, a lot of people have extended SPH to incompressible fluids like air and water. The basic approach is to have repulsive/attractive forces between the particles when their auras overlap. If incompressibility is to be enforced, very stiff spring forces have to be introduced, almost like a rigid link.

In practice, this means that you have to be careful about the *time step*: the amount of time separating two snapshots of the roaming bugs in the dark. If you are not careful the bugs will *blow up*. They will wander all over the place as far as they can from each other. This creates infinite values.

This is not cool for the computer Slave since it can only handle a finite number of bits. So, the way the Slave handles these cases is to just give up. "Geez these numbers are too big, take it easy Master. Instead of your big numbers I will call them *NaNs* and you deal with them. Even better if you fix up your code so they do not show up at all." A number called an *NaN*, which stands for *Not a Number* is the kiss of death. Once a NaN appears when running your code it will slow it down and do all kinds of funny stuff. But there are ways to catch NaNs and make sure they do not happen.

Our users do not like NaNs. Mathematicians call this an *instability*. Coders call this "useless garbage and go fix your code dude." Coders have an affinity to the Slave who has to digest their code.

An interesting side effect of SPH is that fluids can be bouncy like Jell-O. But less damped and more lively. This is not very realistic but this effect can be cool in fluid animation. The biggest issue with a simple vanilla implementation of SPH is that it can be unstable. But a lot of researchers have tackled this problem.*

This book will not include SPH code. Sorry. You can find the code on the Internet, however. Or you can write your own. Have fun.

I just briefly described a few so-called Lagrangian approaches to fluid motion. Remember you can measure the change by following the flow. Go with the flow.

To summarize: The interaction of the bugs determines a velocity for each bug and their crawling follows that velocity field. At the same time, these bugs have to get along: not too close and not too far.

Now let's turn our attention to grids.

6.1.2 Grids

The best advice I've received is to be yourself. The best artists do that.

FRANK GEHRY (FAMOUS TORONTO-BORN ARCHITECT)

Grids are just a way to partition space into cells. Think of grids as one of those hideous apartment buildings with identical tiny apartments. Usually, they are built to house the poor and newly arrived immigrants. In French, they are called *cages à lapin* (rabbit cages). Now each bug is trapped in its tiny apartment, and it can only interact with its neighboring bugs through its six walls. Yes we also include the floor and the ceiling. This is depicted in Figure 6.5

---

* I implemented the standard SPH in 1991 and it was incredibly unstable. I gave up. I like big time steps. Kudos to the people who made it work. Back then I asked J.J. Monaghan from Australia who co-invented the technique to send me some of his papers. He sent them to "Jos Stam, Toronto, Canada." Amazingly his papers got to me. Thanks Monaghan! I sincerely mean it. Toronto is the third largest city in North America for those of you who do not know this fact. We have more humans than wolves and bears in this fine city even though it is located in funky Canada.

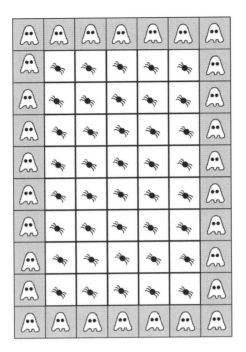

FIGURE 6.5   Bugs stuck in their apartments surrounded by ghosts

for bugs trapped in a 2D apartment building. In this case, the bugs can only interact with their four neighbors.

They interact exactly like the women computers mentioned earlier. Let's say each wall, ceiling, and floor has a tiny hole so the bugs can pass messages back and forth. For example, "My velocity arrow is such and such what is yours?" No privacy for these bugs. Not true for the lonely bugs that live in "internal boundary apartments." They can sleep all day and night.

We also included a layer of *ghost apartments*. They do not really exist. But we added them so the bugs with an actual view also have four neighbors. The ghost apartments with their ghost bugs will not block their views.* But it will make it easier to handle what happens at the boundaries. The ghost in an adjacent apartment is sometimes like a mirror image of the bug. It does everything the bug does but in reverse. Actually, it is kind of freaky to have a ghost neighbor like that. But this is not always the case. The ghost can act in different ways. Another example is that the ghost neighbor could be blowing air in the bug's face all day. Or the ghost can grab the poor bug and throw him out of the window.

---

* What about the ghosts? Well they do not exist anyway, so who cares.

FIGURE 6.6   Three funky hipster bug apartment buildings.

Grids do not have to be as regular as this. We can imagine funkier apartments for the bugs. Three examples are depicted in Figure 6.6. These apartments are for hipster bugs and are most likely built by famous architects like Gaudi or Libeskind. We could have come up with even crazier grids. But I think I made my point. Notice that the grids can have curved walls *à la* Frank Gehry.

In a grid representation, the bug is actually not allowed to move at all. The bug is just sitting in the center of his apartment on a revolving stool.* So it can face any angle. The bug is also holding an arrow whose length can change over time. The evolution of the bug's arrow is a function of the arrows of their bug neighbors. This is shown in Figure 6.7. The top three bugs show the evolution of a single bug's orientation and arrow length over time. Notice that the color of the bug can also change over time as well. This could be indicative of the amount of heat in the apartment, the levels of carbon dioxide and what not.

In the bottom of the figure, we show how bugs exchange information with their neighbors through their walls.

This grid representation is called *cell centered* or *collocated* because both the bug's color and their velocity arrow are defined at the center of the cell. This representation makes the computer implementation easier

---

* In three dimensions, the stool would have to be more complicated. Like something you can find at an amusement park.

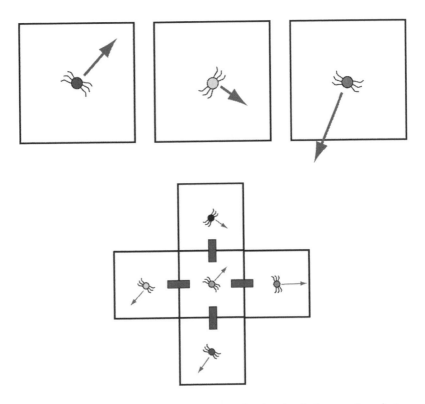

FIGURE 6.7 Evolution of a bug's arrow and color (top). Interactions between neighbors through the walls.

and simpler. Indeed, we will give a full implementation in code for the case of these poor bugs that are stuck in the *cages à lapin* surrounded by ghosts.

Another grid representation has the lateral velocities defined at the wall boundaries. This representation is actually more natural and can be understood as fluxes defined at the walls of the bug's apartment. This representation is usually known as a *staggered grid* or a *MAC* grid in fluid dynamics speak. This is an acronym for *Marker And Cell*. MAC is normally the preferred representation, and we have used it to explain continuity and the incompressibility conditions earlier (see Figures 6.9 and 6.10). This is the representation that is most commonly used for grids. We used MAC in our computer implementation of the fluid animation feature called *Fluid Effects* in our MAYA animation software.

This representation is depicted in Figure 6.8, where each bug has a horizontal and a vertical velocity defined at the walls that it shares with its

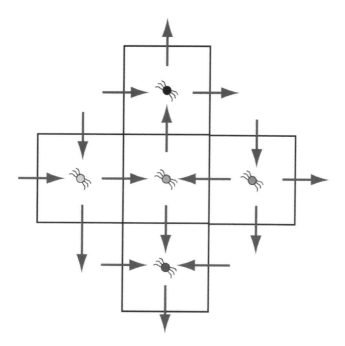

FIGURE 6.8   In a staggered grid, velocities are defined at the walls and other quantities are defined at the bugs.

neighbors. The bugs are being very neighborly. The staggered approach also extends to the more hipster apartments depicted in Figure 6.6 earlier, even though the walls have funkier shapes.

To summarize: In a grid representation, bugs are stuck in their apartments and can only exchange information with their neighbors. Properties of the fluid are only defined in each bug's apartment.

Now we will briefly discuss cases where bugs are allowed to leave their apartments. In some cases the bugs have to return home but in other cases the bugs can take over their neighbor's apartments.

6.1.3 Bugs Moving through Grids

Most people are aware of the particle/wave duality in quantum mechanics. Particles and waves are mathematical abstractions. Sometimes using particles makes sense and sometimes using waves makes sense. They are just models that complement each other.

But really when you think about it: what is a particle that has zero size and what is a wave made of? It is all mathematical abstract nonsense that happens to be useful in physics. Take a second to think about that.

To paraphrase John Von Neumann: no one understands what a particle or a wave is. We just get used to the math and then pretend that we understand it. But it works!

This analogy is just a dandy (pretentious?) way to illustrate that one can combine models that describe a phenomenon from different points of view. That is why I describe bugs crawling between apartment buildings. I can feel and see them and therefore I can describe them.

Earlier we talked about free-roaming polite bugs and poor neighborly bugs stuck in their apartments. Why not combine these two situations into one? That is when the bugs can move from one apartment to the other. Like some sort of commune of the 1960s in California or a kibbutz in Israel. I like this approach as it is social and model agnostic at the same time.

We will present two such approaches.

6.1.4 Semi-Lagrangian

I will start with my favorite technique which is officially called *semi-Lagrangian*: half of a French mathematician and philosopher. This method is also called the *method of characteristics*.

This is how the semi-Lagrangian technique works.

As shown in Figure 6.9, we have two identical apartment buildings. The one on the left is filled with bugs and the building on the right is initially empty. Let's say the landlord decided to relocate all the bugs because the

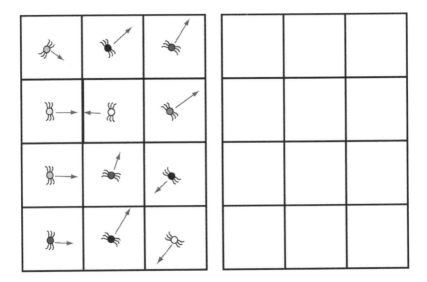

FIGURE 6.9 Semi-Lagrangian transport of bugs between two apartment buildings.

first building has an asbestos problem. The bugs have to eventually end up in their matching apartment in the second building, which is asbestos free. The landlord is clearly a bit of a psychopath and a control freak. But he offers a lower rent in the newly cleanly built apartment building if the bugs follow his request.

The landlord's crazy request is as follows.

You guys are now free to leave your stool. And roam around. One condition, however: follow your arrow multiplied by some number in the opposite direction. You will end up in another apartment. Now mix the colors of the bugs in the neighboring apartments and recolor yourself. Also compute your new arrow from the neighbor's arrows. And *voilà!* Welcome to your new apartment that is asbestos free and cheaper.

This is a transport mechanism.

Colors and vectors are transported from the *old* apartments to the *new* apartments.

Figure 6.10 shows how this works for one of the bugs. But it will work for all bugs as long as each bug leaves a note behind describing their former color and arrow. The bugs' new arrow and color is a blend of the neighboring ones. The blend is a function of how close the bug is to its respective new neighbors. As you can see from Figure 6.7, the bug now has a different

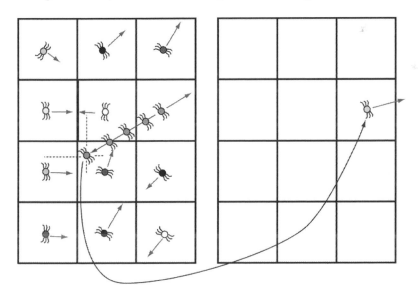

FIGURE 6.10 One bug crawls into neighboring apartments and blends both the arrows and the colors of the final neighbor. The bug then moves into its new apartment.

FIGURE 6.11   Three different ways to interpolate a point in between two known data points.

color and a different arrow. Mathematicians call this blending procedure *interpolation.**

Interpolation just means: you have two values and you want to know the values in between. This is shown in Figure 6.11. The black dots are the known values and the red one is the unknown whose value we are trying to figure out. As can be seen in the figure, many options are available. We usually like the simplest one shown on the left of the figure, which is just a straight line. On the other hand, if information of the rate of change is available at the known points, then one can use a more clever interpolation scheme as shown in the middle and right-hand side of Figure 6.11. Really it is about relating the information at some particular points to points in between them.

That is how we get the unknown from the known.

For example, we have that

$$1.2 = 0.8 \times 1.0 + 0.2 \times 2.0$$

Which means that 1.2 lies between 1.0 and 2.0. 1.2 is closer to 1.0 than 2.0. Therefore the number that multiplies 1.0 is bigger than the number that multiplies 2.0. These numbers are called *weights*. Notice that the weights satisfy the following: $0.8 + 0.2 = 1.0$ and that they are always positive and smaller than 1.0. In fact, $0.8 = 1.0 - 0.2$. In this case, we used linear interpolation as shown on the left-hand side of Figure 6.11. In general, for linear interpolation we have that

value in between $= (1 - $ distance to 1$) \times$ value 1 $+ ($distance to 1$) \times$ value 2.

In the case of our bugs that crawl in 2D apartments they end up with four neighbors: $b1$, $b2$, $b3$, and $b4$. Now we have a 2D problem and the interpolation is as follows:

---

* When classmates and I first heard this word in a math class in Geneva, Switzerland, we all chuckled. Whoa INTERPOL? Cool like in *International Police*.

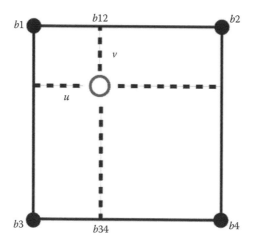

FIGURE 6.12   Linear interpolation in two dimensions.

$$\text{bug color} = (1 - u) \times (1 - v) \times b1 + u \times (1 - v) \times b2 + (1 - u) \times v \times b3 + u \times v \times b4.$$

This is shown in Figure 6.12. This formula is really an application of the 1D interpolation formula applied twice. In Figure 6.12, u denotes the horizontal distance to $b1$ and v denotes the vertical distance to $b1$. To see the link between 2D interpolation and 1D interpolation, we can introduce the following two intermediary 1D interpolations:

$$b12 = (1 - u) \times b1 + u \times b2$$
$$b34 = (1 - u) \times b3 + u \times b4$$
$$\text{Bug color} = (1 - v) \times b12 + v \times b34$$

This procedure can be carried out in three dimensions as well using the same principle. Try it. In fact it works for any dimension. The 1D interpolation can be extended to any dimension through a process that goes by the fancy name of a *tensor product*. Coders will also notice that the second version is more efficient than the first one.

Why?

6 ×'s versus 8 ×'s, 3 +'s versus 4 +'s and 3 −'s versus 4 −'s. The less ×'s, +'s and −'s, the faster your code is. Usually the less code, the faster your program will run.* Software called *Optimizers* that reads your code will

---

* Yes, yes, yes, I know about loop unrolling. But Mister Optimizer automatically takes care of that. Can you imagine if you had to unroll your loops yourself?

sometimes take care of this for you. Optimizers take your code and output other code that supposedly runs faster. But remember an Optimizer is only as smart as the person who wrote it. That is an upper bound. Even worse is when Mister Optimizer creates code that does something different than you intended it to do: "Cool. It is faster but it does not do what my Pet wanted it to do."

This can be the source of many so-called Heisenbugs named after Werner Heisenberg, one of the founders of quantum mechanics quoted previously. The Heisenberg principle states that the velocity and the position of a particle cannot be measured exactly at the same time in the quantum world.

The reason being is that to localize a particle you have to bombard it with some wave with a specific velocity. That is going to mess up the position. And similarly when measuring the velocity, you are going to mess up the velocity by bombarding it with particles. Bottom line: if you look at something it is going to affect whatever you are looking at. That is the Heisenberg principle in a nutshell.

In the world of computer coding, one sometimes gets a different behavior when Mister Optimizer is involved. Your code all of a sudden does not do what you want it to do. But as soon as you try to inspect the code: insert a breakpoint or add a print statement, the behavior is kosher again. This is frustrating since breakpoints and prints slow down the code. But anyone who has gone through this experience will understand what a *Heisenbug* is and the art it takes to deal with them. It helps to work with many smart coders who are just down the hall and who are willing to help you out.

To summarize: In a semi-Lagrangian framework, bugs leave their apartments to invade neighboring apartments following their arrows back in time. They then gather information through interpolation from their neighbors and change their colors and vectors accordingly. At the end, every bug is happy and lives in an asbestos-free and cheaper apartment.

Let's now turn to another hybrid approach.

6.1.5 PIC

PIC stands for *Particle In Cell*. In our terminology it would be *BIA: Bugs In Apartments*.

PIC involves both bugs and apartments just like the semi-Lagrangian methods described earlier.

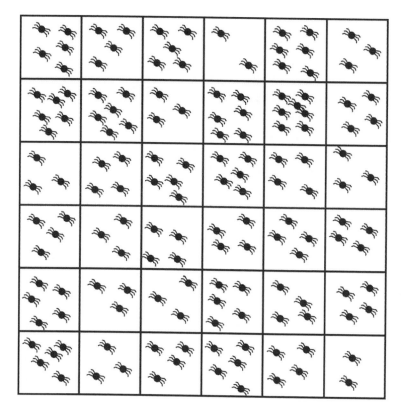

FIGURE 6.13   Bugs in cells.

Frank Harlow came up with the PIC method for fluids in the 1960s for (there was early work for plasmas). This method requires many bugs per apartment for it to work well. How many? Well that is up to the Master again who writes the code. Figure 6.13 shows the situation. Many bugs are now sharing apartments. Their number is not fixed just bounded by the Master. Some apartments have more bugs than others.

This is how PIC works.

Velocities are defined on the grid, either collocated or staggered. Just like in the grid-based methods we discussed previously. Each bug interpolates its velocity from its neighboring apartments. The bug then uses this velocity to wander to another apartment.

This time forward in time. No psychopathic landlord involved.

The bug then alters the velocity of its new neighbor apartments. This is depicted in Figure 6.14. We assigned a different color to each bug so they are easier to keep track of. The top left shows their initial configuration

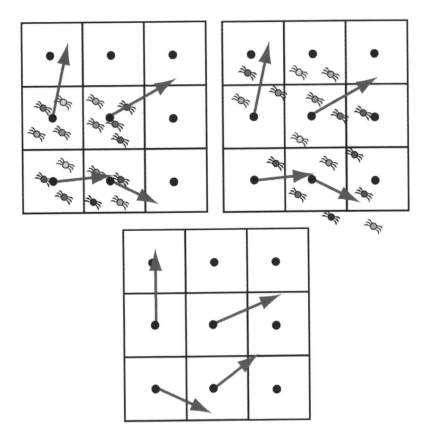

FIGURE 6.14   PIC's three steps.

with bugs in their apartments and their velocities. The top right shows their track to other apartments based on the velocities. And the bottom shows how the velocities are updated in each apartment due to the arrival of the new (or old) bugs with their new velocities. Of course new bugs (not shown) can come from apartments not depicted in Figure 6.14. They could come from the left wall, for example. Also two bugs have left the portion of the building that we are showing.

The bottom line is: we really only care about the velocities. You can think of the bugs as being little minions that carry around velocities from one place to another. However, in computer animation, the bugs can be useful to define the surface when simulating a liquid-like water. Unlike smoke, a liquid has a well-defined surface that separates the air from the liquid. Both are fluids but usually only the motion of the liquid is animated. So the bugs are floating and swimming in the liquid but not flying in the air.

This is kind of like the semi-Lagrangian approach except that there are more bugs and they move forward in time.

Again this is a transport problem: values in the apartments are updated using crawling bugs.

The grid, on the other hand, takes care of continuity (what flows in has to come out) and diffusion (stuff gets blurred). We will get to how to solve these effects on a grid below.

I have never implemented a PIC solver or its prettier cousin the FLIP solver. And of course there are many variants with their secret sauces. There is code to get you started on the Internet. Since I did not write it, I will not include it in this book.

To summarize: Moving bugs are great for accounting for the transport of a fluid, but grids are better for accounting for continuity and diffusion. By combining these techniques we get PIC.

CHAPTER 7

Intermezzi

Intermezzo is an Italian word which stands for some sort of performance that fits in between the main acts of an opera or a concert. This usually gives people time to go to the washroom, stretch their legs, or get another drink. The other people who do not have these needs remain entertained by frivolous acts and performances. But sometimes they are more fun than the main acts.

The following are four *Intermezzi. Enjoy*!

7.1 INTERMEZZO UNO: LINEAR SYSTEMS

Yuzz	Wum	Um	Humpf	Fuddle	Glikk	Nuh	Snee

| Quan | Thnad | Spazz | Floob | Zatz | Jogg | Flunn | Itch |

| Yekk | Vroo | Hi! | - |

FROM DR. SEUSS'S BOOK: *ON BEYOND ZEBRA*

In order to understand the following fluid solver code, it is helpful to grasp the concept of a linear system of equations.

If you are familiar with this material feel free to skip this *Intermezzo* and go to the washroom.

If you are not familiar with linear systems, no worries linear systems are one of the simplest problems to solve in mathematics.

For starters I think anyone who is reading this book can solve this single linear equation without any effort

$$5 \times x = 7.$$

This equation asks which unknown thing x multiplied by 5 equals 7.

The solution for the unknown thing is obviously the following fraction:

$$x = \frac{7}{5}.$$

Now the unknown thing becomes a known thing.

This result can also be written as follows:

$$x = \frac{1}{5} \times 7 = (5)^{-1} \times 7.$$

It might seem silly to write it in this way, but when we get to larger systems of linear equations it is helpful to keep this very simple example in mind.

Why do we always use the symbol x for the unknown? Why ex?

Apparently, it comes from the Arabic word for *thing*: شيء It is pronounced something like *she'en* in Arabic.* Because the Spanish who were invaded partially by the Arabs starting in 711 did not have a sound for "sh", they instead used "xei" and related it to the way the Greek symbol "chi" is pronounced. Chi is usually spelled as χ. It was then translated into the usual x once the rest of Europe caught up with this cool stuff from a faraway land. Algebra comes from the Arabic word *Al-Jabra*, which I have been told loosely translates into a "reunion of broken parts": الجبر. Poetry meets mathematics or mathematics meets poetry. To me it is the same, both present a beautiful realm in a different way. Both have constraints on what one can create in that realm.

Al-Jabra is the name of a mathematical treatise written in the year 820 in Baghdad, now part of Iraq.

To find an unknown thing you have to inverse something known and multiply it with the known. That is how you get the unknown from the known. That sounds a bit like interpolation, doesn't it? But it is different. It is a little bit more complicated but not too complicated.

As we have seen earlier, 1D linear equations are easily solved for a single unknown thing.

Now let's turn to a larger system like†:

$$4x + 6y = 0$$

$$3x + y = -10.$$

In this case, we have to solve for two unknown things that we labeled x and y that have to satisfy the two equations simultaneously.

By the way, I hated this stuff in high school. I am not a number cruncher. We have dumb computers for doing that. But let's go through the exercise of solving this puzzle.

---

* I do not speak or read Arabic. I heard the pronunciation through Google translate. There is where I also got the beautiful scriptures for *thing* and *Al-Jabra*. To me the fact that the sign for *thing* is as complicated as the *reunion of broken parts* is a complete mystery.

† We omit the "×" multiplication symbol. It is silently implied. $3 \times x = 3x$. It saves space and there is less confusion between the two exes.

One strategy to solve these equations is to first solve for y from the second equation in terms of x and then substitute that result in the first equation to find x. Then we go back to our second equation and solve for y.

Let's go and do it.

From the second equation we get that

$$y = -10 - 3x$$

Therefore, by substituting this expression for y in the first equation we have that

$$4x + 6(-10 - 3x) = 0$$

$$4x - 60 - 18x = 0$$

$$-14x - 60 = 0$$

$$x = -\frac{60}{14} = -\frac{30}{7}$$

That is just straightforward high school math. Hence, we now know the value for x and consequently we can find the value for y by substitution:

$$y = -10 + 3 \times \frac{30}{7} = \frac{-70 + 90}{7} = \frac{20}{7}$$

So, after all these boring computations we conclude that the solution is $x = \frac{-30}{7}$ and $y = \frac{20}{7}$.

Our two unknowns are now two knowns.

Since I am bad at this stuff let's make sure this is the right solution as I do not want to embarrass myself in my own book. All we have to do is just plug in the solution back into the equations and see if they are satisfied.

$$4\left(\frac{-30}{7}\right) + 6\left(\frac{20}{7}\right) = \frac{-120 + 120}{7} = 0$$

$$3\left(\frac{-30}{7}\right) + \left(\frac{20}{7}\right) = \frac{-90 + 20}{7} = \frac{-70}{7} = -10.$$

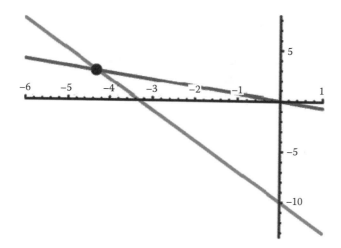

FIGURE 7.1   The solution of a 2D linear system can be computed geometrically.

Yes they are satisfied! High fives! Every smart reader of this book is now shaking their head.

Now let's make this a bit more fun, at least to me.

Let's first look at these linear equations from a geometrical point of view.

The two equations aforementioned define two lines in the plane and their intersection is the solution to the equations. This is illustrated in Figure 7.1. You can verify that the coordinates of the point of intersection matches the result we just painfully derived. Isn't it more fun to draw two lines rather than going through a series of calculations?

I think so.

By the way this geometrical approach can be generalized to any dimension not just two. In three dimensions, three 2D planes intersect in one point. Well okay not always, like in the case when some of them are parallel. That is when it gets tricky. Mathematicians call these cases *degenerate dimensions*. For four dimensional linear systems, we intersect four 3D *hyperplanes*. For N dimensional systems we intersect N (N–1)-dimensional hyperplanes.

Do not ask me how to visualize them. That is someone else's job.

That is why we introduce *matrices*. Matrices are like apartment buildings that contain numbers, not bugs. They are useful to solve linear problems. The 2D linear system earlier can be written using a matrix as:

$$\begin{pmatrix} 4 & 6 \\ 3 & 1 \end{pmatrix} \begin{pmatrix} x \\ y \end{pmatrix} = \begin{pmatrix} 0 \\ -10 \end{pmatrix}$$

In plain speak: a known thing called a matrix multiplies an unknown thing called a vector, which has to be equal to a known vector. It generalizes the simple 1D problem mentioned earlier. The solution is now

$$\begin{pmatrix} x \\ y \end{pmatrix} = \begin{pmatrix} 4 & 6 \\ 3 & 1 \end{pmatrix}^{-1} \begin{pmatrix} 0 \\ -10 \end{pmatrix}$$

This seems more posh than the usual high school derivation. The caveat of course is: what is the inverse of a matrix? For a number which is a special case of a matrix it is just one over the number as long as that number is not zero. Degenerates cases like that are a pain, but there are known ways to deal with them without anyone getting hurt.

Computing inverses of matrices is crucial to animating fluids. We will see that in practice you do not have to *explicitly* compute the inverse.

We have just replaced common numbers with matrices and vectors. Mathematicians take the liberty of treating them as another type of *number*. They are not the familiar numbers we are used to, but you can multiply them and invert them just like our familiar numbers.

Why stick to only two unknowns and two by two apartment buildings? This approach also works for 3D equations: in this case our unknowns are x, y, and z. What about bigger systems? We seem to be running out of characters. We could use the other roman characters but we are left with only 23 of them. Dr. Seuss in another genius book called *On Beyond Zebra* introduced other symbols coming out of his imagination to extend the roman characters. But even Dr. Seuss was running out of symbols. Mathematicians borrow heavily from Greek symbols and Hebrew symbols. But that is still not enough.

The way out of this conundrum is to *label* a single character. Let's use the Arabic *thing* character x, which is the most popular character for an unknown that we are trying to figure out from known things. A label is just a way to distinguish between identical looking things. Imagine being in a former communist country where every shampoo bottle has the same shape. Which one would you buy? No advertisements back then. Well you would check out the labels. That is the same for our unknowns. Each x now has a label attached to it. Usually, it works as follows: "thing one," "thing two," thing three," "thing four," "thing five," "all the intermediate things," "the size of my linear system."

Actually, when we discussed diffusion if you remember we already introduced the label notation.

But let me repeat it. Repetition is a good way to understand stuff. At least that works for me.

Instead of (x, y) we write $\mathbf{x} = (x_1, x_2)$. We can generalize this and now we can deal with big systems of equations. Let's say the size is $N = 1{,}000{,}234{,}000{,}120$ then our vector of unknowns can be written as follows:

$$\mathbf{x} = (x_1, x_2, x_3, x_4, x_5, \ldots, x_N).$$

Mathematicians are lazy but they are smart and that is why they can be lazy. I did not write out all 1,000,234,000,120 labeled things.* The "..." does the trick. It means that you are smart enough to figure it out, you can see the pattern. If you are bored you can always complete the entire sequence. But why bother? In fact I could have listed only two things separated by the "...": the first one has the label "1" and the last one has the label "the size of my linear system."

Now that we know how to label vectors of any size how do we label matrices? If you think of a matrix as an apartment building it is pretty obvious that you need the floor number and the apartment number on that floor. That is two numbers. *Bingo!* We can write a matrix using two labels. Also our apartment buildings are square. No hipsters are allowed in. Each floor has as many apartments as the number of floors.

Therefore our matrix of size N can be written as follows:

$$\mathbf{A} = \begin{pmatrix} a_{11} & \cdots & a_{1N} \\ \vdots & \ddots & \vdots \\ a_{N1} & \cdots & a_{NN} \end{pmatrix}.$$

Similarly, the known vector on the right-hand side can be written as (it should be a column vector really):

$$\mathbf{b} = (b_1, \ldots, b_N).$$

---

* My editor would be happy since I would then meet the quota of pages that I promised to write.

And here comes the expression for a general linear system:

$$\mathbf{A}\,\mathbf{x} = \mathbf{b}.$$

How do you multiply a vector by a matrix? It should be obvious from the simple 2D example.

But here is the rule just in case:

$$\begin{pmatrix} a_{11} & a_{12} \\ a_{21} & a_{22} \end{pmatrix} \begin{pmatrix} x_1 \\ x_2 \end{pmatrix} = \begin{pmatrix} a_{11}\,x_1 + a_{12}\,x_2 \\ a_{21}\,x_1 + a_{22}\,x_2 \end{pmatrix}.$$

The matrix multiplies a vector in order to produce another vector.

That is how simple linear systems are.

And it works for any size.

And the solution is readily available:

$$\mathbf{x} = \mathbf{A}^{-1}\,\mathbf{b}.$$

That is it.

Of course that is not it. We still have to compute the inverse of the matrix, we need another *Intermezzo*.

To summarize: Matrices and vectors are useful to solve linear problems. Matrices are kind of like numbers as you can add, subtract, multiply, and sometimes divide them. There is one crucial difference, however; that is, that matrices do not always **commute**: **AB−BA** is not always equal to zero.*

7.2 INTERMEZZO DUE: THE GENERAL SOLUTION OF A LINEAR SYSTEM

[I was advised] to read Jordan's *Cours d'Analyse*; and I shall never forget the astonishment with which I read that remarkable work, the first inspiration for so many mathematicians of my generation, and learnt for the first time as I read it what mathematics really meant.

GODFREY HAROLD HARDY (FAMOUS ENGLISH MATHEMATICIAN)

---

* Heisenberg used this result to derive his uncertainty principle. The funny fact is that Heisenberg did not know that his operators were in fact infinite-dimensional matrices. He did not know about matrices! Fellow mathematicians, when he showed his results to them, they were like: "Dude those are matrices."

If a Jordan canonical form of a matrix is familiar to you than you can skip this *Intermezzo* and go to the washroom.

This *Intermezzo* starts with a bombastic statement.

> There is a fundamental result in mathematics that says that every matrix can be put in a *Jordan canonical form*. This result is named after the French mathematician, Camille Jordan (1838–1922), not after a country in the Middle East.

This result basically says that

> For each matrix there is a linear transform that will put it into a much simpler form.

It is vague but it captures the gist. We will make it more concrete.

Let me explain this concept with a simple example of an ellipse living in the plane. Ellipses can have various shapes and orientations as shown in Figure 7.2a. The circle is a special case. In general, an ellipse is defined by the lengths of its principal directions and also by a rotation angle.'

In the bottom of Figure 7.2, we show the same ellipse represented using different reference frames illustrated by the two arrows in the center of the ellipse. If the arrows are aligned with the principal axes of the ellipses (Figure 7.2b, right) then the description of the ellipse is much simpler.

The two descriptions are equally valid. Just one of them is simpler. Simple is good because it involves less boring math and more fun math.

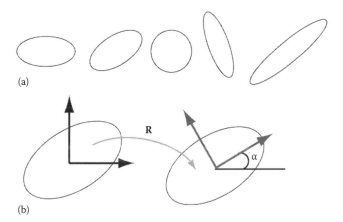

(a)

(b)

FIGURE 7.2 Examples of ellipses in the plane (a) and two descriptions of the same ellipse (b).

How do you describe an ellipse? There are really many ways. But let's take the example of a circle of unit length first which is a special case of an ellipse. In this case the two principal axes have identical lengths: equal to one in this case. The unit circle can be defined as the set of all points that are at a distance of one from the center of the circle. If x and y are the coordinates of a point in the plane, then according to Pythagoras the following identity has to hold:

$$x^2 + y^2 = 1$$

What does this have to do with matrices?

Well we can alternatively write this relationship as follows:

$$(x \quad y)\begin{pmatrix} 1 & 0 \\ 0 & 1 \end{pmatrix}\begin{pmatrix} x \\ y \end{pmatrix} = 1$$

There you go: here is a lucky boring matrix squeezed in between two unknown vectors. They are identical twins actually: one is lying down and one is standing up straight.

In fancy vector notations this becomes

$$\mathbf{x}^T \, \mathbf{A} \, \mathbf{x} = 1.^*$$

In the case of the circle, the matrix is called the *identity matrix*. It is the equivalent of the number "1" for matrices. Hence the name, you multiply a vector by the identity matrix and you get the same vector back. For numbers, for example, we have the obvious fact that $1 \times 2345 = 2345$. This is the reason that 1 is not considered a prime number by the way. It would contradict the "unique prime decomposition theorem."

Any number multiplied by one gives us back the same number. I think most people are taught that in grade school.

---

* What about that "*T*" superscript? It is used to denote the transpose of a vector. This is a matter of convention. I like my vectors to stand upright by default: a column of numbers. To get a row of numbers you just rotate your tall and thin vector by −90°. And *voila!* You get the transpose of a vector: a vector lying on its back. Just to make it clear what this equation says

$$(x \quad y)\begin{pmatrix} 1 & 0 \\ 0 & 1 \end{pmatrix}\begin{pmatrix} x \\ y \end{pmatrix} = (x \quad y)\begin{pmatrix} x \\ y \end{pmatrix} = x^2 + y^2$$

For noncircular ellipses the corresponding matrix is not as simple. However, it can be made simple through a particular linear transformation: a rotation in the plane.*

We will spend a little bit more time on this problem.

This exercise shows the beauty of abstraction in mathematics.

It is the art of replacing concrete things by nonsensical abstract symbols that have to satisfy certain rules. You apply these rules to these nonsensical symbols and you get results. Then these results can be applied to a variety of concrete problems. That is the power of abstraction. Recall the Arabic origin of the word *Algebra*: it is a "reunion of broken parts."

The general equation of an ellipse in the plane is

$$A x^2 + 2Bxy + Cy^2 = 1$$

In matrix form this can be written as

$$(x \quad y)\begin{pmatrix} A & B \\ B & C \end{pmatrix}\begin{pmatrix} x \\ y \end{pmatrix} = 1$$

Our matrix is now not as simple as in the case of the unit circle. The equation stands for any ellipse after all. But the matrix is special, it is *symmetrical*. What that means is that if you take the mirror image of the matrix along its left to right diagonal you get the same matrix. More concretely

$$\begin{pmatrix} A & B \\ B & C \end{pmatrix} = \begin{pmatrix} A & B \\ B & C \end{pmatrix}^T.$$

This is not always the case. Consider the following nonsymmetrical matrix:

$$\begin{pmatrix} 3 & 6 \\ 10 & 1 \end{pmatrix} \neq \begin{pmatrix} 3 & 10 \\ 6 & 1 \end{pmatrix}.$$

---

* Here is the exact expression if you need to know: $\mathbf{R}(\alpha) = \begin{pmatrix} \cos(\alpha) & \sin(\alpha) \\ -\sin(\alpha) & \cos(\alpha) \end{pmatrix}$.

In Figure 7.2b, we show how to put our matrix in a simpler form. All we have to do is to find the rotation matrix that transforms the black frame on the left into the red frame on the right. The right frame is nicer since it is aligned with the principal axes of the ellipse. All we are doing is just changing our frame of reference. The ellipse has not changed. We are just looking at it in a different way.

We just changed the description of something without changing it.

The new coordinates are obtained from the old ones through the rotation transformation:

$$\begin{pmatrix} x' \\ y' \end{pmatrix} = \mathbf{R}(\alpha) \begin{pmatrix} x \\ y \end{pmatrix}$$

In these new coordinates the equation of the ellipse becomes

$$(x' \quad y') \begin{pmatrix} \dfrac{1}{a^2} & 0 \\ 0 & \dfrac{1}{b^2} \end{pmatrix} \begin{pmatrix} x' \\ y' \end{pmatrix} = 1$$

And guess what? The numbers a and b are the lengths of the principal axes of the ellipse. So, what we have done through a rotation is to simplify the ellipsoidal matrix to a *diagonal* matrix. This is an apartment building that is empty except for the rooms that have the same number as the floor it is on. Lots of empty rooms, everyone will sleep well.

Hence, for our ellipsoidal matrix we have that

$$\begin{pmatrix} A & B \\ B & C \end{pmatrix} = \mathbf{R}^T \begin{pmatrix} \dfrac{1}{a^2} & 0 \\ 0 & \dfrac{1}{b^2} \end{pmatrix} \mathbf{R}$$

This is where the beauty of abstraction kicks in. We can write this result for any symmetrical matrix **A**.

There is a transformation **R** and diagonal matrix **D** such that

$$\mathbf{A} = \mathbf{R}^T \mathbf{D} \mathbf{R}$$

Well we just showed that our ellipse matrix is equivalent to a diagonal matrix. We just changed how we view things and *voilà!*

We used ellipses just to visualize the transformation and the subsequent simplification.

We now present a higher-dimensional example. Like this matrix of size 10×10:

$$\begin{bmatrix} 2 & -1 & 4 & -3 & 6 & 7 & 8 & 2 & 5 & -2 \\ -1 & 3 & -7 & 8 & 2 & -3 & -5 & 1 & 0 & 4 \\ 4 & -7 & 1 & 5 & 9 & 4 & -4 & -3 & 8 & -1 \\ -3 & 8 & 5 & 7 & -4 & 1 & 5 & 3 & 7 & 3 \\ 6 & 2 & 9 & -4 & 5 & -6 & 7 & -8 & 1 & -4 \\ 7 & -3 & 4 & 1 & -6 & -1 & 4 & 6 & 0 & 2 \\ 8 & -5 & -4 & 5 & 7 & 4 & 6 & 1 & 4 & 0 \\ 2 & 1 & -3 & 3 & -8 & 6 & 1 & -4 & 2 & 6 \\ 5 & 0 & 8 & 7 & 1 & 0 & 4 & 2 & 1 & -3 \\ -2 & 4 & -1 & 3 & -4 & 2 & 0 & 6 & -3 & -8 \end{bmatrix}$$

There exists a linear transformation that will turn this matrix into the following simpler diagonal form:

$$\begin{bmatrix} 1.6362 & 0 & 0 & 0 & 0 & 0 & 0 & 0 & 0 & 0 \\ 0 & 8.9481 & 0 & 0 & 0 & 0 & 0 & 0 & 0 & 0 \\ 0 & 0 & 13.930 & 0 & 0 & 0 & 0 & 0 & 0 & 0 \\ 0 & 0 & 0 & 19.872 & 0 & 0 & 0 & 0 & 0 & 0 \\ 0 & 0 & 0 & 0 & 25.620 & 0 & 0 & 0 & 0 & 0 \\ 0 & 0 & 0 & 0 & 0 & -3.0797 & 0 & 0 & 0 & 0 \\ 0 & 0 & 0 & 0 & 0 & 0 & -7.8420 & 0 & 0 & 0 \\ 0 & 0 & 0 & 0 & 0 & 0 & 0 & -12.452 & 0 & 0 \\ 0 & 0 & 0 & 0 & 0 & 0 & 0 & 0 & -13.986 & 0 \\ 0 & 0 & 0 & 0 & 0 & 0 & 0 & 0 & 0 & -20.646 \end{bmatrix}$$

To compute this matrix I used the symbolic math package called *Maple*. I love these symbolic packages as they take care of the boring math. If a computer can do the math than you know it is boring math. My contribution was to make sure that the 10×10 matrix is indeed symmetrical. That's it. Then I just told Maple to compute the *eigenvalues* of the matrix, and Bingo, it returned the values on the diagonal of the matrix. I truncated them too. The numbers on the diagonal are not the exact values.

Eigenvalues? *Eigen* is German for *self* or *own*. Not that that is a very helpful fact to know. These values are specific to the matrix and are owned by it. Not really. Different matrices can have the same eigenvalues. But they are basically the same as in the case of our ellipse. However, they have different eigenvectors.

Why bother with this math involving German-sounding names and transformations? Well it can help you to compute the inverse of a matrix. Inverting a diagonal matrix is just like inverting numbers. All you have to do is invert every number on the diagonal. For example:

$$
\begin{pmatrix} 14 & 0 & 0 \\ 0 & 3 & 0 \\ 0 & 0 & -6 \end{pmatrix}^{-1} = \begin{pmatrix} \dfrac{1}{14} & 0 & 0 \\ 0 & \dfrac{1}{3} & 0 \\ 0 & 0 & -\dfrac{1}{6} \end{pmatrix}.
$$

The beauty is that solving for inverses is now as simple as the case of a single number. Of course we have not mentioned how to compute this magical transform that takes our dense matrix to the nicer diagonal matrix. The Maple software took care of that for our 10D linear system. To compute the transform usually involves computing *eigenvectors*. We are not going to dwell too much on this subject. I just wanted to mention that through clever mathematics any linear system can be brought into a simpler linear system. This all works out nicely if the magical transform can easily be computed. That is the key. We will see that for fluids living on donuts the transform is well known and it is called the *Fourier transform*.

Everything I said is valid for symmetrical matrices of any size, not only 3×3 or 10×10.

What about arbitrary matrices that are not symmetrical?

Camille Jordan, the French mathematician I mentioned at the beginning of this section, took care of that. He proved that for any arbitrary matrix you can find a linear transformation that decomposes the matrix into a bunch of *Jordan blocks*.

FIGURE 7.3   Jordan (in background) with two Jordan blocks (foreground). In this case, there are two blocks and they are bounded by red rectangles. One has a size of 3×3 and another has a size of 4×4. (Modified from Public Domain.)

Figure 7.3 shows a picture of Camille Jordan with two blocks superimposed on his face representing some 7×7 matrix. In this case there are two blocks. The first block is of size 3×3 and the second one is of size 4×4. Notice that the matrix is in general almost diagonal except for the pesky number ones on the heads of some of the diagonal numbers.

Jordan's achievement is monumental.

It is amazing that all matrices can be reduced to this simple form. Symmetrical matrices are a special case where all Jordan blocks have a size of 1×1. No one has a pesky one on their head in this case.

That is it for linear systems then, right?

No it is still not it.

In theory, yes, but in practice we do not normally compute the Jordan canonical form for linear systems. Not for fluid animation at any rate. But it is very cool to know that this result is rock solid and has a mathematically rigorous proof.*

---

* I have used it in some of my other research on *subdivision surfaces*. I used the fact that taking powers of matrices is the same as taking powers of the Jordan blocks, which are much simpler to compute.

To summarize: Any matrix can be put into a simpler form. A diagonal matrix for symmetrical matrices and for general matrices is the Jordan canonical form: blocks with ones on their heads. This can help to invert and understand matrices.

7.3 INTERMEZZO TRE: CIRCULANT MATRICES AND THE FOURIER TRANSFORM

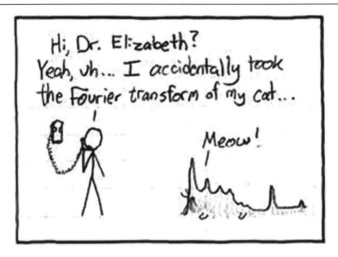

CREATED BY RANDALL MUNROE CHECK OUT HIS STUFF AT HTTP://XKCD.COM

Before we move on let me describe a beautiful result that will help us solve the motion of fluids on donuts. Remember those pesky bugs crawling all over your yummy morning donut.

This involves the all mighty *Fourier transform*. If you are already familiar with this most well-known transform of all transforms you can skip this *Intermezzo* and go stretch your legs.

It is not usually explained in the following manner, at least not to engineers I believe. This is how it was roughly explained in one of my Abstract Algebra classes 27 years ago. This is from fuzzy memory.

The Fourier transform on the other hand is heavily used by engineers.

We have to know about things called *roots of unity* first. This can be explained with algebraic things or using geometrical figures.

Let's start with the algebraic approach involving things. In this case the problem becomes: "which things, when raised to some given power are equal to one." Warning: there are going to be a lot of *ones* in the following paragraphs.

The simplest case is

$$z = 1.$$

Wow, that was easy. Only one solution: only one is equal to one. It seems almost absurd to have an equation for such a simple fact, but to some people it looks impressive.

Next we can try

$$z^2 = 1.$$

Now we have two solutions: $z = -1$ and $z = 1$. Minus one times minus one is equal to one and one times one is equal to one. That was kind of easy too.

Alright, what about

$$z^3 = 1.$$

Now it gets more interesting. We should have three solutions right? The number one is of course one of them since one times one times one times one equals one. What about the two other things? It is not going to be minus one this time because minus one times minus one times minus one is equal to minus one, not one. Got that?

We are stuck only if we consider the numbers that we are used to. The way out of this trap is to just add another dimension. We extend our numbers stuck on a 1D line into 2D numbers. This is just like the vectors in the plane we described earlier. Two-dimensional numbers are really the sweet spot for these types of problems. Three-dimensional numbers are useless. But 4D numbers called *quaternions* are useful to describe rotations and other stuff. Game developers use them, for example. We do not need them in this book. The basic relations of quaternions were engraved on Broome Bridge in Dublin, Ireland, by Hamilton when he discovered them on a stroll through the city. Hamilton was an Irish mathematician. Check it out when you happen to be in Dublin. Not your usual tourist attraction. Most people go to Temple Bar or the Guinness Brewery. But check it out nevertheless if you get a chance.

Generally, the 2D numbers we need are called *complex numbers* or *imaginary numbers*. In my opinion, these are badly chosen names for these numbers because they actually make everything simpler, not more complex. There is nothing imaginary about them either. They should be called *awesome numbers* instead.

I am not going to present the basic theory of awesome numbers (I mean *cough!* complex numbers) as there are thousands of excellent books that do a wonderful job explaining why they are so awesome. I encourage readers to look it up. This is a book about fluid animation after all not about awesome numbers. But awesome numbers can help to animate awesome-looking fluids on donuts.

I am just going to stick to awesome numbers (vectors) that are of length one: the vectors centered at the origin whose tip lies on a unit circle. In the previous examples, we had our unknown thing z raised to the power one, power two, and power three and we wanted to find the unknown things when raised to these powers to be equal to the awesome number one. The awesome number one in the awesome system of numbers is the vector of length one that lies on the horizontal line and points to the right.

Geometrically for a given power n the solutions are all the vectors that are a multiple of the angle of 360° divided by n. So for $n = 1$ it is just the vector of length one that points in the positive direction because a rotation of 360° will bring it back to itself. For $n = 2$ we of course have the usual vector of length one but also the vector in the opposite direction because it is a rotation of 180 which is half of 360.* So far, our solutions live in the familiar 1D numbers domain. But they are embedded in the 2D space of awesome numbers. They are a subset. Most awesome numbers eschew the lowly 1D numbers stuck on their infinite line.

For $n = 3$ it gets more interesting. Now our rotation angle is $360°/3° = 120°$. Again we have our vector of unit length but also the rotated ones. They are depicted on the left side of Figure 7.4. Next to the $n = 3$ (cubic) case, we also depict the solutions for $n = 4, 5, 10$. The pattern is pretty obvious. The solutions are evenly spaced like the spokes on a bicycle wheel. In each case, the red vectors can be brought to align with the black one by rotating them counterclockwise a number of times with an angle equal to $360/n$. The "number of times" is a number between zero and $n-1$.

---

* Those of you who paid attention so far will recall that this is why Euler's beautiful formula is true.

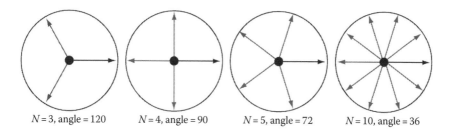

$N = 3$, angle = 120 $N = 4$, angle = 90 $N = 5$, angle = 72 $N = 10$, angle = 36

FIGURE 7.4   Roots of unity for degrees 3, 4, 5, and 10.

What is the connection between raising some number to a given power and the roots of unity?*

To take the power of a unit awesome number you just multiply its angle with respect to the awesome one vector times the power. Remember an awesome unit vector is defined by a rotation angle with respect to the awesome one number.

Let us do it for the power three. Remember I am a *freak* and I like to explain things with simple examples.

$$3 \times 0 = 0$$

$$3 \times 120 = 360 = 0$$

$$3 \times 240 = 720 = 0.$$

This seems like crazy math but really that is not the case. Remember these angles are like bicycle spokes or the hands on your wristwatch.

They rotate and circulate.

They eventually end up at the same spot. Not like usual numbers that run off to infinity. *Hilbert's infinite hotel* trick doesn't apply in this case. "Sorry we are full we cannot move guests around because we are fully booked because this is a finite hotel." Down the street you will find Hilbert's infinite hotel which has cheaper rates. Hilbert's hotel always has a vacant room. All you have to do is move the guest from room 1 to room 2, move the guest from room 2 to room 3, move the guest from room 3 to room 4, and so on. This is a bit of a pain for the guests but hey the rates are cheap. Pack lightly when you intend to check in at "Hilbert's infinite hotel."

---

* For those of you who know this kind of math it is because: $(e^{i2\pi j/n})^n = e^{i2\pi j} = 1$. With $j = 0, \ldots n-1$.

The wristwatch is a good analogy. When you adjust your watch for 12 hours you end up with the same time. When I travel to China, I do not have to adjust my watch since there is a 12-hour time difference between China and Toronto. I mention China, not a specific city or region because they are all on the same time zone.

It does not help to get over your jet lag however. The Air Canada flight from Beijing to Toronto leaves at 6 p.m. and gets you back at 6 p.m. the same day.

In Figure 7.4 (left), the black vector needs to be rotated zero times by 120°, and the first red vector needs to be rotated counterclockwise two times by 120° to align it with the black one. The second red vector has to be rotated only counterclockwise once by 120° to align it with the black one.

Just from visually inspecting Figure 7.4, one can notice some interesting properties of the roots of unity. Every root has a partner root, which is its reflection with respect to the horizontal axis. In this ballroom you are also allowed to be your own partner. Awesome one is allowed to dance with itself. If the degree n is an even number like 4 and 10 then every root has a partner pointing in the opposite direction. All these facts can be rigorously proved. But they are pretty self-evident from Figure 7.4.

Also their total sum is always equal to zero. For an even number of roots this is pretty obvious: every root cancels out his/her partner root. For odd number roots it works out as well.

Keep these roots of awesome one in mind.

We will now turn to circulant matrices and later bring back our waltzing roots of unity to join the party.

There is a good reason why these matrices are called circulant and they are intimately related to our roots of unity that live on a circle.

To construct circulant matrices we start with a vector of any size. To clear any confusion I have to state that awesome numbers can be represented by 2D vectors. The vectors that are multiplied by the circulant matrices on the other hand can be vectors of arbitrary size that sometimes contain awesome numbers.

Just to make it more concrete we will start with a vector of size three:

$$(a,b,c).$$

The numbers a, b, and c can have arbitrary values.

One example could be

$$(1, -40, 1024).$$

From this vector we can create what is usually called a *circulant matrix*. The way you construct such a matrix is to fill the rows with a right-shifted version of the vector to create a matrix. In our example, you get the following 3×3 matrix:

$$\mathbf{A} = \begin{pmatrix} a & b & c \\ c & a & b \\ b & c & a \end{pmatrix}.$$

Figure 7.5 shows how to construct the circulant matrix from a vector. The figure uses the same pattern of unitary roots as shown in Figure 7.4 in the case of three roots. This time we label each root with the numbers stored in the vector.

This is how it works.

We fill in each row of the matrix counterclockwise from each circle starting from the awesome one. Subsequently, we rotate the labels counterclockwise and fill out the remaining four rows similarly. Hopefully, this process is clear from comparing Figure 7.5 and the circulant matrix earlier.

It is pretty easy to spot the pattern in the matrix as well: identical numbers flowing diagonally from left to right.

Let us go back to the roots of unity for a power of three. These roots can be labeled from the second root denoted by ω. This root raised to any power

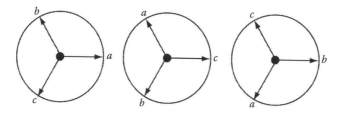

FIGURE 7.5   The rows of a 3×3 circulant matrix are obtained by counterclockwise rotations.

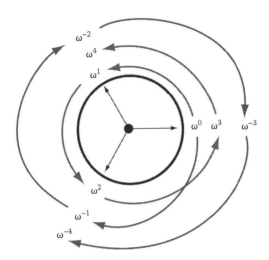

FIGURE 7.6 All the roots of unity for the case of a power 3 can be obtained by taking powers of the second root denoted by ω^1.

in the awesome system of numbers gives us all the roots. In fact $\omega^0 = 1$: returns the awesome number one which is the first root. In Figure 7.6, we show that all the roots of unity can be obtained by taking the powers from the second root of unity.

This root is usually denoted by the symbol ω. It comes from the Greek alphabet and is pronounced *omega*. It also looks pretty. Taking powers of this pretty symbol gives us all the roots of unity as shown in Figure 7.6. If we follow the red arrows we get all the roots counterclock wise. On the other hand, if we follow the blue arrows we get all the roots clockwise. The only difference is that in one case we take positive powers (red) while in the other case (blue) we take negative powers. This can go on forever.

Notice that $\omega^3 = 1$. This is the case for all powers that are multiples of three.

Therefore, all the following numbers are all equal to the awesome number one.

$$1 = \ldots, \omega^{-6}, \omega^{-3}, \omega^0, \omega^3, \omega^6, \ldots$$

Another important property is that the sum of the roots of unity is equal to zero. Geometrically, if you connect all the roots of unity you get a regular polygon. In this case it is a triangle. But it works for all other cases as well.

Looking at Figure 7.4 we can easily construct regular polygons that connect the roots of unity: we get a triangle (3), a square (4), a pentagon (5), and a decagon (10). For the general case of n roots you get what mathematicians call an *n-gon*. No fancy Greek this time.

The center of mass of an arbitrary regular polygon is clearly zero
Mathematically, for our degree three example we have that

$$1 + \omega + \omega^2 = 0.$$

Now here enters the magic.

For circulant matrices the transform, which by the way is also a matrix, is constructed as follows for the 3×3 case:

$$\mathbf{F} = \frac{1}{\sqrt{3}} \begin{pmatrix} 1 & 1 & 1 \\ 1 & \omega & \omega^2 \\ 1 & \omega^2 & \omega^4 \end{pmatrix}.$$

Using the properties of the roots shown in Figure 7.6 and by following the red arrows we can rewrite this matrix as follows:

$$\mathbf{F} = \frac{1}{\sqrt{3}} \begin{pmatrix} 1 & 1 & 1 \\ 1 & \omega & \omega^2 \\ 1 & \omega^2 & \omega \end{pmatrix}.$$

For circulant matrices this magical transform will make it diagonal. The transform takes us into the nice clean space where the matrix is diagonal. But how do we get back to the messy hood? We replace every power of the root ω by its inverse. We now follow the blue arrows in Figure 7.6. We get that

$$\mathbf{F}^{-1} = \frac{1}{\sqrt{3}} \begin{pmatrix} 1 & 1 & 1 \\ 1 & \omega^2 & \omega \\ 1 & \omega & \omega^2 \end{pmatrix}.$$

Sanity check: Let's verify that the transform times the inverse gives us the identity matrix. Remember the identity matrix? That is the matrix that has only 1s on the diagonal.

Here is the math:

$$\mathbf{F}^{-1}\,\mathbf{F} = \frac{1}{\sqrt{3}}\begin{pmatrix} 1 & 1 & 1 \\ 1 & \omega^2 & \omega \\ 1 & \omega & \omega^2 \end{pmatrix}\frac{1}{\sqrt{3}}\begin{pmatrix} 1 & 1 & 1 \\ 1 & \omega & \omega^2 \\ 1 & \omega^2 & \omega \end{pmatrix}$$

$$= \frac{1}{3}\begin{pmatrix} 3 & 1+\omega+\omega^2 & 1+\omega^2+\omega \\ 1+\omega^2+\omega & 3 & 1+\omega+\omega^2 \\ 1+\omega+\omega^2 & 1+\omega^2+\omega & 3 \end{pmatrix} = \begin{pmatrix} 1 & 0 & 0 \\ 0 & 1 & 0 \\ 0 & 0 & 1 \end{pmatrix}.$$

All those off-diagonal identical terms are equal to zero because the roots of unity add up to zero. Recall the regular polygons and the corresponding algebraic relation:

$$1+\omega+\omega^2 = 0.$$

All is good. We now have a recipe to compute the corresponding diagonal matrix **D** from the circulant matrix **A**.

To simplify the math we use the result that every 3×3 circulant matrix can be written as

$$\mathbf{A} = a\mathbf{I} + b\mathbf{S} + c\mathbf{S}^2.$$

This is just a way of using algebra to rewrite the circulant matrix. The **S** matrix just models a shift. In fact it is equal to

$$\mathbf{S} = \begin{pmatrix} 0 & 1 & 0 \\ 0 & 0 & 1 \\ 1 & 0 & 0 \end{pmatrix} \text{ and therefore } \mathbf{S}^2 = \mathbf{S}\times\mathbf{S} = \begin{pmatrix} 0 & 0 & 1 \\ 1 & 0 & 0 \\ 0 & 1 & 0 \end{pmatrix}.$$

Go ahead and verify this fact at home.

The important point here is that this result is true for any vector (a,b,c). From some simple algebra, we conclude that the corresponding diagonal matrix is equal to

$$\mathbf{D} = \mathbf{F}^{-1}\,\mathbf{A}\,\mathbf{F} = a\,\mathbf{F}^{-1}\mathbf{F} + b\,\mathbf{F}^{-1}\mathbf{S}\mathbf{F} + c\,\mathbf{F}^{-1}\mathbf{S}^2\,\mathbf{F}.$$

I made it simple by considering only small 3×3 matrices. For larger systems you have to take more powers of the matrix $\mathbf{S}$.

For the 3×3 case when working out the math we get that

$$
\mathbf{D} = \begin{pmatrix} a & 0 & 0 \\ 0 & a & 0 \\ 0 & 0 & a \end{pmatrix} + \begin{pmatrix} b & 0 & 0 \\ 0 & b\omega & 0 \\ 0 & 0 & b\omega^2 \end{pmatrix} + \begin{pmatrix} c & 0 & 0 \\ 0 & c\omega^2 & 0 \\ 0 & 0 & c\omega \end{pmatrix}
$$

$$
= \begin{pmatrix} a+b+c & 0 & 0 \\ 0 & a+b\omega+c\omega^2 & 0 \\ 0 & 0 & a+c\omega+b\omega^2 \end{pmatrix}.
$$

That is it.

There are our magical transformations and the resulting diagonal matrix.

I know this has been a bit heavy on the cool math. However, the only numbers we used were 1, 2, 3, and $\sqrt{3}$. All the rest was algebra that applies to many more numbers, even awesome ones. This is the kind of math I love. And perhaps I have spent a little too much space on explaining the discrete Fourier transform. The theory is beautiful and very useful at the same time: a double whammy.

To summarize: The Fourier transform provides the magical transformation from circulant matrices to diagonal matrices. The Fourier transform and its inverse can be written explicitly and elegantly in closed form. We presented it for the special case of 3×3 matrices. But the theory can be extended in a straightforward manner for larger systems. In fact it works for any circulant matrix of any size. How cool is that?

7.4 INTERMEZZO QUATTRO: NUMERICAL SOLUTION OF LINEAR SYSTEMS

Mathematics is the science of what is clear by itself.

CARL GUSTAV JACOB JACOBI (GREAT GERMAN
MATHEMATICIAN)

When I have clarified and exhausted a subject, then I turn away from it, in order to go into darkness again.

CARL FRIEDRICH GAUSS (FAMOUS GERMAN
MATHEMATICIAN)

I will try to make this a short *Intermezzo* as there are thousands of excellent books on this topic that explain this material really well. My hope is to give enough information in order for the reader to understand some of the code as follows.

To reiterate: if you are familiar with this material skip this *Intermezzo* and get a drink. Take a break. I recommend a Chinotto or a Campari on the rocks.

Thus far, we have seen that any matrix can be transformed in a simpler form involving Jordan blocks. For circulant matrices this transformation is explicitly given by the discrete Fourier transform.

Now welcome to the messy world of numerical matrices. Welcome to downtown and make sure you carry a computer that is password protected.

Numerical matrices contain computer numbers. Computer numbers are not like *ideal* mathematical numbers. They are finite. They have finite precision. They have to because the computer can only handle a finite number of bits. Remember? Numerical numbers are tricky. But I will not dwell on this topic in this book. Someone ought to write a book on this subject and enlighten us all once and for all on this tricky stuff. In my experience, you deal with them like you deal with strangers whose language you barely speak. You get used to them, learn from their behavior, and you try not to get in trouble.

There are many packages commercial and free for all that manipulate numerical matrices. These packages can compute fun things like the German eigenvectors and eigenvalues, but also the inverses, transposes, pseudo-inverses, Russian Choleski decompositions, and what not for numerical matrices. Their output usually consists of numerical vectors, matrices, or even a single number as in the case of the determinant of a matrix. For example, if the determinant of your matrix is zero then you know that it is degenerate, it has a nontrivial null space. Or said differently, the matrix's kernel is nonzero. This is crazy talk. But that is how mathematicians talk and it makes complete sense if you know the lingo.

These numerical packages compute numerical unknowns from numerical knowns. Everything is done in the computer. No blackboards or whiteboards are involved and no black coffee.

Computer coders are great at naming these numerical packages. Here is a sample: BCSLIB-EXT, MA57, MUMPS, Oblio, PARDISO, SPOOLES, SPRSBLKLLT, TAUCS, UMFPACK, WSMP, and so on. This is for real.

Welcome to geek central.

I do not use any of these packages.* Not because I am lazy but because I am lucky. I like to write code instead of mashing various downloaded codes together and have them work with the latest Ubuntu Linux release, even having to rebuild the kernel in some cases. I have nothing against Linux by the way. It is just another hood to code in. I have written code there without getting hurt. But if you download code that was not written in your hood it can be painful.

Why am I lucky? This is why:

Linear systems in fluid animation are sparse.

We already observed in *Intermezzo duo* that any matrix can be transformed into a simple form, thanks to the French mathematician Camille Jordan. These matrices comprised of simple Jordan blocks are sparse. These matrices have very few elements that are not equal to zero. In fact they are almost vectors: quasi-vectors. It seems like a waste of space to write sparse matrices in matrix form. So much space wasted on lowly zeroes.

The linear systems in fluid animation are simple to start with. Their matrices contain mostly zeroes. They are sparse. They can be made sparser with Jordan's help. But this is not necessary. Computing Jordan blocks is a messy business unless you are lucky and you want to solve a fluid on a donut. In the latter case you can use the almighty Fourier transform and all your Jordan blocks are of size one.

Here is an example of a sparse matrix of size 10×10:

$$
\begin{pmatrix}
* & * & 0 & 0 & 0 & 0 & 0 & 0 & 0 & 0 \\
* & * & * & 0 & 0 & 0 & 0 & 0 & 0 & 0 \\
0 & * & * & * & 0 & 0 & 0 & 0 & 0 & 0 \\
0 & 0 & * & * & * & 0 & 0 & 0 & 0 & 0 \\
0 & 0 & 0 & * & * & * & 0 & 0 & 0 & 0 \\
0 & 0 & 0 & 0 & * & * & * & 0 & 0 & 0 \\
0 & 0 & 0 & 0 & 0 & * & * & * & 0 & 0 \\
0 & 0 & 0 & 0 & 0 & 0 & * & * & * & 0 \\
0 & 0 & 0 & 0 & 0 & 0 & 0 & * & * & * \\
0 & 0 & 0 & 0 & 0 & 0 & 0 & 0 & * & *
\end{pmatrix}.
$$

---

* I am such a liar. I used FFTW from MIT because it so cool. More about that in the following when we discuss bugs crawling on donuts.

The "*" stand for any number that is not zero, they visualize the sparseness. They do not stand for unknown things that we have to solve for. They are not exes you dumped or who dumped you. They are just a visual aid to figure out the structure of a matrix. The actual numbers are irrelevant as long as they are nonzero.

How do you measure sparseness? One measure of sparseness could be the number of "*" divided by the number of 0's? Consequently, this means that the following 20×20 matrix is sparser than the 10×10 matrix aforementioned.

$$
\begin{pmatrix}
* & * & 0 & 0 & 0 & 0 & 0 & 0 & 0 & 0 & 0 & 0 & 0 & 0 & 0 & 0 & 0 & 0 & 0 & * \\
* & * & * & 0 & 0 & 0 & 0 & 0 & 0 & 0 & 0 & 0 & 0 & 0 & 0 & 0 & 0 & 0 & 0 & 0 \\
0 & * & * & * & 0 & 0 & 0 & 0 & 0 & 0 & 0 & 0 & 0 & 0 & 0 & 0 & 0 & 0 & 0 & 0 \\
0 & 0 & * & * & * & 0 & 0 & 0 & 0 & 0 & 0 & 0 & 0 & 0 & 0 & 0 & 0 & 0 & 0 & 0 \\
0 & 0 & 0 & * & * & * & 0 & 0 & 0 & 0 & 0 & 0 & 0 & 0 & 0 & 0 & 0 & 0 & 0 & 0 \\
0 & 0 & 0 & 0 & * & * & * & 0 & 0 & 0 & 0 & 0 & 0 & 0 & 0 & 0 & 0 & 0 & 0 & 0 \\
0 & 0 & 0 & 0 & 0 & * & * & * & 0 & 0 & 0 & 0 & 0 & 0 & 0 & 0 & 0 & 0 & 0 & 0 \\
0 & 0 & 0 & 0 & 0 & 0 & * & * & * & 0 & 0 & 0 & 0 & 0 & 0 & 0 & 0 & 0 & 0 & 0 \\
0 & 0 & 0 & 0 & 0 & 0 & 0 & * & * & * & 0 & 0 & 0 & 0 & 0 & 0 & 0 & 0 & 0 & 0 \\
0 & 0 & 0 & 0 & 0 & 0 & 0 & 0 & * & * & * & 0 & 0 & 0 & 0 & 0 & 0 & 0 & 0 & 0 \\
0 & 0 & 0 & 0 & 0 & 0 & 0 & 0 & 0 & * & * & * & 0 & 0 & 0 & 0 & 0 & 0 & 0 & 0 \\
0 & 0 & 0 & 0 & 0 & 0 & 0 & 0 & 0 & 0 & * & * & * & 0 & 0 & 0 & 0 & 0 & 0 & 0 \\
0 & 0 & 0 & 0 & 0 & 0 & 0 & 0 & 0 & 0 & 0 & * & * & * & 0 & 0 & 0 & 0 & 0 & 0 \\
0 & 0 & 0 & 0 & 0 & 0 & 0 & 0 & 0 & 0 & 0 & 0 & * & * & * & 0 & 0 & 0 & 0 & 0 \\
0 & 0 & 0 & 0 & 0 & 0 & 0 & 0 & 0 & 0 & 0 & 0 & 0 & * & * & * & 0 & 0 & 0 & 0 \\
0 & 0 & 0 & 0 & 0 & 0 & 0 & 0 & 0 & 0 & 0 & 0 & 0 & 0 & * & * & * & 0 & 0 & 0 \\
0 & 0 & 0 & 0 & 0 & 0 & 0 & 0 & 0 & 0 & 0 & 0 & 0 & 0 & 0 & * & * & * & 0 & 0 \\
0 & 0 & 0 & 0 & 0 & 0 & 0 & 0 & 0 & 0 & 0 & 0 & 0 & 0 & 0 & 0 & * & * & * & 0 \\
0 & 0 & 0 & 0 & 0 & 0 & 0 & 0 & 0 & 0 & 0 & 0 & 0 & 0 & 0 & 0 & 0 & * & * & * \\
* & 0 & 0 & 0 & 0 & 0 & 0 & 0 & 0 & 0 & 0 & 0 & 0 & 0 & 0 & 0 & 0 & 0 & * & *
\end{pmatrix}.
$$

Bottom line: sparseness just means you do not have to store your entire matrix in memory because most of the entries are zero. So, really in this case you are dealing with vectors not matrices. No one wants to waste memory on the zero minions.

Apart from sparseness, there is another reason why I am lucky. You can tell this from the two matrices just shown. The reason is that:

Matrices in fluid animation have very regular patterns.

Sparseness and regularity make it much easier to solve the linear systems encountered in fluid animation.

All sparse matrices are not necessarily regular. And all regular matrices are not necessarily sparse.

Here are two examples.

$$
\begin{bmatrix} \text{sparse} \\ \textit{but} \\ \text{not regular} \end{bmatrix} =
\begin{pmatrix}
* & 0 & * & 0 & 0 & 0 & 0 & 0 & 0 & * & * & * \\
0 & 0 & 0 & * & * & 0 & 0 & 0 & 0 & 0 & 0 & 0 \\
* & * & 0 & 0 & 0 & 0 & 0 & 0 & 0 & 0 & 0 & 0 \\
0 & 0 & 0 & 0 & 0 & 0 & 0 & 0 & 0 & 0 & * & 0 \\
* & * & 0 & 0 & 0 & 0 & 0 & * & 0 & 0 & 0 & 0 \\
0 & 0 & 0 & 0 & 0 & 0 & 0 & * & 0 & 0 & 0 & 0 \\
* & * & * & * & * & 0 & 0 & 0 & 0 & 0 & 0 & 0 \\
0 & 0 & 0 & 0 & 0 & 0 & * & * & 0 & 0 & 0 & 0 \\
0 & 0 & 0 & * & 0 & 0 & 0 & 0 & 0 & 0 & * & 0 \\
0 & 0 & 0 & 0 & 0 & 0 & 0 & * & * & 0 & 0 & 0 \\
* & 0 & 0 & 0 & 0 & 0 & 0 & 0 & 0 & 0 & * & 0 \\
0 & 0 & 0 & 0 & 0 & 0 & 0 & 0 & 0 & * & 0 & *
\end{pmatrix}
$$

$$
\text{Vs} \begin{bmatrix} \text{regular} \\ \textit{but} \\ \text{not sparse} \end{bmatrix} =
\begin{pmatrix}
* & 0 & * & * & * & * & * & * & * & * \\
* & * & 0 & * & * & * & * & * & * & * \\
* & * & * & 0 & * & * & * & * & * & * \\
* & * & * & * & 0 & * & * & * & * & * \\
* & * & * & * & * & 0 & * & * & * & * \\
* & * & * & * & * & * & 0 & * & * & * \\
* & * & * & * & * & * & * & 0 & * & * \\
* & * & * & * & * & * & * & * & 0 & * \\
* & * & * & * & * & * & * & * & * & 0 \\
0 & * & * & * & * & * & * & * & * & *
\end{pmatrix}.
$$

The bottom line is that when you have to wrestle with a sparse but nonregular matrix, you probably will be better off hiring a wrestler from a sparse matrix library. On the other hand, if you have to wrestle a nonsparse but regular matrix get a wrestler from your local mathematics department. For circulant matrices, you would have to go to Grenoble in France and ask to see *Monsieur* Fourier (never mind that he is dead). If on the other hand, no clever math dude can figure it out you will have to go to your local Walmart and buy a numerical dense matrix solver software package. The greeter at the entrance will point you to the right aisle. "It is right next to the gun and ammo on aisle 15."

However, in fluid animation we are lucky. Our matrices are both sparse and regular. Therefore, we can write our own code and stay away from Walmart. I have nothing against Walmart by the way; they have cheap black T-shirts that fit me.

Let us consider a simple example as usual to see how a sparse regular linear system can be solved.

The following is the depicted heat transfer in a 1D bar. We have two boundaries. The left-hand side is heated at a constant temperature of 1 (pick your unit) and the right-hand side is held at a constant temperature of 0 (using the same units as 1). Units do not matter in this example.

The setting is pretty straightforward. We have a bar that is heated at one end and is cooled at the other end and we want to know how the temperature evolves over time. Figure 7.7 depicts the situation. We know that eventually the bar will have a steady distribution of temperature. Not constant in this case because both ends are fixed with a fixed temperature.

This is a diffusion process. Remember those crawling bugs? In this case they are stuck on a line.

Let us assume that we discretize the problem as depicted in Figure 7.7 with 8 nodes. There is nothing special about the number eight. This example of course works for any number of nodes. Nodes 1 and 8 are fixed. The temperature of node 1 is fixed to be 1 and the temperature of node 8 is fixed to be 0. That leaves us with six unknowns: node 2, node 3, node 4, node 5, node 6, and node 7.

We are interested only in the final steady state of the temperature not the evolution of temperature over time.

The temperature is higher on the left-hand side of the bar than on the right-hand side of the bar. These values are fixed once and for all. We are interested in computing the six unknown values in between.

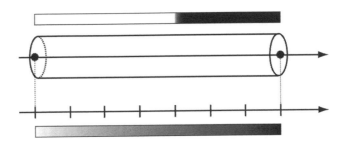

FIGURE 7.7   Heat flow in a 1D bar.

This is the corresponding linear system:

$$
\begin{pmatrix}
- & 2 & 1 & 0 & 0 & 0 & 0 \\
1 & - & 2 & 1 & 0 & 0 & 0 \\
0 & 1 & - & 2 & 1 & 0 & 0 \\
0 & 0 & 1 & - & 2 & 1 & 0 \\
0 & 0 & 0 & 1 & - & 2 & 1 \\
0 & 0 & 0 & 0 & 1 & - & 2
\end{pmatrix}
\begin{pmatrix}
x_2 \\ x_3 \\ x_4 \\ x_5 \\ x_6 \\ x_7
\end{pmatrix}
=
\begin{pmatrix}
-1 \\ 0 \\ 0 \\ 0 \\ 0 \\ 0
\end{pmatrix}.
$$

The matrix is sparse and regular. Not that sparse in this case. But larger systems will become sparser and sparser since there will be more zeroes as was shown in the examples earlier. It is definitely regular. I think that is pretty clear.

The solution is actually known precisely in this case:

$$
\begin{pmatrix}
x_2 \\ x_3 \\ x_4 \\ x_5 \\ x_6 \\ x_7
\end{pmatrix}
=
\begin{pmatrix}
\dfrac{6}{7} \\[4pt]
\dfrac{5}{7} \\[4pt]
\dfrac{4}{7} \\[4pt]
\dfrac{3}{7} \\[4pt]
\dfrac{2}{7} \\[4pt]
\dfrac{1}{7}
\end{pmatrix}.
$$

The steady state is a linear interpolation between the left-end temperature 1 and the right-hand temperature of 0. Try to verify this at home by multiplying the known regular-sparse matrix with the previously unknown vector that is now known in order to get the known vector on the right.

Why bother trying to solve this problem numerically since we already know the answer?

In my experience, this is a good strategy when implementing computer code for solvers. Think of these as sanity checks. If your code does not reproduce the sequence of six numbers for this problem, then there is something wrong with the implementation of your linear solver. Sorry, end of argument: your code is wrong. That is why mathematics is useful in writing halal code.

On the other hand, sometimes faulty code can result in amazing unexpected visual effects. In our business of computer animation we call this: "a bug has just turned into a feature."

Customer: "This is so cool!"

Coder: "Thanks. But it is wrong."

If the coolness of the bug does not break anything else in the software, we can always introduce a switch between the *cool behavior* and the *right behavior*. Turning the switch on or off is up to the user also known as the customer. Yes, a customer. Some people still pay for software, especially if it has cool bugs.

Geez and now you also have to find a name for your newly introduced switch. Like "Psychedelic Effect Number 4320" or "Psychedelic Chickens Sliding down Mount Everest." The guys writing the documentation for the software are like: what? A more boring name would be "New Incompressibility."

I am not a big fan of this approach. But if the faulty code turns out to reveal something new about how we think about a problem, then I am a big fan of this approach. Remember the motto: *if it looks good it is good*. On the other hand, I think we have to understand why it looks good. That is what my job in research is all about. If not you are just throwing dirt code on a wall and scraping off whatever sticks.

When working with computer numbers we solve these linear equations *iteratively*. We start with a guess and then refine it using many steps until we are satisfied that we are near the solution. Depending on the application this nearness condition can vary.

We will consider two techniques in this *Intermezzo*: the *Jacobi iteration* and *Gauss–Seidel iteration*. They are named after three German mathematicians: Carl Gustav Jacob Jacobi (1804–1851), Carl Friedrich Gauss (1777–1855), and Philipp Ludwig von Seidel (1821–1896). They are all depicted in Figure 7.8.

FIGURE 7.8 Jacobi, Gauss, and Seidel.

Just to clarify: *iteration* is the process of computing a sequence of vectors. Each vector is obtained from the previous one, starting with an initial vector $\mathbf{x}^{(0)}$. From that a sequence of vectors is obtained:

$$\mathbf{x}^{(0)} \to \mathbf{x}^{(1)} \to \mathbf{x}^{(2)} \to \mathbf{x}^{(3)} \to \mathbf{x}^{(4)} \to \mathbf{x}^{(5)} \to \mathbf{x}^{(6)} \to \mathbf{x}^{(7)} \to \mathbf{x}^{(8)} \to \mathbf{x}^{(9)} \to \cdots \to \mathbf{x}^{(\infty)}.$$

If all goes according to the game plan then we have in the end that

$$\mathbf{A}\,\mathbf{x}^{(\infty)} = \mathbf{b}.$$

How to obtain one iterate from the other is the art of solving linear systems iteratively. In fact, we only have to explain one step in this chain since the same rule applies to all steps separated by an arrow.*

Therefore all we have to explain is a single step:

$$\mathbf{x}^{(known)} \to \mathbf{x}^{(unknown)}.$$

Again: we are trying to get the unknown from the known. Jacobi and Gauss–Seidel have two different ways of doing this.

Jacobi updates the unknowns only using the knowns. Gauss–Seidel updates the unknowns from the knowns and the unknowns that have already been turned into knowns.

---

* This is not always the case for more sophisticated linear solvers.

Their behavior and implementation differs: Jacobi is easy to do in parallel and Gauss–Seidel eats up less memory and converges faster.

There are many ways of explaining these methods. Let us use an algebraic approach, first in cartoon matrix math and then making it explicit for our heated bar. The idea is to separate a matrix into three regions: "the diagonal," "the lower left," and the "upper right." Visually, it is something like this:

$$
\begin{pmatrix}
* & * & 0 & 0 & 0 & 0 & 0 & 0 & 0 & 0 \\
* & * & * & 0 & 0 & 0 & 0 & 0 & 0 & 0 \\
0 & * & * & * & 0 & 0 & 0 & 0 & 0 & 0 \\
0 & 0 & * & * & * & 0 & 0 & 0 & 0 & 0 \\
0 & 0 & 0 & * & * & * & 0 & 0 & 0 & 0 \\
0 & 0 & 0 & 0 & * & * & * & 0 & 0 & 0 \\
0 & 0 & 0 & 0 & 0 & * & * & * & 0 & 0 \\
0 & 0 & 0 & 0 & 0 & 0 & * & * & * & 0 \\
0 & 0 & 0 & 0 & 0 & 0 & 0 & * & * & * \\
0 & 0 & 0 & 0 & 0 & 0 & 0 & 0 & * & *
\end{pmatrix}
=
\begin{pmatrix}
* & 0 & 0 & 0 & 0 & 0 & 0 & 0 & 0 & 0 \\
0 & * & 0 & 0 & 0 & 0 & 0 & 0 & 0 & 0 \\
0 & 0 & * & 0 & 0 & 0 & 0 & 0 & 0 & 0 \\
0 & 0 & 0 & * & 0 & 0 & 0 & 0 & 0 & 0 \\
0 & 0 & 0 & 0 & * & 0 & 0 & 0 & 0 & 0 \\
0 & 0 & 0 & 0 & 0 & * & 0 & 0 & 0 & 0 \\
0 & 0 & 0 & 0 & 0 & 0 & * & 0 & 0 & 0 \\
0 & 0 & 0 & 0 & 0 & 0 & 0 & * & 0 & 0 \\
0 & 0 & 0 & 0 & 0 & 0 & 0 & 0 & * & 0 \\
0 & 0 & 0 & 0 & 0 & 0 & 0 & 0 & 0 & *
\end{pmatrix}
$$

$$
+
\begin{pmatrix}
0 & 0 & 0 & 0 & 0 & 0 & 0 & 0 & 0 & 0 \\
* & 0 & 0 & 0 & 0 & 0 & 0 & 0 & 0 & 0 \\
0 & * & 0 & 0 & 0 & 0 & 0 & 0 & 0 & 0 \\
0 & 0 & * & 0 & 0 & 0 & 0 & 0 & 0 & 0 \\
0 & 0 & 0 & * & 0 & 0 & 0 & 0 & 0 & 0 \\
0 & 0 & 0 & 0 & * & 0 & 0 & 0 & 0 & 0 \\
0 & 0 & 0 & 0 & 0 & * & 0 & 0 & 0 & 0 \\
0 & 0 & 0 & 0 & 0 & 0 & * & 0 & 0 & 0 \\
0 & 0 & 0 & 0 & 0 & 0 & 0 & * & 0 & 0 \\
0 & 0 & 0 & 0 & 0 & 0 & 0 & 0 & * & 0
\end{pmatrix}
+
\begin{pmatrix}
0 & * & 0 & 0 & 0 & 0 & 0 & 0 & 0 & 0 \\
0 & 0 & * & 0 & 0 & 0 & 0 & 0 & 0 & 0 \\
0 & 0 & 0 & * & 0 & 0 & 0 & 0 & 0 & 0 \\
0 & 0 & 0 & 0 & * & 0 & 0 & 0 & 0 & 0 \\
0 & 0 & 0 & 0 & 0 & * & 0 & 0 & 0 & 0 \\
0 & 0 & 0 & 0 & 0 & 0 & * & 0 & 0 & 0 \\
0 & 0 & 0 & 0 & 0 & 0 & 0 & * & 0 & 0 \\
0 & 0 & 0 & 0 & 0 & 0 & 0 & 0 & * & 0 \\
0 & 0 & 0 & 0 & 0 & 0 & 0 & 0 & 0 & * \\
0 & 0 & 0 & 0 & 0 & 0 & 0 & 0 & 0 & 0
\end{pmatrix}
$$

We can condense this into a more compact notation as follows:

$$\mathbf{A} = \mathbf{D} + \mathbf{L} + \mathbf{R}.$$

As shown earlier, the inverse of the diagonal matrix D is easy to compute. Just take the inverse of all the diagonal elements. This allows us to write

$$\mathbf{A}\,\mathbf{x} = \mathbf{D}\,\mathbf{x} + \mathbf{L}\,\mathbf{x} + \mathbf{R}\,\mathbf{x}.$$

To cut to the chase we will show how both Jacobi and Gauss–Seidel determine unknowns from knowns using this decomposition:
  Jacobi:

$$\mathbf{x}^{(unknown)} = \mathbf{D}^{-1}(\mathbf{b} - \mathbf{L}\,\mathbf{x}^{(known)} - \mathbf{R}\,\mathbf{x}^{(known)}).$$

Gauss–Seidel:

$$\mathbf{x}^{(unknown)} = \mathbf{D}^{-1}(\mathbf{b} - \mathbf{L}\,\mathbf{x}^{(unknown)} - \mathbf{R}\,\mathbf{x}^{(known)}).$$

A subtle difference for sure, but it makes a big difference in practice. I wrote a simple piece of code that solves the heat transfer in a bar with eight nodes using the C++ language. This code tries to solve the linear heat equation up to three decimal places. In this case, the Jacobi approach requires 54 iterations to achieve that precision while Gauss–Seidel requires 29 iterations to achieve the same precision. The values of the nodal values are shown in Figure 7.9: on the left for Jacobi and on the right for Gauss–Seidel.
  Clearly, Gauss–Seidel outperforms Jacobi.
  However, Jacobi is easier to implement on parallel architectures like the GPU. Gauss–Seidel also has the problem that there is an order bias. If you reshuffle the order of the nodes you will get a different sequence on the right-hand side of Figure 7.9. This is usually not a problem when we seek a steady-state solution.
  Here is the code that created the numbers in Figure 7.9 in its entirety.

```
#include <stdio.h>
const int max_iterations = 10000000;
const double tolerance = 1e-3;
const double rhs[8] = {0.0,-1.0,0.0,0.0,0.0,0.0,0.0,0.0};

static double abs (double a) {
  return (a >= 0.0 ? a: -a);
}
static void initialize (double * a) {
  for (int i=0; i<8; i++) {a[i] = 0.0;}
}
static void copy (double * a, double * b) {
  for (int i=0; i<8; i++) {a[i] = b[i];}
}
```

```
static double difference (double * a, double * b) {
 double d = 0.0;
 for (int i=0; i<8; i++) {d += abs (a[i] - b[i]);}
 return (d);
}
static void iterate (double * a, double * b, double * c) {
 initialize (a); initialize (c);
 for (int k=0; k<max_iterations; k++) {
 printf ("%3d: ", k);
 for (int i=1; i<=6; i++) {
 a[i] = (rhs[i] - b[i-1] - c[i+1]) * (-0.5);
 printf ("%5.3f ", abs(a[i]));
 } printf ("\n");
 double err = difference (a, c); copy (c, a);
 if (err < tolerance) {break;}
 }
}
int main (int argc, char ** argv)
{        '
 double unknown[8], known[8];
 printf ("\nJacobi iterations:\n\n"); iterate (unknown,
known, known);
 printf ("\nGauss-Seidel iterations:\n\n"); iterate
(unknown, unknown, known);
 return (1);
}
```

We had to include the *stdio* header file so that our Slave can communicate the results to the **Human** or **Pet** through a **printf**. The header file is hood and device agnostic and will take care of all the messy details. It helps the **Compiler** (remember him?) to figure out how to generate ones and zeroes that instruct the Slave how to read and print stuff. The text will be printed pretty much in any hood and pretty much on any device. To nonexperts *stdio* sounds like a cheesy 1970s nightclub in Manhattan or a European hair gel. To the *cognoscenti* it stands for *standard input/output*.

Notice that we did not use a matrix type because of the *regularity* and the *sparseness* of our matrix. There are only vectors for (1) the right-hand side, (2) the known, and (3) the unknown. We padded the right-hand side of vector rhs left and right with a zero to make the inner loops simpler. So the vector is of size 8 not 6. The two added values correspond to the ghost values we mentioned earlier.

```
 0 : 0.500 0.000 0.000 0.000 0.000 0.000
 1 : 0.500 0.250 0.000 0.000 0.000 0.000
 2 : 0.625 0.250 0.125 0.000 0.000 0.000
 3 : 0.625 0.375 0.125 0.063 0.000 0.000
 4 : 0.688 0.375 0.219 0.063 0.031 0.000
 5 : 0.688 0.453 0.219 0.125 0.031 0.016
 6 : 0.727 0.453 0.289 0.125 0.070 0.016
 7 : 0.727 0.508 0.289 0.180 0.070 0.035
 8 : 0.754 0.508 0.344 0.180 0.107 0.035
 9 : 0.754 0.549 0.344 0.226 0.107 0.054
10 : 0.774 0.549 0.387 0.226 0.140 0.054
11 : 0.774 0.581 0.387 0.263 0.140 0.070
12 : 0.790 0.581 0.422 0.263 0.167 0.070
13 : 0.790 0.606 0.422 0.294 0.167 0.083
14 : 0.803 0.606 0.450 0.294 0.189 0.083
15 : 0.803 0.627 0.450 0.320 0.189 0.094
16 : 0.813 0.627 0.473 0.320 0.207 0.094
17 : 0.813 0.643 0.473 0.340 0.207 0.104
18 : 0.822 0.643 0.492 0.340 0.222 0.104
19 : 0.822 0.657 0.492 0.357 0.222 0.111
20 : 0.828 0.657 0.507 0.357 0.234 0.111
21 : 0.828 0.668 0.507 0.370 0.234 0.117
22 : 0.834 0.668 0.519 0.370 0.244 0.117
23 : 0.834 0.676 0.519 0.381 0.244 0.122
24 : 0.838 0.676 0.529 0.381 0.252 0.122
25 : 0.838 0.683 0.529 0.390 0.252 0.126
26 : 0.842 0.683 0.537 0.390 0.258 0.126
27 : 0.842 0.689 0.537 0.397 0.258 0.129
28 : 0.845 0.689 0.543 0.397 0.263 0.129
29 : 0.845 0.694 0.543 0.403 0.263 0.132
30 : 0.847 0.694 0.549 0.403 0.267 0.132
31 : 0.847 0.698 0.549 0.408 0.267 0.134
32 : 0.849 0.698 0.553 0.408 0.271 0.134
33 : 0.849 0.701 0.553 0.412 0.271 0.135
34 : 0.850 0.701 0.556 0.412 0.274 0.135
35 : 0.850 0.703 0.556 0.415 0.274 0.137
36 : 0.852 0.703 0.559 0.415 0.276 0.137
37 : 0.852 0.705 0.559 0.418 0.276 0.138
38 : 0.853 0.705 0.562 0.418 0.278 0.138
39 : 0.853 0.707 0.562 0.420 0.278 0.139
40 : 0.854 0.707 0.563 0.420 0.279 0.139
41 : 0.854 0.708 0.563 0.421 0.279 0.140
42 : 0.854 0.708 0.565 0.421 0.280 0.140
43 : 0.854 0.710 0.565 0.423 0.280 0.140
44 : 0.855 0.710 0.566 0.423 0.281 0.140
45 : 0.855 0.710 0.566 0.424 0.281 0.141
46 : 0.855 0.710 0.567 0.424 0.282 0.141
47 : 0.855 0.711 0.567 0.425 0.282 0.141
48 : 0.856 0.711 0.568 0.425 0.283 0.141
49 : 0.856 0.712 0.568 0.425 0.283 0.141
50 : 0.856 0.712 0.569 0.425 0.283 0.141
51 : 0.856 0.712 0.569 0.426 0.283 0.142
52 : 0.856 0.712 0.569 0.426 0.284 0.142
53 : 0.856 0.713 0.569 0.426 0.284 0.142
54 : 0.856 0.713 0.570 0.426 0.284 0.142
```

```
 0 : 0.500 0.250 0.125 0.063 0.031 0.016
 1 : 0.625 0.375 0.219 0.125 0.070 0.035
 2 : 0.688 0.453 0.289 0.180 0.107 0.054
 3 : 0.727 0.508 0.344 0.226 0.140 0.070
 4 : 0.754 0.549 0.387 0.263 0.167 0.083
 5 : 0.774 0.581 0.422 0.294 0.189 0.094
 6 : 0.790 0.606 0.450 0.320 0.207 0.104
 7 : 0.803 0.627 0.473 0.340 0.222 0.111
 8 : 0.813 0.643 0.492 0.357 0.234 0.117
 9 : 0.822 0.657 0.507 0.370 0.244 0.122
10 : 0.828 0.668 0.519 0.381 0.252 0.126
11 : 0.834 0.676 0.529 0.390 0.258 0.129
12 : 0.838 0.683 0.537 0.397 0.263 0.132
13 : 0.842 0.689 0.543 0.403 0.267 0.134
14 : 0.845 0.694 0.549 0.408 0.271 0.135
15 : 0.847 0.698 0.553 0.412 0.274 0.137
16 : 0.849 0.701 0.556 0.415 0.276 0.138
17 : 0.850 0.703 0.559 0.418 0.278 0.139
18 : 0.852 0.705 0.562 0.420 0.279 0.140
19 : 0.853 0.707 0.563 0.421 0.280 0.140
20 : 0.854 0.708 0.565 0.423 0.281 0.141
21 : 0.854 0.710 0.566 0.424 0.282 0.141
22 : 0.855 0.710 0.567 0.425 0.283 0.141
23 : 0.855 0.711 0.568 0.425 0.283 0.142
24 : 0.856 0.712 0.569 0.426 0.284 0.142
25 : 0.856 0.712 0.569 0.426 0.284 0.142
26 : 0.856 0.713 0.570 0.427 0.284 0.142
27 : 0.856 0.713 0.570 0.427 0.285 0.142
28 : 0.856 0.713 0.570 0.427 0.285 0.142
29 : 0.857 0.713 0.570 0.428 0.285 0.143
```

FIGURE 7.9   Jacobi output (left) and Gauss–Seidel output (right).

This code is easy to generalize to higher-dimensional systems. Try this at home. If you cut and paste this code and know how to compile C++ code in your hood you are all set. It is also easily turned into *pure* C.

To summarize: Very simple code can help you to solve a linear system. These systems are very common in science and it is amazing that such simple code can solve them, thanks to Jacobi, Gauss, and Seidel. Note you do not have to store the matrix explicitly. No space is wasted on useless zeroes. The code shown earlier demonstrates that.

End of story for the solution of linear systems.

Again sorry to disappoint: this is not the end of the story. These methods are simple but they do not converge to the solution very rapidly. It takes many steps to get close to the solution. Geeks like things that are rapid. No *slow food* for programmers. Actually, they have liquid protein mixes now for programmers so they don't waste time and chill out at a decent restaurant for lunch or dinner.

Sure Gauss–Seidel is better than Jacobi. But there is better stuff out there.

For example:

Conjugate Gradient, Preconditioned Conjugate Gradient, GMRES, Multi-Grid, Preconditioned Multi-Grid, and so on. These are all very cool techniques that I have used and they are covered in thousands of books.

Look this stuff up.

CHAPTER 8

A Simple Fluid Solver

Simplicity is the ultimate sophistication.

LEONARDO DA VINCI (THE ULTIMATE
RENAISSANCE MAN)

It is now prime time to present a simple fluid solver that I wrote about 15 years ago. It is based on the techniques that I first crammed into a paper presented in 1999 at the annual SIGGRAPH conference. The story I like to tell, which is true by the way, is that it was the paper with the lowest scores that got accepted that year at the conference.

Allow me to reiterate.

In academia you submit a paper which then gets assigned to expert reviewers who in turn judge your paper, write a review, and give it a score. Two of these reviewers are part of a committee who make the final decision whether your paper is accepted or rejected at the conference. Since SIGGRAPH is the premier conference in computer graphics, it is very prestigious to get your paper accepted there. The acceptance rate is usually about 20% or 30% of all submitted papers. For academics, having papers accepted at SIGGRAPH is important in order to get a job or even better, a job for life at a university. This is called tenure. For real, a well-paid job for life. This is a kind of cynical however. Mostly researchers want to get a paper at SIGGRAPH so they can share and present their work to a large audience and also share their contributions. It is all about sharing something you have worked really hard on. At least that is what I want to believe.

I created a simple solver.

But what do we mean by saying something is simple? Remember Kolmogorov and his turbulence model mentioned earlier? According to Kolmogorov, a problem is simple (not complex) when the computer code that solves the problem is small. Here is the catch though. What programming language should we choose? I can create a language, of course called *JosStamBogusFluidLanguage*, where there is only one instruction called `Solve _ Fluid`. We are all done. Yay! But it is one line of code written in a bogus language invented by yours truly. No one is impressed.

That of course is a cheat. No matter what language we use it all gets translated down into zeroes and ones. But only our Slave likes zeroes and ones. The Compiler turns our program written in our favorite programming language into these pesky 0s and 1s.

The solver I will describe was first presented at *GDC* 2003 in San Jose, California. *GDC* stands for Game Developer Conference, and it is usually held yearly somewhere in the San Francisco Bay area. I will present the solver in *pure C* language. It uses all the concepts introduced in the previous sections and intermezzi.* Pure C is my favorite language. This language is the closest thing to programming languages called *assembly languages*.

Assembly languages give you a lot of control to create 0s and 1s. No human I know can type in 0s and 1s and create a program that performs a certain task. I often stray away from those types who are able to perform such a task unless they are fun to hang out with and also know about French philosophers or Seattle rock bands.

Coding in Assembly is cool because you are closer to the Slave. Like a secret language that less geeky and more sophisticated programmers will not understand. Let them wrestle with their C++ templates. If the last sentence does not make any sense to you, consider yourself lucky. But there will be one template class in the following text.

The problem with Assembly is that it is mostly Slave dependent. It depends on the hardware. So you spend weeks coding for the iPad in Assembly (good luck!) and then someone wants your App to be ported to the Surface, and you have to code it all over again in another Assembly (good luck again!).

---

* The original paper was called "Real-Time Fluid Dynamics for Games." You can find it on the web by Googling the title.

Pure C is cool because you are close to the Slave but not too close. You are not dealing with just one Slave but potentially with many Slaves at the same time living in different hoods.

In Figure 8.1 we show a simple C program (left) translated into binary code and assembly language.* Figure 8.1 is interesting as it shows that the C code on the left is pretty readable, while the Assembly version on the right is not (to most mere mortals!). The binary version of the code is also shown. They are the numbers on the left-hand side or the right-hand side. They are hexadecimal numbers. Look it up. Hint "E" equals "1110" in binary and is equal to 14 in the decimal system. I was taught this in grade one in Geneva by the way as part of the *new math* movement pioneered by the Swiss philosopher and linguist Jean Piaget. We used to spot him riding his bike in our neighborhood in Geneva in the 1970s.

This program computes the so-called *Fibonacci numbers*. This is how they are computed. You start with 1 and 1. Then repeatedly the numbers are computed by adding together the two previous numbers. The sequence goes like this:

1 1 2 3 5 8 13 21 34 55 89 144 233 377 610 987 1597 2584 4181 6765 10946 17711 28657 46368 75025 121393 196418 317811 514229 …

These numbers grow really fast and have many interesting properties. The ratio of two consecutive Fibonacci numbers *converges* to the golden ratio that is equal to $1+\sqrt{5}/2 \cong 1.61803…$ You can use those German eigenvectors and eigenvalues to prove this. Look it up. The golden ratio also shows up in ancient Greek architecture to construct esthetically pleasing buildings. The golden ratio shows up in surprising ways all over mathematics.

I think everyone will agree that the pure C code is easier to decipher. However, note that for this particular example the pure C code is much smaller than this particular compiled Assembly version. Also the C code is more readable. That is the whole point. We do not want get too close to the Slave.

I can sense some people yawning reading this. Yes okay tell me something I don't know. However, clarifying things is always helpful, I think.

To summarize: We made it clear what simple code is. In the end, it is equal to the number of ones and zeroes that are served to the Slave for breakfast. No one codes in Assembly language anymore. No one types in

---

* This was created with the following wonderful tool available on the web: http://assembly.ynh.io/

```
#include <stdio.h>
static void Fibonacci ( int N ) {
  int i, F0=1, F1=1, F=0, Ftemp;
  printf ( "1 1 ");
  for ( i=2 ; i<N ; i++ ) {
    F = F0 + F1;
    Ftemp = F; F0 = F1; F1 = Ftemp;
    printf ( "%d ", F );
  }
  printf ( "\n" );
}
int main ( int argc, char ** argv ) {
  Fibonacci ( 30 );
  return 0;
}
```

```
                              .Ltext0:
                  .section  .rodata
           .LC0:
0000 31203120              .string   "1 1 "
00
           .LC1:
0005 25642000              .string   "%d "
                  .text
           Fibonacci:
           .LFB0:
                  .cfi_startproc
0000 55               pushq     %rbp
                  .cfi_def_cfa_offset 16
                  .cfi_offset 6, -16
0001 4889E5             movq      %rsp, %rbp
                  .cfi_def_cfa_register 6
0004 4883EC30           subq      $48, %rsp
0008 897DDC             movl      %edi, -36(%rbp)
000b C745F001           movl      $1, -16(%rbp)
  000000
0012 C745F401           movl      $1, -12(%rbp)
  000000
0019 C745F800           movl      $0, -8(%rbp)
  000000
0020 BF000000           movl      $.LC0, %edi
  00
0025 B8000000           movl      $0, %eax
  00
002a E8000000           call      printf
  00
002f C745EC02           movl      $2, -20(%rbp)
  000000
0036 EB35              jmp       .L2
           .L3:
0069 8345EC01           addl      $1, -20(%rbp)
0038 8B45F4             movl      -12(%rbp), %eax
003b 8B55F0             movl      -16(%rbp), %edx
003e 01D0              addl      %edx, %eax
0040 8945F8             movl      %eax, -8(%rbp)
0043 8B45F8             movl      -8(%rbp), %eax
0046 8945FC             movl      %eax, -4(%rbp)
0049 8B45F4             movl      -12(%rbp), %eax
004c 8945F0             movl      %eax, -16(%rbp)
004f 8B45FC             movl      -4(%rbp), %eax
0052 8945F4             movl      %eax, -12(%rbp)
0055 8B45F8             movl      -8(%rbp), %eax
0058 89C6              movl      %eax, %esi
005a BF000000           movl      $.LC1, %edi
  00
005f B8000000           movl      $0, %eax
  00
0064 E8000000           call      printf
  00
           .L2:
006d 8B45EC             movl      -20(%rbp), %eax
0070 3B45DC             cmpl      -36(%rbp), %eax
0073 7CC3              jl        .L3
0075 BF0A0000           movl      $10, %edi
  00
007a E8000000           call      putchar
  00
007f C9               leave
                  .cfi_def_cfa 7, 8
0080 C3               ret
                  .cfi_endproc
           .LFE0:
```

(a)

FIGURE 8.1   C code (a) and the corresponding Assembly code (b).   (*Continued*)

```
                              .globl    main
                main:
                .LFB1:
                              .cfi_startproc
        0081 55               pushq     %rbp
                              .cfi_def_cfa_offset 16
                              .cfi_offset 6, -16
        0082 4889E5           movq      %rsp, %rbp
                              .cfi_def_cfa_register 6
        0085 4883EC10         subq      $16, %rsp
        0089 897DFC           movl      %edi, -4(%rbp)
        008c 488975F0         movq      %rsi, -16(%rbp)
        0090 BF1E0000         movl      $30, %edi
             00
        0095 E866FFFF         call      Fibonacci
             FF
        009a B8000000         movl      $0, %eax
             00
        009f C9               leave
                              .cfi_def_cfa 7, 8
        00a0 C3               ret
                              .cfi_endproc
                .LFE1:
                .Letext0:
```

(b)

FIGURE 8.1 *(Continued)*   C code (a) and the corresponding Assembly code (b).

zeroes and ones anymore. The bottom line is the size of the executable that Slave has to digest.

Now let's all watch a math horror flick.

8.1 A MATH HORROR FLICK: OPERATOR SPLITTING

I can't really make fun of zombies. They're not liars. They're not cheats.

GEORGE ROMERO (AMERICAN FILM MAKER KNOWN
FOR HIS EPIC ZOMBIE MOVIES)

The title probably sounds like nonsense to most people. Operator splitting sounds like a nasty thing to do to operators. But really what it means is to take a complicated problem and split it up into simpler parts. No one gets hurt in the process. Not that I know of.

It is sort of the opposite of the meaning of the Arabic word *algebra*. Now we solve for each broken part and assemble it in a reunion. We do not solve for the reunion and then resolve the broken parts. But some of the broken parts use algebra. Math is multifaceted.

What have we learned about fluids so far? One can crudely summarize it as follows. Things are moved around, things are diffused, things are stirred around by forces, and things have to conserve mass.

Okay.

The strategy in *operator splitting* methods is to solve each effect separately and then iterate this process over discrete intervals of time to get an animation of a fluid.

In my experience, this is a good strategy to solve problems. Understand the parts and solve them separately and consequently; interesting emergent behaviors will result from their interactions.

8.2 CODE PLEASE?

The best programs are written so that computing machines can perform them quickly and so that human beings can understand them clearly. A programmer is ideally an essayist who works with traditional aesthetic and literary forms as well as mathematical concepts, to communicate the way that an algorithm works and to convince a reader that the results will be correct.

DONALD ERVIN KNUTH (FAMOUS COMPUTER
SCIENTIST AND PROFESSOR AT STANFORD)

Here we go. I assume that you are familiar with the C language. If not you might get the gist of how to write a fluid solver in about 100 lines of readable C code. And hey maybe you will get hooked on some pure grade C. That would be cool. Figure 8.2 shows me giving a keynote talk

FIGURE 8.2 Future Game On, Paris, September 10, 2010 (photo by Jason de la Roca). Yeah, that is me on the right with my fuzzy claw.

and showing the code that fits on a single PowerPoint slide at a gamer conference in Paris on September 10, 2010.

Let us start with the data structures. Those are the parts of the computer memory that will store our densities and our velocity fields. To simplify things, we assume that we are only solving for densities being moved around in a fluid field with a constant density. Whoa?

There is a common misunderstanding about fluid densities that I have encountered when presenting this material in my talks that I have to clear right up front.

When I say density, I mean the density of something like perfume or dog farts being infused, transported, and diffused in a fluidlike air or water. The density of the fluid is fixed once and for all in our simple example code. It is equal to the number one, yes "1," in our solver. In standard units, this is close to the density of air. But as we saw earlier, it does not matter since we can always rescale our numbers in a manner consistent to another system of units.

One more time, when I say density, it is the density of something immersed in the fluid—not the density of the fluid. I hope that at this point you will shake your head and think: "Yes, alright man I got it. Can we move on a little?"

We are going to describe a fluid solver that lives on a grid. Please refer back to Figure 6.5. Remember the poor bugs stuck in their hideous apartment building surrounded by ghosts? Well, let us turn that into C code. The apartments will be stored in a chunk of memory. Remember we needed two coordinates to label each apartment. But we prefer one coordinate for efficiency reasons. It is simpler and faster.

Here is the solution: we simply chop off each floor and put them side by side to create a motel. This would not work in Paris, there's no space, so we will have to imagine a place in New Mexico perhaps. This transformation is illustrated in Figure 8.3. The relationship between the labeling of the hotel rooms and the motel rooms is pretty straightforward:

$$\text{Index}_{Motel} = \text{room}_{Hotel} + N \times \text{floor}_{Hotel}.$$

Here, N is the number of rooms on one floor of the hotel, and it is also the number of floors of the hotel. In Figure 8.3, $N = 4$. As an example, room (3,2) in the hotel corresponds to room 11 in the motel. This is what mathematicians call a *one-to-one mapping*. It should be pretty obvious how to

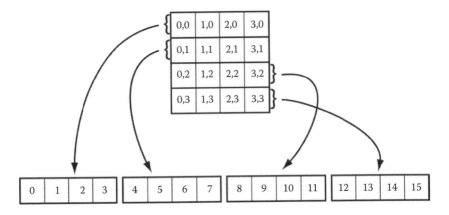

FIGURE 8.3 Mapping from a 2D grid to a 1D grid.

get back to the hotel given the motel room number. Can you figure it out? I am feeling generous so I'll give you the solution in pure C code:

```
int room_number = motel_number%N;
int floor_number = motel_number/N;
```

This is how you get two numbers out of one number. What is "%"? The creators of pure C decided that this symbol stands for the reminder of a division: high school stuff.

All this mapping business is there just to explain that we will only have 1D arrays of type *float*. But they are proxies (substitutes) for our higher dimensional grids. They make the code more readable. That's it.

Let us get back to our data structures. Data and memory are especially important on game consoles since memory is limited. You do not want to waste it.

We use floats as our numerical substitutes for ideal mathematical numbers. We need six arrays: two for the density, two for the horizontal component, and two for the vertical component of the velocity: $2 + 2 + 2 = 6$. Here is how it is done in C:

```
static float u[size], v[size], u_prev[size],
  v_prev[size];
static float dens[size], dens_prev[size];
```

In the case of the fluid solver the size is equal to $(N+2)*(N+2)$. Why the plus two? That is because we have to include the ghost cells so that our boundary conditions are met. What about `static`? That is just so that Slave is not confused if another piece of code included in the software uses the same name. The name will only exist in this file. This avoids arguments of the following type:

> *Slave.* "Back off Master two. That data is owned by Master one."

> *Master Two.* "Well just ask your Master one to use `static` on his data. Wow he must be a rookie. Where did you guys meet anyway?"

> *Slave.* "How arrogant you are Master two. Maybe you should use `static` on *your* data."

We can model our mapping between hotels and motels using something called a *macro* in the C language. Actually, macro is shorthand for *macroinstruction*. A macro turns small stuff into bigger stuff. Programmers are like mathematicians and are lazy so they create things that automatically create code for them. The macro is the least sophisticated of these techniques. And I will stick to it. No templates right now in this book. Templates can be very useful however but do not abuse them.

Here is how you can define a macro to model the relation between hotels and motels:

```
#define IX(i,j) ((i)+(N+2)*(j))
```

For example, if N=34565 then

```
IX(31119,23) = (31119) + (34567)*(23) = 826,160.
```

But it can also work for N=3 or any other number.

Let us now introduce another macro that will make it easier to go through our grids and update them. Here it is:

```
#define FOR_EACH_CELL for ( j=1 ; j<=N ; j++ ) {\
                          for ( i=1 ; i<=N ; i++ ) {
#define END_FOR }}
```

We also need a macro to swap array pointers. A pointer is just the address of the start of an array in memory. Here is the macro:

```
#define SWAP(x0,x) {float *tmp=x0;x0=x;x=tmp;}
```

In the code that follows, we have simplified things somewhat. Some people might wonder what happened to the grid spacing. This is usually denoted by the symbol "h." In our solver we are assuming that we are dealing with a unit square domain: each side is of size one. Therefore:

```
h = 1/N, h^2 = 1/N^2, 1/h = N and 1/h^2 = N^2.
```

Keep this in mind in trying to understand the code. This has confused many people but taking these shortcuts makes the code more compact.

8.2.1 Moving Densities

We first describe code that moves and diffuses densities in a static velocity field. The beauty is that we can reuse the same code to animate the velocity field as well. Historically, I first wrote the density animation code from a given static velocity field and then realized it could be applied to the velocity field as well.

That was another epiphany.

The procedure is shown in Figure 8.4. We start with an initial array of densities specified by the Human or the Pet. This is called an initial value problem in mathematics. Then the density evolves through three steps in our solver: we add densities, diffuse the densities, and then move the density through the fixed (for now) velocity field. That is operator splitting for you.

Let us go through each step and show the corresponding code.

Step 1: Add Sources to the density! This is simple: we just add densities to the grid. For example, human or pet could be using a mouse, a stylus, or

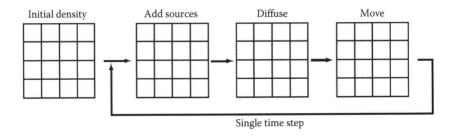

FIGURE 8.4   Schematic depiction of how the density grid is updated over fixed time steps.

their fingers or paws to add densities to some locations in the grid. Or it could be generated using some procedure. Like: "every 5 frames put some density in the middle cell of the grid." In code:

```
void add_source ( int N, float * x, float * s,
  float dt )
{
    int i, size = (N+2)*(N+2);
    for ( i=0 ; i<size ; i++ ) x[i] += dt*s[i];
}
```

Step 2: Diffuse the density! We encountered this before and we will use an implicit technique to solve the resulting linear system. If you do not know what I am talking about go back to Intermezzo Quattro.

The process of diffusion is depicted in Figure 8.5 where a single cell of density is diffused over a time step "dt" throughout the grid.

We will use a linear Gauss–Seidel solver because it converges faster than a Jacobi solver. If you are converting this to parallel code you might want to use Jacobi or *red-black* Gauss–Seidel.

In Intermezzo Quattro, we already gave an implementation for the diffusion of temperature in a rod. But here is an implementation that is more general in pure C. It depends on two variables: "a" and "c." These two variables will allow us to *solve* all the linear systems in our fluid solver. The variable "b" models how the ghosts should behave, more about that in the following text.

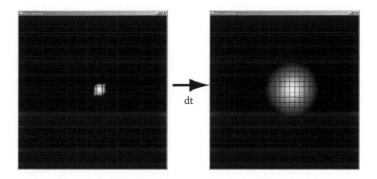

FIGURE 8.5   A single diffusion for the density step of the solver.

Here is the code for the linear solver using Gauss–Seidel iterations:

```
void lin_solve(int N, int b, float *x, float *x0,
  float a, float c) float c)
{
  int i, j, n;
  for ( n=0 ; n<20 ; n++ ) {
    FOR_EACH_CELL
      x[IX(i,j)] = (x0[IX(i,j)]+a*(x[IX(i-1,j)]+
      x[IX(i+1,j)]+x[IX(i,j-1)]+x[IX(i,j+1)]))/c;
    END_FOR
    set_bnd ( N, b, x );
  }
}
```

In this code initially the array "x0" is the known and the array "x" is initially the unknown, which becomes a known array through iteration.

Why 20 iterations? Well you are free to pick any number you want. The larger the number of iterations, the slower but the more precise your solution will be. The smaller the number of iterations, the faster the code will be and the less precise it will be. For the grid sizes, I was using in the late 1990s when I wrote this code it was sort of a compromise between these two behaviors. Feel free to experiment.

Of course there are more principled ways to choose the number of iterations. For example, it could be based on how close the known is to the unknown. But with Gauss–Seidel you will have to wait a long time. If you want some good speed, check out the stuff that I mentioned in Intermezzo Quattro. In fact the code in that Intermezzo the iterations were based on an error criterion. Of course it was set pretty low. But it was just to make a point.

What about "set_bnd" and "b"? In hindsight I could have called them "set_ghost_cells" and "ghost_type." But I wrote this before I discovered the existence of ghosts. Just kidding.

Here is "set_bnd." It just fills the boundary ghost cells from the interior cells.

There are three options for the ghost values. Here they are

(0) *Ghost*: do exactly what your neighbor does.

(1) *Ghost*: do exactly the opposite that your horizontal neighbor does.

(2) *Ghost*: do exactly the opposite that your vertical neighbor does.

That is what the following code implements. Only case (0) is used for the density code. Conditions (1) and (2) are used in the following velocity solver to ensure that no flow escapes our apartments.

```
void set_bnd(int N, int b, float *x)
{
  int i;
  for ( i=1 ; i<=N ; i++ ) {
    x[IX(0  ,i)]=b==1 ? -x[IX(1,i)]  : x[IX(1,i)];
    x[IX(N+1,i)]=b==1 ? -x[IX(N,i)]  : x[IX(N,i)];
    x[IX(i,0  )]=b==2 ? -x[IX(i,1)]  : x[IX(i,1)];
    x[IX(i,N+1)]=b==2 ? -x[IX(i,N)]  : x[IX(i,N)];
  }
  x[IX(0  ,0  )]=0.5f*(x[IX(1,0  )]+x[IX(0  ,1)]);
  x[IX(0  ,N+1)]=0.5f*(x[IX(1,N+1)]+x[IX(0  ,N)]);
  x[IX(N+1,0  )]=0.5f*(x[IX(N,0  )]+x[IX(N+1,1)]);
  x[IX(N+1,N+1)]=0.5f*(x[IX(N,N+1)]+x[IX(N+1,N)]);
}
```

Notice how we first fill the four boundaries. And then the ghosts in their fancy corner apartments are just an average of the values of their neighbor ghosts. Ghosts do not have any free will. They are ghosts after all. I will explain the meaning of "b" when we get to flow fields using this routine.

Using this code, we can write a routine that diffuses density in a stable manner.

```
void diffuse(int N, int b, float *x, float *x0, float
diff, float dt) float dt)
{
  float a=dt*diff*N*N;
  lin_solve ( N, b, x, x0, a, 1+4*a );
}
```

We will use this routine again to handle viscosity for the fluid's velocity. That is the beauty of this.

Step 3: Move the density! Here is the most fun part. How do you move a density through a fixed velocity field? This is like me and a whole other horde of tourists wandering through Venice as mentioned previously. The setting is depicted in Figure 8.6. The velocity field in red is fixed. The figure shows the evolution of the density over a single time step. Two things

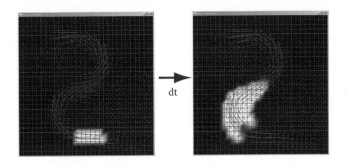

FIGURE 8.6 One step of a density (in white) being moved by a static fluid field (in red).

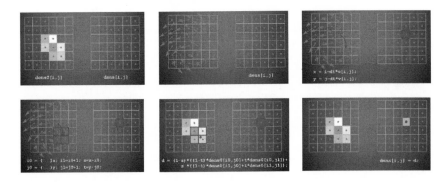

FIGURE 8.7 Transport of densities in a grid using the semi-Lagrangian technique.

to notice: (1) the density flows along the velocity field and (2) the density seems to spread out. The first property is exactly what we want. The second one is an artefact of the semi-Lagrangian technique that we use in this code. No free lunch. This technique is stable but it adds artificial diffusion. The simple code uses the semi-Lagrangian method.

We already described this technique earlier using bugs and psychopathic landlords. Now let us translate that into C code.

Figure 8.7 shows the six steps involved and the corresponding C code. Think of the shades of grey as now being a density of bugs.

Like we mentioned earlier, we need two grids: the initial density stored in dens0 and the moved density in the array dens. We break this moving business down into six steps.

1. Current density on the left and the new densities on the right which we are going to update.

2. We show the velocity field that is used to transport the density field.

3. This is how we transport the center of a cell using the simplest possible technique to other grid cells.

4. We determine where the cell ends up and find the four neighbors.

5. Once we have the four neighbors we can interpolate the density values.

6. Yay! We have the new interpolated density value and we transport it to the same location in the new grid.

That's it.

This is really the coolest part of the solver. The other parts are just text book linear algebra mathematics dressed in tight code. At least to me and most hackers*: writing tight and fast code is cool.

Okay, here is the code that moves densities around.

```
void advect(int N, int b, float *d, float *d0, float
  *u, float *v, float dt)
{
    int i, j, i0, j0, i1, j1;
    float x, y, s0, t0, s1, t1, dt0;
    dt0 = dt*N;
    FOR_EACH_CELL
        x = i-dt0*u[IX(i,j)]; y=j-dt0*v[IX(i,j)];
        if (x<0.5f) x=0.5f; if (x>N+0.5f) x=N+0.5f;
          i0=(int)x; i1=i0+1;
        if (y<0.5f) y=0.5f; if (y>N+0.5f) y=N+0.5f;
          j0=(int)y; j1=j0+1;
        s1=x-i0; s0=1-s1; t1=y-j0; t0=1-t1;
        d[IX(i,j)] = s0*(t0*d0[IX(i0,j0)]+t1*d0[IX
          (i0,j1)])+s1*(t0*d0[IX(i1,j0)]+t1*d0[IX(i1,j1)]);
    END_FOR
    set_bnd ( N, b, d );
}
```

---

* I am not talking about hackers that break into someone else's computer and steal their data, plant viruses, and commit other acts of shameless vandalism. These guys are just losers and give coders a bad name. True hackers only care about crafting the most elegant and rapid code that solves a problem.

Step 4: Let's put it all together! This is the code to solve for the density given a fixed nonevolving vector field

```
void dens_step ( int N, float * x, float * x0,
  float * u, float * v, float diff, float dt )
{
    add_source ( N, x, x0, dt );
    SWAP ( x0, x ); diffuse ( N, 0, x, x0, diff, dt );
    SWAP ( x0, x ); advect ( N, 0, x, x0, u, v, dt );
}
```

If you have a vector field available on a grid, this is one way to evolve densities over time. You can create a lot of nifty swirly effects over time.

Go wild. Please.

You do not have to stick to a single density by the way, of course not. You can evolve different densities using the same velocity field. I wrote programs that evolve the densities for the red, green, and blue components of the density and then mixed them together to create psychedelic effects. Also you can have different densities *react* between each other, like in chemical reactions.

This density solver is really a building block to create many cool effects.

The code for a density solver moving in a fluid flow can be used to compute the motion of the fluid itself. Our density solver will still work but now the fluid velocity is just assumed to be static only for the current frame.

To summarize: We provided simple code to describe the evolution of a density immersed in a static velocity field. The beauty is that this code can be reused to solve the motion of fluids.

Next, we describe how we reuse the code given previously to solve for the fluid's velocity.

8.2.2 Moving Fluids That Change Themselves: Nonlinearity

Recall the result first found by Euler: fluids move themselves. That is why they are complicated and nonlinear and hard to solve. We just covered the case of fluids frozen in time moving densities immersed in them.

We provided the code.

Actually, the situation shown in Figure 8.4 applies to the evolution of the velocity of the fluid as well. This is depicted in Figure 8.8.

It perfectly mirrors the density solver. That was a key insight.

This was another epiphany.

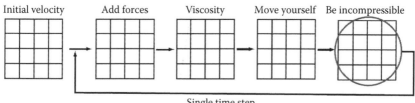

Single time step

FIGURE 8.8   A single step of the solver for the velocity of a fluid is very similar to the solver for the density shown in Figure 8.4. Except for that big red circle.

And that is why I presented it in this manner.

Forces are added by human fingers or pet paws. Then, depending on the property of the fluid, the velocities will be diffused through the effect of viscosity. Finally the velocity will move itself. Forces of course can also be a function of temperature (buoyancy), mass densities (gravity) or chemical reactions and other effects cooked up by a coder or an animator.

The density solver code can be reused to animate the velocity of the fluids.

Are we done then?

Not quite. There is another step not present in the density solver that is circled in red in Figure 8.8. The velocity flow has to be incompressible. Remember Euler's first result: what flows in has to flow out. We also mentioned the fundamental result of Helmholtz and Hodge: every vector field can be written as the sum of an incompressible vector (which we want) and a gradient field (which we do not want).

The key is to compute the gradient part of the velocity field and then subtract it from the field itself.

This involves three substeps.

1. Compute the amount of nonincompressibility in each cell.

2. Compute the pressure for each cell that will fix that.

3. Subtract the gradient of this pressure field from the original nonincompressible fluid.

Substep 1 just computes the difference between inflow and outflow. If it is zero: cool we are all done. But in general, this is not the case because the previous four steps shown in Figure 8.8 do not guarantee this property.

Substep 2 is the tricky part. We have to solve a linear equation to get the unknown pressure field from the known nonincompressibility. This is the so-called *Poisson equation*. But no worries. We can solve it using the linear solver that we used to handle the diffusion of the density. I am not going to write down the Poisson equation, because I promised you that I was not going to use a single partial differential equation in this book. But the equation basically says: "What is the pressure whose gradient will make our flow incompressible?" I cheated again. I mentioned the word gradient. But recall that it is just the direction of steepest negative descent or positive ascent when you are skiing.

You can also view it as a *projection*. Think of incompressible vector fields as special fields living in the whole infinite space of all imaginable vector fields. Think of Plato's cave mentioned earlier or the process of creating an image from a 3D representation. Plato's shadows are projections. Projection is a process where you reveal one aspect of something. For a specific fluid we reveal its incompressible side.

Substep 3 is easy. We just subtract the gradient of the pressure from the vector field. The gradient is just the difference in pressure between adjacent cells.

Here is the code.

```
void project(int N, float * u, float * v, float * p,
  float * div)
{
    int i, j;
    FOR_EACH_CELL
        div[IX(i,j)] = -0.5f*(u[IX(i+1,j)]-u[IX(i-1,j)]+
                    v[IX(i,j+1)]-v[IX(i,j-1)])/N;
        p[IX(i,j)] = 0;
    END_FOR

    set_bnd ( N, 0, div ); set_bnd ( N, 0, p );
    lin_solve ( N, 0, p, div, 1, 4 );

    FOR_EACH_CELL
        u[IX(i,j)] -= 0.5f*N*(p[IX(i+1,j)]-p[IX(i-1,j)]);
        v[IX(i,j)] -= 0.5f*N*(p[IX(i,j+1)]-p[IX(i,j-1)]);
    END_FOR

    set_bnd ( N, 1, u ); set_bnd ( N, 2, v );
}
```

In this code we also make sure to populate the ghost apartments, I mean boundary grid cells.

The solver code for the evolution of the fluid's velocity is

```
void vel_step(int N, float *u, float *v, float *u0,
float *v0, float visc, float dt)
{
  add_source ( N, u, u0, dt ); add_source ( N, v,
    v0, dt );
  SWAP ( u0, u ); diffuse ( N, 1, u, u0, visc, dt );
  SWAP ( v0, v ); diffuse ( N, 2, v, v0, visc, dt );
  project ( N, u, v, u0, v0 );
  SWAP ( u0, u ); SWAP ( v0, v );
  advect ( N, 1, u, u0, u0, v0, dt );
  advect ( N, 2, v, v0, u0, v0, dt );
  project ( N, u, v, u0, v0 );
}
```

Pretty cool no?

Notice that the projection step is called twice: before and after advection. Semi-Lagrangian advection works better if the velocity field is close to incompressible. Advection on the other hand messes up incompressibility so it does not hurt to apply an incompressibility step afterwards. Sounds like a recipe doesn't it?

It is.

Please feel free to play around with these basic pieces in different orders. I won't provide fancy mathematical proofs that this all converges to a solution. Every piece is stable so you will get something interesting that looks fluidlike. This is unless computer errors are introduced in the code of course. But even then, as we have seen earlier, some customers might like the effects created by these defects.

Alright, here is the full version of the solver without my fuzzy scary claw:

```
#define IX(i,j) ((i)+(N+2)*(j))
#define SWAP(x0,x) {float * tmp=x0;x0=x;x=tmp;}
#define FOR_EACH_CELL for ( j=1 ; j<=N ; j++ ) {\
                        for ( i=1 ; i<=N ; i++ ) {
#define END_FOR }}
void add_source(int N, float *x, float *s, float dt)
{
  int i, size=(N+2)*(N+2);
```

```
    for ( i=0 ; i<size ; i++ ) x[i] += dt*s[i];
}
void set_bnd(int N, int b, float *x)
{
  int i;
  for ( i=1 ; i<=N ; i++ ) {
    x[IX(0 ,i)]=b==1 ? -x[IX(1,i)]  : x[IX(1,i)];
    x[IX(N+1,i)]=b==1 ? -x[IX(N,i)]  : x[IX(N,i)];
    x[IX(i,0 )]=b==2 ? -x[IX(i,1)]  : x[IX(i,1)];
    x[IX(i,N+1)]=b==2 ? -x[IX(i,N)]  : x[IX(i,N)];
  }
  x[IX(0  ,0  )]=0.5f*(x[IX(1,0  )]+x[IX(0  ,1)]);
  x[IX(0  ,N+1)]=0.5f*(x[IX(1,N+1)]+x[IX(0  ,N)]);
  x[IX(N+1,0  )]=0.5f*(x[IX(N,0  )]+x[IX(N+1,1)]);
  x[IX(N+1,N+1)]=0.5f*(x[IX(N,N+1)]+x[IX(N+1,N)]);
}
void lin_solve(int N, int b, float *x, float *x0,
float a, float c)
{
  int i, j, n;
  for ( n=0 ; n<20 ; n++ ) {
    FOR_EACH_CELL
      x[IX(i,j)] = (x0[IX(i,j)]+a*(x[IX(i-1,j)]+
        x[IX(i+1,j)]+x[IX(i,j-1)]+x[IX(i,j+1)]))/c;
    END_FOR
    set_bnd ( N, b, x );
  }
}
void diffuse(int N, int b, float *x, float *x0,
float diff, float dt)
{
  float a=dt*diff*N*N;
  lin_solve ( N, b, x, x0, a, 1+4*a );
}
void advect(int N, int b, float *d, float *d0, float *u,
   float *v, float dt)
{
  int i, j, i0, j0, i1, j1;
  float x, y, s0, t0, s1, t1, dt0;
  dt0 = dt*N;
  FOR_EACH_CELL
    x=i-dt0*u[IX(i,j)]; y=j-dt0*v[IX(i,j)];
    if (x<0.5f) x=0.5f; if (x>N+0.5f) x=N+0.5f; i0=(int)
      x; i1=i0+1;
    if (y<0.5f) y=0.5f; if (y>N+0.5f) y=N+0.5f; j0=(int)
      y; j1=j0+1;
    s1=x-i0; s0=1-s1; t1=y-j0; t0=1-t1;
    d[IX(i,j)] = s0*(t0*d0[IX(i0,j0)]+t1*d0[IX(i0,j1)])+
                 s1*(t0*d0[IX(i1,j0)]+t1*d0[IX(i1,j1)]);
```

```
      END_FOR
      set_bnd ( N, b, d );
}
void project(int N, float * u, float * v, float * p,
    float * div)
{
    int i, j;
    FOR_EACH_CELL
        div[IX(i,j)] = -0.5f*(u[IX(i+1,j)]-u[IX(i-1,j)]+
                        v[IX(i,j+1)]-v[IX(i,j-1)])/N;
        p[IX(i,j)] = 0;
    END_FOR
    set_bnd ( N, 0, div ); set_bnd ( N, 0, p );
    lin_solve ( N, 0, p, div, 1, 4 );
    FOR_EACH_CELL
        u[IX(i,j)] -= 0.5f*N*(p[IX(i+1,j)]-p[IX(i-1,j)]);
        v[IX(i,j)] -= 0.5f*N*(p[IX(i,j+1)]-p[IX(i,j-1)]);
    END_FOR
    set_bnd ( N, 1, u ); set_bnd ( N, 2, v );
}
void dens_step(int N, float *x, float *x0, float *u,
    float *v, float diff, float dt)
{
    add_source ( N, x, x0, dt );
    SWAP ( x0, x ); diffuse ( N, 0, x, x0, diff, dt );
    SWAP ( x0, x ); advect ( N, 0, x, x0, u, v, dt );
}
void vel_step(int N, float *u, float *v, float *u0, float
    *v0, float visc, float dt)
{
    add_source ( N, u, u0, dt ); add_source ( N, v,
        v0, dt );
    SWAP ( u0, u ); diffuse ( N, 1, u, u0, visc, dt );
    SWAP ( v0, v ); diffuse ( N, 2, v, v0, visc, dt );
    project ( N, u, v, u0, v0 );
    SWAP ( u0, u ); SWAP ( v0, v );
    advect ( N, 1, u, u0, u0, v0, dt ); advect ( N, 2, v,
        v0, u0, v0, dt );
    project ( N, u, v, u0, v0 );
}
```

I know that to some of you this code looks even scarier than the Holy Scriptures. But you can actually find English words in the program. If you know English you can get the gist of this program. To programmers these characters are clear to them if they know how to program in C or some other dialect of it. To the Slave it is crystal clear after we invite Mister Compiler to join the party and translate it all into zeroes and ones.

This code compiles *as is* by the way. Your geeky friend in your hood can help you if needed.

This figure is just slightly bigger than the fancy equations shown in Figures 3.23 and 3.24. The code is entirely self-contained. It does not rely on any external libraries. Some people think that makes it *elegant*. I do.*

To summarize: We provided code for the evolution of the velocity field by reusing code from the simple density solver. We however needed to provide additional code to make the velocity incompressible. But luckily we were able to reuse the linear solver code with different parameters.

8.3 BUGS CRAWLING ON DONUTS, THE FFT, AND ~60 LINES OF C CODE

> Two things are infinite: the universe and human stupidity; and I am not sure about the universe.
>
> ALBERT EINSTEIN

In this section, I will present a custom-made solver for a flow that lives on a Donut. It is based mostly on the theory of Monsieur Fourier. Refer to Intermezzo Tre aforementioned. Also it is useful to go back to Figure 3.28 and see how a 2D square can be wrapped around a donut.

This is not just an academic exercise or something out of a mathematical cabinet of curiosity.

Because our squares are actually donuts, they can be used as wallpaper. We solve a fluid on a small square and then we can replicate it over an entire wall because the fluids seamlessly fit across opposite boundaries. This tiling is shown in Figure 8.9 where a single snapshot of a donut fluid is replicated four times. The repetition is pretty obvious in this case. But this is just a single snapshot of an animated sequence. Remember visually, fluids like air are nowhere to be seen. Only their effects are visible on things being stirred around by them. So, even though the four tiles on the right-hand side of Figure 8.9 look repetitive, their influence on the motion of things is not necessarily visible. Also keep in mind that we are only showing a single snapshot in time of the fluid.

---

* It is also readable. If you are as old as I am, you might remember the one liners published in the *Amiga World* magazine that could only handle 256 characters. One of them was a one liner that ray traced a sphere. Search for *obfuscated code* on the Internet and you will know what I mean by *readable code*.

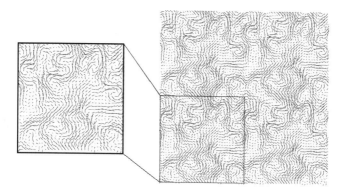

FIGURE 8.9   Fluids on donuts can be tiled infinitely all over the entire plane.

The fluid's velocity is sort of a background for many effects. Usually the flow is not shown; only its effect on things is obvious. I have said this before but it is an important fact to keep in mind when dealing with fluids using velocity fields.

We can create more out of less.

In fact it is possible to create an infinite fluid out of a finite fluid. It is sort of like how a fractal works but in a different way. Why? We cannot zoom into this fluid infinitely many times. Actually, that is not true. We can make our original fluid as small as we want. For the sake of argument, let us limit the size of the smallest grid to the so-called *Planck length* which is roughly 10^{-35} m. It is the smallest scale handled by physics. Based on size you can scale the velocity field: remember Kolmogorov. Continuous space is a mathematical fiction but mathematics is a good way to abstract things. Fiction is cool and so is the math involved. In practice, we use larger domains for starting grids. Usually of length one by one.

In Intermezzo Tre, we dealt with the discrete Fourier transform. We worked out all the details for a 3×3 matrix. The continuous Fourier transform is what is normally taught at universities, especially to engineers. But it is also a fiction. The discrete Fourier transform is immensely useful in diagonalizing matrices. But in practice the Fourier transform is used because of something called the *FFT: Fast Fourier Transform*. This ingenious technique was discovered by Gauss, the guy depicted in the center of Figure 7.8, in 1805. The FFT was later rediscovered by Cooley and Tukey at IBM in 1965. They were not aware of Gauss's work. That happens all the time in research. Gauss did not publish his result, however. It was found only after his death and published posthumously.

We will not explain the FFT in this work because that would take another Intermezzo and there are thousands of books that explain it in great detail. Look it up if you are interested.

However, I will briefly mention the *FFTW*: the *Fastest Fourier Transform in the West*.* I already apologized in a footnote (how cowardly is that?) that I sometimes use external libraries. FFTW is one of the cool ones. It is written in C and it works for any size, not only powers of two like the original FFT. Hey and it is from MIT.† It is a good stuff, trust me.

In Intermezzo Tre, we saw that Fourier transforms were useful to analytically put circulant matrices (structured but not sparse) into a simple form. But what is a Fourier transform of a fluid? The crucial link is that fluids on donuts wrap around like the circulant matrices. They are related even when we are talking about very different objects. Again, this is the beauty of mathematics.

That is what we will discuss next.

The Fourier transform is used heavily in image processing. This transform gives an alternative picture of a picture that is equivalent to the picture. Got that? A picture, after being Fourier transformed, reveals another aspect of itself. This other view presents the *spectral content* of the picture. This is when the wave numbers come into play that we mentioned earlier. In Figure 8.10, we show four waves and their corresponding wave numbers. The arrow is like the one mentioned in Figure 5.2 in reference with Kolmogorov turbulence. The bigger the vector the more detail in the wave: the smaller the scale. The vector also shows the direction of the wave like that of a wind direction.

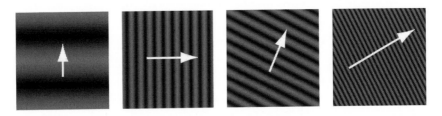

FIGURE 8.10   Four wave vectors and their corresponding waves.

---

* http://www.fftw.org.
† MIT stands for the Massachusetts Institute of Technology. That is where the top brainy kids go to study and do cool geek stuff. I never applied there.

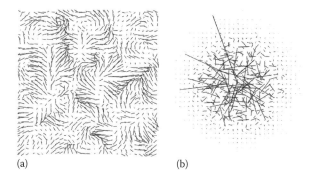

(a)   (b)

FIGURE 8.11   A spatial vector field (a) and its Fourier transform (b).

Figure 8.11 shows a vector field (a) and its Fourier transform (b). The field in the spatial domain is clearly periodic. You can decorate arbitrary sized wallpaper with it. The Fourier transformed field on the right is very different. Most of the action is concentrated in the center. The vectors in the center are actually the largest and then they drop off. Each vector in the Fourier (Figure 8.11b) field says how much the wave vector (one of those in Figure 8.11) contributes to the spatial field. There is a drop off because the field is of finite size, or in the continuous case, the effect of viscosity limits the amount of scales.

It is instructive to look at the similar Fourier transform for pictures. Figure 8.12 shows two pictures and their respective Fourier transforms. Notice that the two pictures are random. They are noisy. But they are not completely random or noisy because their respective Fourier transforms are bounded. The spread is inversely related to the *size* of the structures in the spatial images. Sound familiar? It is similar to a dish of turbulence served *à la* Kolmogorov.

Actually, fields that are fractals never go to zero, but they still drop off with scales. Kolmogorov's turbulence is like that. In practice, we just cut off the Fourier representation when the values decrease with increasing scale.

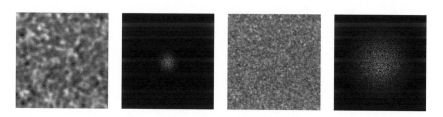

FIGURE 8.12   Two random images and their respective Fourier transforms.

When these values are below a certain threshold dictated by the Master, they are by *fiat* set to zero. Remember Slave can only handle that many bits. Let's not waste time and memory on tiny numbers.

In the Fourier domain, our flows are not as visually appealing as in our usual space.

Usually, the Fourier transform is used to solve for incompressibility for periodic flows living on donuts. Recall the Helmholtz–Hodge decomposition shown in Figure 3.13. In the Fourier domain, this becomes the decomposition depicted in Figure 8.13.

I think this is the best geometrical explanation of the Helmholtz–Hodge decomposition. This was another epiphany for me. Any vector field in the Fourier domain is the sum of the following:

1. An incompressible field whose vectors are all tangent to circles.

2. A gradient field whose vectors are all normal to circles.

Figure 8.14 illustrates this situation. The orange vector is the wave vector **k** defined by a direction and a magnitude. It corresponds to a planar wave as shown in Figure 8.10. At the tip of this wave vector a particular Fourier velocity **v** is shown in black. This corresponds to one of the vectors of the field on the left-hand side of Figure 8.13. This vector field can be decomposed into a tangential component $\mathbf{v}_T$ (in green) and a perpendicular component $\mathbf{v}_N$ (in blue). I know there are a lot of arrows in the figure. But focus on **k** the wave vector and **v** the vector in Fourier space. The components of the Fourier vector (green/blue) are just the coordinates with respect to the circle.

This is similar to our ellipse example described in Intermezzo Due earlier. In this case, we have that $\mathbf{v}=\mathbf{v}_T+\mathbf{v}_N$, therefore $\mathbf{v}_T=\mathbf{v}-\mathbf{v}_N$. This is

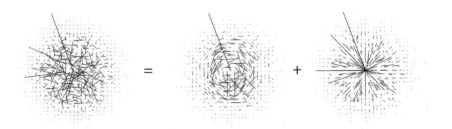

FIGURE 8.13   The Helmholtz–Hodge decomposition in the Fourier domain.

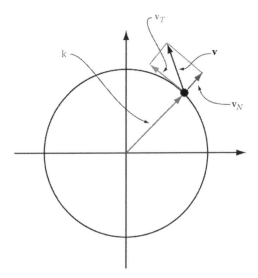

FIGURE 8.14 Every vector in the Fourier domain is separated into a tangential component and a perpendicular component.

essentially the Helmholtz–Hodge decomposition. In plain speak: we get an incompressible vector field by projecting the original field onto the line tangential to the circle defined by the wave vector. Just so you can understand the following code let's go over the mathematical steps of a projection for a single vector **v**. We are given a tangential vector **T** and we want to project our vector on this tangential vector. Every tangential vector has an evil twin which is perpendicular to itself. We call it **N** because it is *normal* to the tangential vector. The vector v_N is obtained by projecting the vector **v** onto the normal vector **N**:

$$v_N = v * N.$$

The star "*" this time stands for a dot product between vectors. The dot product is pretty simple; it takes two vectors and turns them into a number. For example:

$$(a,b) * (c,d) = ac + bd.$$

But also:

$$(a,b,c,d,e,f) * (g,h,i,j,k,m) = ag + bh + ci + dj + ek + fm.$$

Hopefully these two examples clarify what a dot product between vectors is. It works for any dimension.

To get the tangential part of the vector we just have to subtract the normal component of the original vector from itself:

$$\mathbf{v_T} = \mathbf{v} - \mathbf{v_N} = \mathbf{v} - \mathbf{v}^*\mathbf{N}.$$

This is another, simpler way to describe the Helmholtz–Hodge result. It is simpler because we looked at this problem from the Fourier point of view.

If you have digested the code described earlier for a simple solver, then the code in Figure 8.15 should be pretty easy to swallow. I have even added some code showing how to talk to the FFTW library. First you have to initialize some of their data structures. Also I introduced a FFT macro which takes care of direct and inverse transforms using the FFTW library. The size of the grid is hard coded to 32×32. But it does not have to be. Any rookie programmer can change the code to allow any sizes. Even better, you can turn it into an input specified by a Human or a Pet. By the way, you do not have to use the FFTW. It should be pretty clear how to modify the code with your favorite fast Fourier transform. I decided to include the low level stuff anyway for the FFTW. Why? Because FFTW is a cool solver and can handle any grid size. I restricted the size to an even number as you can tell from the code. It makes some of the math easier. If you are going to use FFTW, it is up to you to get it working in your hood. Installing libraries, like adding up numbers, bores me to death. It's the kind of stuff you keep for sleepy Friday mornings.

This looks complicated and simple at the same time. Well, at least to me.

Anyone who has written code will agree that it is simple for what it is able to achieve. A noncoder will just shrug and view this code as some other abstract nonsense like the Lagrangian of the standard model. The difference is that you can make it work on your laptop with the help of your geeky girlfriend/boyfriend. She or He will get it to work in your hood.

The most difficult part is to go back and forth between the FFTW data structures and our velocity arrays. It took me awhile to get it right. But I give these relations here for free for this particular piece of code. Use it in any other application that requires simulating something on a torus. The basic idea is:

```
#include <srfftw.h> /* Heresy! */

#define SIZE 32
#define SIZE2 (SIZE*SIZE)
#define SIZE2P ((SIZE+2)*(SIZE))

static float u[SIZE2], v[SIZE2], u0[SIZE2P], v0[SIZEP2];
static int rfftwnd_plan plan_rc, plan_cr;

#define FFT(s,n,u) \
if (s==1) rfftwnd_one_real_to_complex ( plan_rc, (fftw_real    *)u, (fftw_complex *)u );\
else      rfftwnd_one_complex_to_real ( plan_cr, (fftw_complex *)u, (fftw_real    *)u )

int init_solve ( int n )
{
    int i;

    if ( n%2 ) return 0;

    plan_rc = rfftw2d_create_plan ( n, n,  FFTW_REAL_TO_COMPLEX, FFTW_IN_PLACE );
    plan_cr = rfftw2d_create_plan ( n, n,  FFTW_COMPLEX_TO_REAL, FFTW_IN_PLACE );

    for ( i=0 ; i<n*n ; i++ ) u[i] = v[i] = 0;
    for ( i=0 ; i<(n+2)*n ; i++ ) u0[i] = v0[i] = 0;

    return 1;
}

#define floor(x) ((x)>=0.0?((int)(x)):(-((int)(1-(x)))))

void fourier_solve ( int n, float * u, float * v, float * u0, float * v0, float visc, float dt )
{
    float x, y, x0, y0, f, r, U[2], V[2];
    int i, j, i0, j0, i1, j1, s, t;

    for ( i=0 ; i<n*n ; i++ ){
        u[i] += dt*u0[i]; u0[i] = u[i];
        v[i] += dt*v0[i]; v0[i] = v[i];
    }

    for ( x=0.5/n,i=0 ; i<n ; i++,x+=1.0/n ){
        for ( y=0.5/n,j=0 ; j<n ; j++,y+=1.0/n ){
            x0 = n*(x-dt*u0[i+n*j])-0.5; y0 = n*(y-dt*v0[i+n*j])-0.5;
            i0 = floor(x0); s = x0-i0; i0 = (n+(i0%n))%n; i1 = (i0+1)%n;
            j0 = floor(y0); t = y0-j0; j0 = (n+(j0%n))%n; j1 = (j0+1)%n;
            u[i+n*j] = (1-s)*((1-t)*u0[i0+n*j0]+t*u0[i0+n*j1])+
                          s *((1-t)*u0[i1+n*j0]+t*u0[i1+n*j1]);
            v[i+n*j] = (1-s)*((1-t)*v0[i0+n*j0]+t*v0[i0+n*j1])+
                          s *((1-t)*v0[i1+n*j0]+t*v0[i1+n*j1]);
        }
    }

    for ( i=0 ; i<n ; i++ )
        for ( j=0 ; j<n ; j++ )
            { u0[i+(n+2)*j] = u[i+n*j]; v0[i+(n+2)*j] = v[i+n*j]; }

    FFT(1,n,u0); FFT(1,n,v0);

    for ( i=0 ; i<=n ; i+=2 ){
        x = 0.5*i;
        for ( j=0 ; j<n ; j++ ){
            y = j<=n/2 ? j : j-n;
            r = x*x+y*y;
            if ( r==0 ) continue;
            f = 1 / ( 1 + r*dt*visc);
            U[0] = u0[i  +(n+2)*j]; V[0] = v0[i  +(n+2)*j];
            U[1] = u0[i+1+(n+2)*j]; V[1] = v0[i+1+(n+2)*j];
            u0[i  +(n+2)*j] = f*( (1-x*x/r)*U[0]     -x*y/r *V[0] );
            u0[i+1+(n+2)*j] = f*( (1-x*x/r)*U[1]     -x*y/r *V[1] );
            v0[i  +(n+2)*j] = f*(   -y*x/r *U[0] + (1-y*y/r)*V[0] );
            v0[i+1+(n+2)*j] = f*(   -y*x/r *U[1] + (1-y*y/r)*V[1] );
        }
    }

    FFT(-1,n,u0); FFT(-1,n,v0);

    f = 1.0/(n*n);
    for ( i=0 ; i<n ; i++ )
        for ( j=0 ; j<n ; j++ )
            { u[i+n*j] = f*u0[i+(n+2)*j]; v[i+n*j] = f*v0[i+(n+2)*j]; }
}
```

FIGURE 8.15   Entire code to simulate a fluid on a torus using the FFT.

1. Transform your data from the spatial domain to the Fourier domain.

2. Solve your problem in the Fourier domain.

3. Transform your data back from the Fourier domain to the spatial domain.

In our donut fluid solver, we use the Fourier transform to turn the Helmholtz–Hodge decomposition—which is *global* in the spatial domain—into a *local* projection in the Fourier domain. A global thing has been turned into a local thing. The cost we have to pay for this is that we have to transform our data to the Fourier domain. That transformation however is global. So superficially nothing has been gained. But thanks to the fast Fourier transform this is not true. The global Fourier transform can be made faster computationally. Think again of our ellipse example aforementioned. By changing the point of view—the coordinate system— we made the thing simpler. But we did not alter the thing. It is all about how you look at it. But you have to do it in a rapid way in practice. If not nothing is gained.

This in a nutshell is why the FFT is so cool. Too bad its usage is restricted to donuts. Well not quite. The FFT also works for higher-dimensional donuts, for all spaces that have the property that when you cross a boundary you end up on the opposite boundary of the domain. Some scientists even speculate that our universe is finite in that sense. You go one way and you end up at the same spot. Is that crazy? Maybe. But remember people used to believe the earth was flat. Enough said.

You can use the code in Figure 8.15 *as is*. Other people have done this before. You have to install the FFTW package first however. Talk to your favorite geek in your hood if you cannot do it yourself. Trust me, cool geeks love doing this sort of stuff and will help you out, as long as you buy them a six-pack or a fancy latté.

Notice that we only use the FFTW to enforce incompressibility. The transport/advection step is still done in physical space.

Because I am being generous, the 3D version of the code is shown in Figure 8.16. Like the 2D version it is given *as is*. The reason I included this code is that it is not too hard to convert it to higher dimensions. It would work in 510,384 dimensions. This would involve a lot of typing unless you design some clever macros or templates.

```c
#include <srfftw.h> /* Heresy again!*/

#define SIZE 32
#define SIZE3 (SIZE*SIZE*SIZE)
#define SIZE3P ((SIZE+2)*(SIZE)*(SIZE))

static float u[SIZE3], v[SIZE3], w[SIZE3], u0[SIZE3P], v0[SIZ3P], w0[SIZE3P];

static rfftwnd_plan plan_rc, plan_cr;

#define FFT(s,u) \
if (s==1) rfftwnd_one_real_to_complex ( plan_rc, (fftw_real    *)u,(fftw_complex *)u );\
else      rfftwnd_one_complex_to_real ( plan_cr, (fftw_complex *)u,(fftw_real    *)u )

int init_solve3 ( int n )
{
    int i;

    if ( n%2 ) return 0;

    plan_rc = rfftw3d_create_plan ( n, n, n, FFTW_REAL_TO_COMPLEX, FFTW_IN_PLACE );
    plan_cr = rfftw3d_create_plan ( n, n, n, FFTW_COMPLEX_TO_REAL, FFTW_IN_PLACE );

    for ( i=0 ; i<n*n*n ; i++ ) u[i] = v[i] = w[i] = 0.0f;
    for ( i=0 ; i<(n+2)*n*n ; i++ ) u0[i] = v0[i] = w0[i] = 0.0f;

    return 1;
}

#define floor(x) ((x)>=0.0?((int)(x)):(-((int)(1-(x)))))

void fourier_solve3 ( int n, float * u, float * v, float * w, float * u0, float * v0, float * w0, float visc, float dt )
{
    float x, y, z, f, r, s, t, U[2], V[2], W[2], dtn;
    int idx, idx0, idx1, idx000, idx001, idx010, idx011, idx100, idx101, idx110, idx111;
    int i, j, k, i0, j0, k0, i1, j1, k1;

    for ( i=0 ; i<n*n*n ; i++ ){
        u[i] += dt*u0[i]; u0[i] = u[i];
        v[i] += dt*v0[i]; v0[i] = v[i];
        w[i] += dt*w0[i]; w0[i] = w[i];
    }

    dtn = n*dt;

    for ( i=0 ; i<n ; i++ ){
        for ( j=0 ; j<n ; j++ ){
            for ( k=0 ; k<n ; k++ ){
                idx = i+n*(j+n*k);
                x = i-dtn*u0[idx]; y = j-dtn*v0[idx]; z = k-dtn*w0[idx];
                i0 = floor(x); r = x-i0; i0 = (n+(i0%n))%n; i1 = (i0+1)%n;
                j0 = floor(y); s = y-j0; j0 = (n+(j0%n))%n; j1 = (j0+1)%n;
                k0 = floor(z); t = z-k0; k0 = (n+(k0%n))%n; k1 = (k0+1)%n;
                idx000 = i0+n*(j0+n*k0); idx001 = i0+n*(j0+n*k1); idx010 = i0+n*(j1+n*k0); idx011 = i0+n*(j1+n*k1);
                idx100 = i1+n*(j0+n*k0); idx101 = i1+n*(j0+n*k1); idx110 = i1+n*(j1+n*k0); idx111 = i1+n*(j1+n*k1);
                u[idx] = (1-r) * ( (1-s) * ( (1-t)*u0[idx000] + t*u0[idx001] ) + s * ( (1-t)*u0[idx010] + t*u0[idx011] ) ) +
                           r    * ( (1-s) * ( (1-t)*u0[idx100] + t*u0[idx101] ) + s * ( (1-t)*u0[idx110] + t*u0[idx111] ) );
                v[idx] = (1-r) * ( (1-s) * ( (1-t)*v0[idx000] + t*v0[idx001] ) + s * ( (1-t)*v0[idx010] + t*v0[idx011] ) ) +
                           r    * ( (1-s) * ( (1-t)*v0[idx100] + t*v0[idx101] ) + s * ( (1-t)*v0[idx110] + t*v0[idx111] ) );
                w[idx] = (1-r) * ( (1-s) * ( (1-t)*w0[idx000] + t*w0[idx001] ) + s * ( (1-t)*w0[idx010] + t*w0[idx011] ) ) +
                           r    * ( (1-s) * ( (1-t)*w0[idx100] + t*w0[idx101] ) + s * ( (1-t)*w0[idx110] + t*w0[idx111] ) );
            }
        }
    }

    for ( i=0 ; i<n ; i++ ){
        for ( j=0 ; j<n ; j++ ){
            for ( k=0 ; k<n ; k++ ){
                idx1 = i+n*(j+n*k); idx0 = i+(n+2)*(j+n*k);
                u0[idx0] = u[idx1]; v0[idx0] = v[idx1]; w0[idx0] = w[idx1];
            }
        }
    }

    FFT(1,u0); FFT(1,v0); FFT(1,w0);

    for ( i=0 ; i<=n ; i+=2 )
    {
        x = 0.5f*i;
        for ( j=0 ; j<n ; j++ ){
            y = (float)(j<=n/2 ? j : j-n);
            for ( k=0 ; k<n ; k++ ){
                z = (float)(k<=n/2 ? k : k-n);
                r = x*x+y*y+z*z;
                if ( r==0.0f ) continue;
                f = 1 / ( 1 + r*dt*visc );
                idx0 = i   +(n+2)*(j+n*k);
                idx1 = i+1+(n+2)*(j+n*k);
                U[0] = u0[idx0]; V[0] = v0[idx0]; W[0] = w0[idx0];
                U[1] = u0[idx1]; V[1] = v0[idx1]; W[1] = w0[idx1];
                u0[idx0] = f*( (1-x*x/r)*U[0]    -x*y/r *V[0]    -x*z/r *W[0] );
                u0[idx1] = f*( (1-x*x/r)*U[1]    -x*y/r *V[1]    -x*z/r *W[1] );
                v0[idx0] = f*(   -y*x/r *U[0] + (1-y*y/r)*V[0]    -y*z/r *W[0] );
                v0[idx1] = f*(   -y*x/r *U[1] + (1-y*y/r)*V[1]    -y*z/r *W[1] );
                w0[idx0] = f*(   -z*x/r *U[0]    -z*y/r *V[0] + (1-z*z/r)*W[0] );
```

FIGURE 8.16   Three-dimensional version of the code.   (*Continued*)

```
         w0[idx1] = f*(  -z*x/r *U[1]      -z*y/r *V[1] + (1-z*z/r)*W[1] );
       }
     }
   }

   FFT(-1,u0); FFT(-1,v0); FFT(-1,w0);

   f = 1.0f/(n*n*n);
   for ( i=0 ; i<n ; i++ ){
     for ( j=0 ; j<n ; j++ ){
       for ( k=0 ; k<n ; k++ ){
         idx1 = i+n*(j+n*k); idx0 = i+(n+2)*(j+n*k);
         u[idx1] = f*u0[idx0]; v[idx1] = f*v0[idx0]; w[idx1] = f*w0[idx0];
       }
     }
   }
```

FIGURE 8.16 *(Continued)*   Three-dimensional version of the code.

What would the advection step be in the Fourier space? This is an interesting question that is rarely addressed in fluid dynamics books. Instead of a local spatial phenomenon it becomes a global Fourier phenomenon. Therefore advection is best done in the spatial domain. Why do something in the Fourier domain that is not Fourier friendly. Fourier space is good for some things but not for others. It takes some practice and flair to use this transform adequately. However, a uniform translational advection in the spatial domain corresponds to a rotation in the Fourier domain.

To summarize: We used the Fourier transform to come up with a simple fluid solver on donuts. We cheated a bit as we used a library from MIT called FFTW. The Fourier transform came in very handy to solve for the incompressibility condition for these fluids. Another cool aspect of these fluids is that donuts can be unfolded into an infinite tiling of the plane. You basically get an infinite fluid from a finite one. How cool is that.

8.4 FOUR-DIMENSIONAL TURBULENT VECTOR FIELDS AND TURBULENCE

> There are really four dimensions, three which we call the three planes of Space, and a fourth, Time.
>
> H. G. WELLS (AMERICAN AUTHOR AS QUOTED FROM HIS NOVEL: *THE TIME MACHINE*)

We can reuse this Fourier code to create turbulent textures. Everything shown earlier was illustrated in a 2D space and a corresponding 2D Fourier space.

Remember turbulence?

That stuff that no one understands. We will use Kolmogorov's simple model to create 4D turbulence fields. It is like wallpaper but it wraps in space and in time: four dimensions. They are like a fatter cousin of the fields we have considered so far. These cousins wrap around not only in space but also in time. That is the wickedest part. These fields run forever in time and tile space endlessly as well. This is sort of trippy. It is useful, as you can use these turbulent fields to *decorate* existing velocity fields to generate more swirling detail on top of them.

This is very common in computer graphics. That is how we add detail to the surfaces. It is called *texture mapping*. Instead of modeling all the detail, a surface is modeled at a coarser level and detail is added later on. So, rather than modeling every pore and zit on a virtual character, these are added using a pore and zit map applied to the surface. More from less.

This is the same with a turbulent vector field: it adds detail and liveliness to a coarser fluid velocity field.

This is how it works.

Take a 4D noise sampled on a grid. This just means assign a random vector to each cell in a 4D grid. Then take a 4D Fourier transform. We make the spatial part incompressible using the fast projection. We then multiply this field by a Kolmogorov-like spectrum. Of course, anyone can use their own spectrum invented in their basement. Then we Fourier transform this field back to the spatial domain. *Voilà!* You now have a 4D grid of turbulent vectors. You only have to compute it once and then you can reuse it in your favorite app to add cool details to your flow. This stuff got me my first SIGGRAPH paper and fueled part of the particle system in Alias's Power Animator software and then our MAYA software. This all happened in the early 1990s in Toronto.

```
gen_turb ( v ) {
  for ( it=0 ; it<=Nt/2 ; it++ ) {
    l = it/Nt;
    for ( ix,iy,iz=0 ; ix,iy,iz<Nx,Ny,Nz ;
      ix,iy,iz++ ) {
      kx, ky, kz = ix/Nx, iy/Ny, iz/Nz;
      if ( ix > Nx/2 ) kx = kx - 1.0;
      if ( iy > Nx/2 ) ky = ky - 1.0;
      if ( iz > Nx/2 ) kz = kz - 1.0;
      k2 = kx*kx+ky*ky+kz*kz;
      /* generate random complex vector */
      tx, ty, tz = unif(0.0,2*PI);
      RE(Wx,Wy,Wz) = S(sqrt(k2),1)*cos(tx,ty,tz);
      IM(Wx,Wy,Wz) = S(sqrt(k2),1)*sin(tx,ty,tz);1 3
      /* project onto plane normal to {kx,ky,kz} */
```

```
      Vx = (1-kx*kx/k2)*Wx - kx*ky/k2 *Wy - kx*kz/k2
         *Wz;
      Vy = -ky*kx/k2 *Wx + (1-ky*ky/k2)*Wy - ky*kz/k2
         *Wz;
      Vz = -kz*kx/k2 *Wx - kz*ky/k2 *Wy + (1-kz*kz/
         k2)*Wz;
      /* store and ensure "mirror" symmetries */
      w[ix][iy][iz][it] = {Vx,Vy,Vz};
      w[(Nx-ix)%Nx][(Ny-iy)%Ny][(Nz-iz)%Nz]
         [(Nt-it)%Nt] = {CC(Vx),CC(Vy),CC(Vz)};
    }
  }
  /* "mirror" symmetries at the axis of the
     symmetry */
  for ( it,ix,iy,iz = 0,0,0,0 and Nt/2,Nx/2,Ny/2,Nz/2 )
    {
    IM(vel[ix][iy][iz][it]) = 0.0;
  }
  X(v) = invFFT4(X(w));
  Y(v) = invFFT4(Y(w));
  Z(v) = invFFT4(Z(w));
  /* normalize each component of v in the range
     [-1,+1] */
}
/* In the code we used the following macros:
RE(c) = real part of complex variable
IM(c) = complex part of complex variable
CC(c) = complex conjugate of the variable
X(v) = x component of a vector
Y(v) = y component of a vector
Z(v) = z component of a vector
S(k,t) = Kolmogorov's spectrum
*/
```

Creating flow turbulence is mostly a purely kinematic approach. We only model the thing that affects the thing; not the thing that affects the thing that then affects the thing. That would be dynamics. We model a first-order effect, not a second-order effect. All the babble mentioned above involved mostly dynamics. Although the dynamics are cooler, kinematics can be cool too. Kinematics is the nice neighbor that is more predictable than the eccentric dynamics neighbor two blocks down the road. But dynamics may be more fun to hang out with.

To summarize: Using a 4D Fourier transform, you can create interesting flow texture maps that wrap both in time and in space. You only have to compute this field once and then store the result. These precomputed flows can then be used in many applications.

8.5 DECORATING FLUIDS

Please do not stand too close to my paintings, the smell will make you sick.

REMBRANDT VAN RIJN (LEGENDARY DUTCH MASTER
PAINTER AND ETCHER, 1606–1669)

In the previous section, we described a technique to decorate the fluid's velocity. We described how to modulate the thing that affects the things. We will describe a technique to directly modify the appearance of a fluid's density using evolving texture maps. The idea is to simulate the velocity at some level and then add detail.

First, we have to explicitly define what a texture map is. Let us do it in two dimensions so that we can clearly illustrate this concept.

A texture map is usually a 2D picture of something. A photograph perhaps: a picture of your dog or a picture of some interesting texture you happened to photograph on Jeju Island in South Korea, for example. This picture can then be mapped onto a digital surface. This is illustrated in Figure 8.17. On the left there is a picture of our family poodle "Luke" and on the right is a surface. Both the photograph and the surface are 2D surfaces. The one on the left corresponding to the photograph is flat and undeformed while the surface on the right has been deformed. You can tell from the shading. On the right-hand side of Figure 8.17, we depict

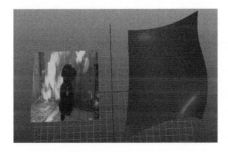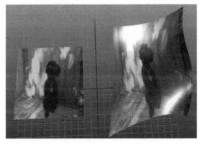

FIGURE 8.17 Left: The texture map and the surface. Right: The texture map applied to the surface.

what happens if our picture is *texture mapped* onto the deformed surface. Generally for each pixel element, a pixel of the texture is mapped to a unique point on the surface. This is really oversimplifying the situation. What if the texture has only a few pixels and the surface is large in comparison? What if the texture map is huge and the surface is tiny in the background? Welcome to the world of optimal sampling. Look it up. This book is not about optimal texture mapping. But it is a fascinating subject.

The point that I am making here is that you can decorate—add detail—to a surface through a mechanism known as texture mapping.

The texture map is often rectangular. Computer graphics people refer to each point in the texture map by two coordinates usually denoted by u and v. These coordinates are often bounded between zero and one. The left bottom corner is (0,0) and gets mapped to the left bottom corner of the surface. The top right corner is (1,1) and gets mapped to the top right corner of the surface. In between: well you just get a mapping in between these two extremes. Notice that the texture map looks distorted on the surface. This is usually an undesirable artefact. But in fluid animation we like this. We want stuff to swirl around and evolve over time and look cool.

So, how do we decorate a fluid with a texture map?*

The key insight is to treat the "u" and the "v" coordinates as density fields that are going to move, diffuse, and wiggle in a vector field. The initial state of the coordinates is depicted in Figure 8.18. Initially, they are just linear ramps. This means there is a one-to-one correspondence between the texture and the fluid when it is in a rest state. Texture coordinates are treated just like the density of perfume, dog farts, or Beijing smog being stirred and diffused in the air, which remember is a fluid. That is how we can dress up fluids in pretty skirts: *Fluides en Jupons*.

I hope that Figure 8.19 illustrates the basic concept. As the u and v coordinates are being moved around, the mapping to the original texture is being affected. Figure 8.19 shows a point at the center of the fluid. Initially its u–v coordinates are (0.5,0.5): it refers to the exact same pixel located at the center of the texture map. However, over time the u–v *densities* evolve because they are immersed in a fluid. The point in the middle now refers to some other u–v coordinate in the original texture map. In this case,

---

* I did not invent this technique from scratch. Nelson Max and Barry Becker in their 1992 paper entitled "Flow Visualization Using Moving Textures" inspired this work. Research is never done in isolation.

FIGURE 8.18   Initial u and v maps treated as density fields.

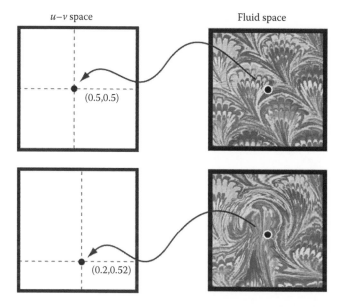

FIGURE 8.19   Texture advection. The u–v coordinates are modified by the fluid. Each cell in the fluid grid has a unique u–v coordinate that corresponds to a point in the texture map.

it's a point in the lower part of the texture. *Et Voila!* This results in the visual illusion of an upward motion.

In fact there is more to this technique that I have to explain.

One problem is that because of numerical diffusion when you run this method for some time everything gets blurred out. In this context, it means that your entire fluid will be equal to a single pixel of the texture map. In the case of the texture map in Figure 8.19, the fluid might end up being all pink just like in the world of Dr. Seuss' *The Cat in the Hat Comes Back*.

To solve this problem, we use three sets of *u*–*v* coordinates. Ugh! This makes everything much slower. But thanks to Moore's law it will be fast at some time in the future. Besides, it creates much cooler animations. And it runs for reasonable resolutions in real-time on an iPhone.

This is how it works.

The idea is to blend three sets of *u*–*v* densities multiplied by a weight at each time frame. The weights add up to one and they evolve over time in a staggered manner.

Figure 8.20 shows one choice of blend functions: 2D teepees. I always go for the simplest stuff because I am lazy. And if that doesn't work I will have to look for something fancier.

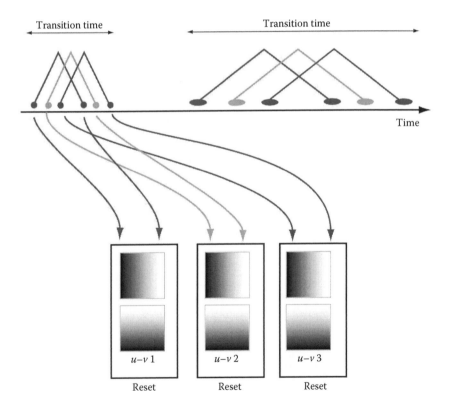

FIGURE 8.20 Weighting different texture maps over time to reduce loss of detail. In this example three texture map coordinates are used.

Figure 8.20 is kind of funky and looks like some crazy triptych or a sanitized version of a Basquiat painting.* I will attempt to explain it in plain English. So why bother with a figure? Well, sometimes it's clearer in words and images. They complement each other. At least that usually works for me.

Three texture coordinates are being evolved over time through a fluid. When the tent function gets to zero, the fluid coordinates are reset as shown in Figure 8.20. No worries; their weight is zero so no one will notice. The other two weights are still alive and well. But then from then on, the defunct texture comes immediately alive after it has been reset and after its weight is set to zero. No worries again; it will rise to power again and then disappear again only to rise again. It is a cyclical process. It could go on forever until your program crashes because of a memory leak, for example.

You do not need three texture maps and a simple tent *teepee* function. I encourage readers to experiment with other combinations at home. I am just saying that this worked out for me. The transition time between texture maps can be easily modeled through a scaling of time. This is depicted on the right-hand side of Figure 8.20. It is just a knob that an animator can use. If it is small, texture coordinates will blend more rapidly and if it is large, texture coordinates will blend at a slower pace. There is no scientific justification for this parameter. Well not that I know of right now. But who cares? This book is about fluid animation. And this technique is way cool. People use it to create nifty effects.

To summarize: Fluids can be dressed up with fancy flowery dresses. Sometimes you get more from less, when it involves mapping a cool texture map with coordinates evolving through the fluid. In addition, these animations can be made livelier by having three sets of u–v coordinates and blending between them over time.

---

* Jean-Michel Basquiat (1960–1988) was from Haitian descent and was born and raised in New York. He is a true 1980s legend. Check out his art.

CHAPTER 9

The Little Computers Who Can Handle Fluids

Intellectual property has the shelf life of a banana.

BILL GATES (COFOUNDER OF MICROSOFT)

Imagine 1999.

Yeah, back when people like me were worried about the Y2K bug because we did not trust the COBOL code that was driving bank transactions and Wall Street trading. Hopefully, a lot of my readers won't even remember that time. I am talking about the time that the small computers were crawling out of their rabbit holes. Thanks to Steve Jobs and Bill Gates. Who doesn't have a *smart phone* today?

Of course nowadays smart phones are everywhere and are taken for granted.

I wrote a fluid simulator for the Pocket PC back in 2000 and showed it at our annual computer graphics conference at SIGGRAPH in 2001 during a speech in front of a large audience and of course elsewhere: in pubs and production houses in swinging Soho in London, in the Metro in Paris, in hotel lobbies and lounges in Los Angeles, good thing I didn't drop my iPAQ in the pool at the Figueroa Hotel, also at family gatherings in Geneva, and so on. The list just goes on.

It is cool to share creations in such an effortless manner with other people. Don't get me wrong. A lot of effort went into creating the App of course. I wrote a lot of code and had to download SDKs and emulators to test and run the code. That takes time and effort. But then you can just show it off in a laid back manner to a wide-ranging audience.

"Check this out man."

Reactions ranged from "awesome stuff dude!" to "what is this rubbish mate?" Good times. To reiterate a point I made earlier: high praise or dumb criticism is better than no reaction at all. Some people get it and some do not.

This section is about how I taught little computers that fit in your pocket to do fluid simulations.

The Palm and the Pocket PC did not have hardware support for floating points. They did not even have fancy graphics interfaces like OpenGL. Still at the time they were cool devices. Even though these devices came out in the late 1990s, it felt like I was back in the 1980s again, yay!

I am going to keep this short.

I felt amused in 2008 when a kid told me after an invited talk: "Why are you showing me a demo on a Palm device that my dad used to figure out his finances?" My response: "Because I can."

I am not going to dwell on how I implemented the basic rendering pipeline of graphics like I did in the late 1990s and in the early 1980s as a teenager. Because now we have *OpenGL ES* that runs on any iOS device. I wasted so much time on re-implementing low-level rendering algorithms. It was fun and I do now understand these algorithms better. Because to code is to really understand something. That is if it runs and works at all. I understand the rendering pipeline. I have coded it many times.

I am now going to open a nasty can of worms that contains **floats, doubles, doubledoubles,** and what not. These are *pretend real numbers*. They are stuck in the discrete realm that the Slave understands and lives in. How do you represent continuous real numbers that the Slave understands?

Bill Kahan is a Toronto-born computer scientist who now lives in Berkeley, California. He won a Turing Award in 1989 partly for coming up with a standard for floating numbers. It is called the *IEEE 754 Standard*. Before that the floating point world was the equivalent of an urban jungle. You would get your code to work with your most favorite *pretend reals* in your hood before finding out that the results would be completely different in another hood that was dealing with another version of *pretend reals*. You were stuck in your hood back then. Professor Kahan took us out of this urban jungle. All computer processors now use the same patois for *real numbers*. Phew! Now consistency, and consistent craziness, can happen in all hoods. That is progress. Respect to Prof. Kahan. His work was a monumental achievement. Chapeau!

Floating points are tricky. Trust me.

I want to introduce *fixed-point* reals instead. They are of course not my invention. I just used them and played with them and had fun with them. They are less tricky and more honest than their IEEE cousins. But they are still tricky. Just in a more predictable way.

Small computers in the late 1990s and PCs in the early 1980s did not support floating point arithmetic on their processors. If you wanted your code to run efficiently you had to use integers. Yes, that's right: a finite number of bits that our Slave can understand, dressed up like in a float dress.

I already spent too much time on this topic. It is *passé*. Let me just show you in Figure 9.1, out of nostalgia, the header file that allows one to implement fixed-point arithmetic instead of floats. To me, it is an achievement that I want to share: albeit a relic from the past. It is a useless piece of code since float operations are actually faster than integers in most cases nowadays. But it is tight and elegant more so than a float dress.

It is very instructive to play with fixed numbers. It shows the kind of traps you can be caught in with float numbers. Try this at home. No one will get hurt.

Using this header file a usual float statement like "x = a*(b/c)" becomes in fixed point "x = XM(a,XD(b,c))." Yeah it is uglier. Besides, you ask, why am I using 16 bits? That was because it was way back in 1999. Observe how I am using the "(long)" type (these babies had 32 bits back then) for multiplication and division. That is why I am using 16 bits. You can make it prettier in C++ or some other object-oriented language by using operator overloading. This has been extremely geeky. If you are into this stuff look it up on the Internet.

Figure 9.2 shows two snapshots of fluids running on a Palm (a) and on an iPAQ Pocket PC (b).

```
/* Each freal in bits is xxxxxxxx.xxxxxxxx That is 16 bits */
#define freal short
#define X1      (1<<8)
#define I2X(i)  ((i)<<8)
#define X2I(x)  ((x)>>8)
#define F2X(f)  ((f)*X1)
#define X2F(x)  ((float)(x)/(float)X1)
#define XM(x,y) ((freal)(((long)(x)*(long)(y))>>8))
#define XD(x,y) ((freal)(((long)(x))<<8)/(long)(y)))
```

FIGURE 9.1   Fixed-point arithmetic implemented using a header file.

 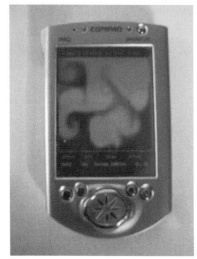

FIGURE 9.2 Two snapshots of fluid animations on a small computer. The Palm (a) and the iPAQ (b).

Actually, the Palm version had an accelerometer SD Card with an API. Remember this was the early naught years. I got this SD card from a Swiss-Italian engineer called Paolo Bernasconi, who worked for a startup company in Silicon Valley called *Motion Sense*. He gave me the API and the SD card. We met at a pub in San Jose, California, for a beer during GDC, the annual gamer conference. I gave a talk there on fluid dynamics.

To summarize: I wrote the first fluid interactive animation app for hand-held devices. I had to use fixed-point arithmetic and my own renderer to have these simulations run on such a small device. I created it basically from scratch: fun times. This was in 2000.

CHAPTER 10

The Smart Phones That Can Handle Fluids

I have conquered an empire but I have not been able to conquer myself.

PETER THE GREAT (CZAR OF RUSSIA, 1672–1725)

Innovation distinguishes between a leader and a follower.

STEVE JOBS (COFOUNDER OF APPLE, 1955–2011)

Now imagine 2007.

Apple comes out with the iPhone: accelerometer built in, support of OpenGL ES, fast processor, Internet access built in, multitouch interface, and so on. Shortly thereafter, the iTouch came out. It was pretty close in coolness to the iPhone. What is not to love? Wow, why did I not buy it in 2007? Because you could not natively write code on the device: only through web apps.

Come on Apple.

All that cool hardware fits in our hand and that we cannot directly access. What a tease. Also I did not want to go the *Jail Break* way. I did not want to get in trouble, and I thought it was the wrong approach.

Then everything changed in early 2008.

Steve Jobs announced that they were releasing a native SDK with an API. I immediately started to download their beta release, bought an iTouch, and started to code a fluid solver on the device. Not only a fluid solver but also other apps like a simulation of hard spheres interacting. Like those poor hamsters stuck in their plastic balls banging into each other.

Writing an app back then was a pain. This is because I had never wandered into the Mac hood before. This was a new neighborhood. Actually, not that different: just a new patois and a lot of glassy condos. But geez these dudes did not make it easy on me. But in the end I was able to write code on one of the most beautiful designed smart phones at the time.

Here is the breakdown of what I had to go through in the new hood:

1. Get an iDevice, in my case an iTouch

2. Get a MacBook Pro or some other Apple computer

3. Learn Xcode

4. Learn Objective C

5. Learn Cocoa (Touch)

6. Learn how to set up an Apple Dev Account

7. Learn how to set up Keychain, Provisioning, etc.

8. Write the app

9. Add Autodesk Marketing Stuff

10. Get the app approved by Apple

Ironically, one of the easiest parts was writing the app (step 8). But in the end I got an Apple app up and running. The app came out officially in early November 2008 on the App Store and was called *Autodesk Fluid*. This was the first app that Autodesk ever released on an iDevice, and I was the *Agent* for all of Autodesk for 2 years. As a bonus I now know how to write code for iOS devices and the Mac. Figure 10.1 shows three different snapshots of the app in action: another triptych of some sorts. The cheesy branding is what I had to put with in order to get my app out there.

This app was free and it got around 300,000 downloads worldwide. For some crazy reason there were 175,000 downloads from the United Kingdom alone in a couple of days. I have no idea what triggered this frenzy. The number of downloads for a certain app is usually an exponential process that decays very rapidly. There are of course exceptions.

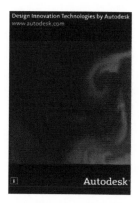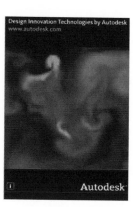

FIGURE 10.1   Three snapshots of the *Autodesk Fluid* app. This was the first app that Autodesk ever released.

At that time, it was the number one free app on the UK App Store. I kept a snapshot of the iTunes UK main page as shown in Figure 10.2. Having that many people download your app is cool. I did not make a single penny out of this app by the way. I did not do it for the money. I just did it to show something cool I created to a wider audience. On the other

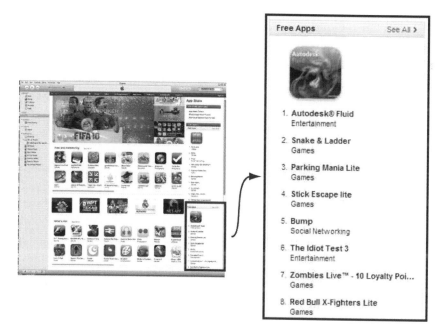

FIGURE 10.2   Autodesk Fluid was the number one free app in the United Kingdom.

hand, you have to be ready to face a lot of *trolling*. Just to give you an idea: "the best part of this app is when I deleted it from my iPhone," "pixelated rubbish," "I wish I could give it a minus one star," and so on. Yes it is hard to be popular in the United Kingdom. Of course there was a lot of praise as well: "this is so sick man!," "cool!," "awesome!" and so on. No bad or hurt feelings by the way. In the end, I created something and I shared it. The trolls are like the little boys who trash your sand castle on the beach. Destroying something makes them feel better.

My experience with the Pocket PC was much easier back in 2000. No approval by Microsoft was necessary. Anyone could just beam their apps to each other just like with the Palm. I always compare iOS to a totalitarian regime that creates beautiful cities. Think of Paris, France, rebuilt by Haussmann under the supervision of Emperor Napoleon III or St. Petersburg built from scratch under the orders of Czar Peter the Great. Both cities have a very coherent look because they were built under the supervision of pretty much a single person. I think of Microsoft Windows more like Toronto, Seattle, or Los Angeles: sort of ugly in appearance but more flexible. Neighborhoods come and go. There is contemporary stuff next to old buildings. There is very little consistency in appearance in these cities.

I prefer to use Apple devices, but I prefer to code in the Windows world. I like to visit Paris, but I prefer to live and work in Toronto.

To summarize: I wrote a fluid app for the iPhone in 2008. The first official app released by the company that I work for: Autodesk. The process was somewhat painful but well worth it. There were 175,000 downloads in the United Kingdom alone in a couple of days.

CHAPTER 11

Fluid FX

Version 2.0 of Autodesk Fluid

Making Fluids fun for the masses.

In 2010, our consumer division at Autodesk decided to create a more sophisticated version of the *Autodesk Fluid app*. Better user interface (UI), the ability to warp texture maps like we described earlier and set things on fire! My original *Autodesk Fluid app* was really a mash up of OpenGL ES and Objective C code that I found on the apple.com website. My fluid code however was still my own. I spent some time optimizing it for the iOS operating system. The beauty of Objective C is that you can include plain good old C in your project. The same is true of C++.

But really under the hood my app was ugly: except of course for the fluid code part.

For *Fluid FX* we actually had expert Mac coders, meetings, product managers, and so on. Not me hacking away alone in my fifth floor cave anymore.

This resulted in *Fluid FX* and other apps for the Mac. You can find them at http://usa.autodesk.com/fx-apps/.

Check it out. This is not a shameless promotion to try to sell stuff and make me rich. I don't get a penny. Like I said before, if you create something cool you want to share it with as many people as possible. Then your work was worth all the time and the effort.

One of the lesser known apps is *Motion FX*. It only runs on the Mac under Lion and upgrades. If you have a Mac and don't want to spend a

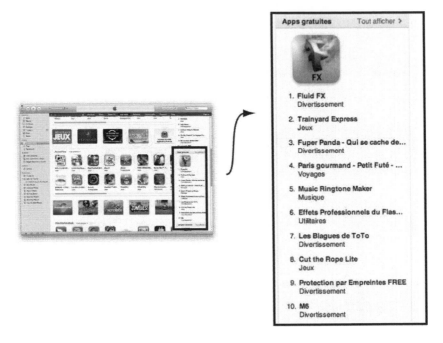

FIGURE 11.1   Here we go again. *Fluid FX* was the number one *App gratuite* in France.

dime, download it. It is free. It uses the camera on your Mac to track your body movements, including eyes, to create a lot of fun animations. You can get it from the link provided earlier. Try this at home and spread the link to your friends. Spread the fun.

This time, *Fluid FX* became the biggest download on the French App Store. This is shown in Figure 11.1.

To summarize: We did it again but better. *Fluid FX*, *Motion FX*, and *Time FX* are all based on the basic code given in this book. Of course a lot of effort has been put into the design of the UI and the proper writing of iOS code. This was a team effort. I thank the entire team for this to happen.

CHAPTER 12

Show Time! MAYA Fluid Effects

माया

MAYA (ILLUSION) IN SANSKRIT

Let us go back in time. As mentioned in the Prolegomenon (Preface) at the beginning of this book, the fluid solver has been put into our flagship animation software called MAYA.

A bit of history is in order.

Once upon a time there was a company called Alias. It was founded in 1984 in Toronto, Canada. Their first products were geared toward the design of modeling shapes.* Legend has it that General Motors bought our software when some of our engineers showed the GM execs a view from inside a virtual car before it was built. Hard to do that with a clay model, isn't it? The software was very *rock "n" roll* back then. Menus would pop up from the bottom, and there was no *undo* feature.

I joined Alias as a part-time employee in 1994 to put some particle stuff into their Power Animator software when I was doing my PhD at the University of Toronto. In 1995, Alias from Toronto and *Wavefront* from sunny Santa Barbara were both acquired by Silicon Graphics from less

---

* Back then in the 1980s our coders could say they were into modeling in nightclubs. Yeah right.

sunny Mountain View and merged to create Alias *wavefront*.* At the same time, people were working on a new revolutionary piece of animation software called MAYA. It was finally released in 1998. This software is used in many production houses and was awarded an Oscar in 2003. And yes, the Oscar is in the lobby of our office in Toronto. Well, a good replica in any case, the real one is stored in a secure vault somewhere. We do not want some visitor to run away with the real thing.

At any rate, in 2000 the company decided to put my fluid solver prototype into MAYA. After an epic meeting in Santa Barbara (remember Duncan?), I went back to Seattle and my colleagues went back to Toronto. After a lot of coding and back and forth meetings, MAYA Fluid Effects came out in 2002 with the MAYA 4.5 release.

One of the biggest hurdles that we faced, as I recall it, was to add *volume rendering* to MAYA in a somewhat efficient way. Volumes are like clouds, smoke, fire, steam, and so on. Not like surfaces. Volumes are three dimensional and they scatter, absorb, and sometimes emit light (think of a flame). This makes modeling their effects much harder than shading a surface. There were also software architectural reasons why it was difficult to add volumes to the rendering engine of MAYA. I had to partly deal with these problems, thank you very much. So I won't dwell further on how it was solved.

But still, Figure 12.1 depicts the situation in a simplified manner. Our volume of fluid, the density, is actually sliced into discrete squares from the point of view of the camera. Then all the illuminations from each slice are blended together from front to back (following the arrow). The situation is a little more complicated in practice, of course. But that is the basic idea.

How to render volumes was a topic part of my PhD thesis. So it was not too much of a challenge to write this code. There is an interplay between dynamics and rendering. Yeah sure you figured out the dynamics (fluid animation), but in the end one still has to render these volumes. I am not going to talk about how to render—create an image—of a volume. There are many good books written on that topic. Look it up if you are interested.

We also added 3D textures to decorate our 3D fluids. Or in some cases just to create a static texture, like in creating background clouds. This is just a pretty straightforward 3D extension of the procedure we explained

---

* At the time there was a contest within the company to find a new name for the merger. At the end, we just added the two names together. This reminds me of the naming of the 1998 soccer stadium in Paris for the World Cup Final. The best that the committee could come up with was *Stade de France*. Come on!

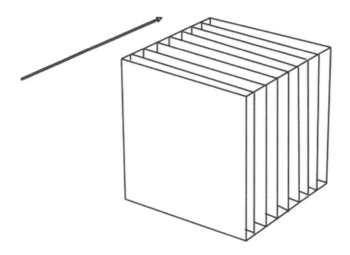

FIGURE 12.1   The rendering of a 3D volume.

above for 2D textures. Just the rendering part is trickier. This is shown in Figure 12.2, which is a still from an animation. The camera is able to *fly through the clouds*. Notice all the subtle effects due to scattering and self-shadowing. There is no emission in this case. The animator through various knobs can control the appearance of the clouds. In Figure 12.2, the animator decided to make them nice and fluffy like cotton balls.

FIGURE 12.2   A volumetric cloud texture map in MAYA.

It is hard to demonstrate the power of MAYA Fluid Effects without showing actual animations. But if you have gone to the movies you have seen their application. Just to name a few: *The Lord of the Rings, Ghost Rider, The Day After Tomorrow, 300, Avengers, Tintin*, and so on. In fact MAYA Fluid Effects got a Technical Achievement Award from the Academy of Movie Picture Arts and Sciences in 2008. I had to wear a tuxedo again.

Following is an important point I want to make. Just to make it crystal clear.

> The artists who create the visuals you see in movies really deserve all the credit for the final shots. We provide the brushes, the tools. When I used to paint with the airbrush, it wasn't Jens Andreas Paasche* who made the painting but he—the inventor—definitely helped me by creating paintings using such a beautiful, elegant and easy to use tool: his airbrush. That was his creation. My paintings using his tools were my creations.

The following figures show many examples using MAYA Fluid Effects created by my friend Duncan Brinsmead who is also my colleague at Autodesk.

Figure 12.3 shows four frames of ink being dropped in a fluid. The forces exerted on the density of ink are to counter gravity. They descend and create an external force on the fluid. The incompressibility of the fluid makes the density curl around and create cool patterns. These four frames do not do justice to the actual animation. But the stills are still cool.

The opposite effect is shown in Figure 12.4. In this case, a nuclear explosion is simulated using a density field and a temperature field. In this case, the motion is upward. We show four frames of the animation. Of course these animations use some spicy magic sauces concocted by Duncan that are not covered by the basic fluid solver.

MAYA Fluid Effects can also be used to create fire-like effects, this is shown in Figure 12.5. It uses a temperature field and a density field that influence the air flow. The color can be controlled by the animator through a ramp.

There are a lot more of effects, of course. We can simulate snow avalanches (Figure 12.6) and liquids (Figure 12.7). The liquid simulations were really hard to implement because of the gain and loss of the mass of

---

* Paasche founded the company in 1906 in Chicago.

FIGURE 12.3   Four frames of an animation created using MAYA Fluid Effects.

FIGURE 12.4   Four frames of a nuclear explosion created with MAYA Fluid Effects.

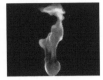

FIGURE 12.5   Four frames of a simple flame created with MAYA Fluid Effects.

FIGURE 12.6   Simulation of a snow avalanche using MAYA Fluid Effects.

FIGURE 12.7   Four frames of a liquid simulation using MAYA Fluid Effects.

the liquid in the advection process. The way we solved these artefacts is somewhat inelegant. We used a reaction-diffusion solver to *straighten* the boundary between the air and the liquid. We also modified the Fish equation to compensate for mass gain and mass loss. We basically make the fluid compressible and divergent where we detect mass gain and mass loss.

Unfortunately, this book will not deal with all the details of liquid simulation in our MAYA software. Why not? It was really sort of a *whack a mole* approach. I hope there is something more elegant out there.

I hope this gives the reader a broad overview of what MAYA Fluid Effects can achieve.

When I was visiting Weta Digital in Wellington, New Zealand, I was talking in French with one of the animators called Mathieu Chardonnet at a local bar. It turned out that he grew up in *La Haute Savoie* next door to Geneva. I used to ski there. After an hour he asked me what I was doing. It turns out that he is a heavy user of MAYA Fluids: so cool.* I love whimsical experiences like that.

Get our MAYA software and try this at home. You can download a free trial of our MAYA software for 30 days. Just search for *free MAYA software* in your favorite search engine.

To summarize: Putting research code into a complex commercial software is not easy. It is a team effort. Volume rendering ended up being a challenge. Putting a basic solver in a powerful software package like MAYA enables people to create a lot of cool visual effects. It has been used in feature movies. We received an Academy Award for it. I had to wear a tuxedo for the second time in my life.

---

* You can find his art at: http://www.krop.com/mathieuchardonnet/

CHAPTER 13

Fluids on Arbitrary Surfaces

The true sign of intelligence is not knowledge but imagination.

ALBERT EINSTEIN (WELL YOU KNOW WHO HE IS)

Previously, we talked about fluids on donuts, also known as tori, which we harnessed using the almighty Fourier transform. Now I will briefly describe a technique to animate fluids on other surfaces: surfaces with more holes or less than donuts. A good example is our good old earth, which is topologically equivalent to a sphere: a big blue round ball with some fluffy clouds floating on it. No holes. But there are surfaces with more holes. Some of those creatures are depicted in Figure 13.1. The creature on the far right is not even a closed surface, but it is has *one hole*.

First I have to describe how these Subdivision Surfaces are created.

How did I create these creatures? That was back in 2002 using our MAYA software in the loft in Seattle. I used subdivision surfaces. This is a technology I worked on. And for some results I created I shared an Academy Award with Ed Catmull and Tony de Rose from Pixar in 2006: these surfaces are used in many movies.

The concept of subdivision surfaces is best explained as a process. First you start with a discrete surface made of polygons. Then like a sadist you chop off corners; in the end after an infinite number of sadistic acts you end up with a nice smooth version of the discrete surface that you

FIGURE 13.1   Four examples of surfaces on which we can model fluids.

started with.* In 1997, I showed that you could save the sadist a lot of time. You don't have to chop off corners. Just compute eigenvalues and eigenvectors. Bring in the German Eigen's to the rescue. From the initial surface you can get directly to the same surface that would have been reached by chopping off corners. Computer graphics researchers had done this before for the initial set of points. I showed that you could do it for all points: even an infinite number of them, directly from the initial set of polygons.

This works not only just in this case. There is a class of subdivision surfaces called "Catmull–Clark subdivision surfaces." They are named after the inventors Ed Catmull and Jim Clark: two computer graphics legends. Catmull started Pixar and Clark founded Silicon Graphics. Their work generalized some smooth surface stuff that only worked for regular quad meshes to arbitrary shapes. This is how it works. It is a recursive process. At each step new points are introduced for each quadrilateral, *quad*, and then all the points are smoothed: the old ones and the new ones.

This is to be repeated *ad infinitum*. In the end, you get a smooth looking surface.

This is illustrated for a cube shrinking into a *sphere* in Figure 13.2. Actually, the limit surface is not a perfect sphere: just an approximation of a sphere. This process is gentler than the sadistic corner cutting procedure described earlier. But in the end you get a nice looking surface, which can have any topology. The gentle approach results in smoother surfaces than the sadist's approach.

I always wanted to combine my subdivision work and my fluid work.

This dream resulted in a 2003 SIGGRAPH publication. Academics were puzzled about why I was wasting my time and not doing something useful for my company. Just minutes before my talk, I was asked to justify why

---

* I am oversimplifying of course. But that is the gist of the subdivision process. This book is not about subdivision surfaces. Look it up if you want more information.

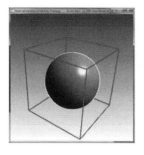

FIGURE 13.2   Three steps of Catmull–Clark subdivision (in red) and the limit surface in blue.

I created this. In my talk I just said: "because it is a cool thing to do"*: Yeah whatever. But really, you never know where research will lead you, and the benefits that will come of it.

This is how I proceeded. I assigned a 2D fluid solver to each initial quad that defines a Catmull–Clark subdivision surface. Using my limit surface technique, I was able to map the fluid solve to the surface. The mapping for three quads of a cube is shown in Figure 13.3.

One tricky aspect of this technique is how to handle exchanges of information between adjacent patches. In order to handle this, we use our ghosts located at the boundary of each quad domain. Remember Figure 6.5 described earlier.

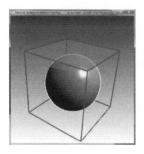
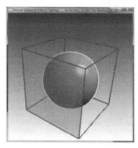
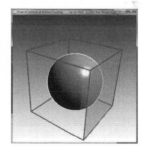

FIGURE 13.3   Using an exact evaluation, each quad from the initial mesh can be mapped to a smooth patch on the surface.

---

* Just as an anecdote. My paper got accepted because of a snowstorm in Colorado. Getting papers accepted at SIGGRAPH is tricky. But who cares, it got accepted. I think it is a beautiful paper. In 2011, I was invited specifically to present these results at IMPA in Rio de Janeiro. I include these results in all my invited presentations on fluid animations.

"Okay neighbor quad I will tell your ghosts what to do at our common border if you tell my ghosts what to do, deal?"

This sounds easy but it is not. It is a lot trickier. I am not going to provide any code here. For that, check out my SIGGRAPH 2003 paper and the follow-up work. I am just going to show some of the results that can be achieved with this technique. Some are depicted in Figure 13.4. These are snapshots from a demo program I wrote, which runs in real time on a decent PC. I showed it in San Diego, California, at SIGGRAPH 2003. These pictures are all rendered using Open GL using transparency and texture maps. Back in 2003 this was considered pretty cool.

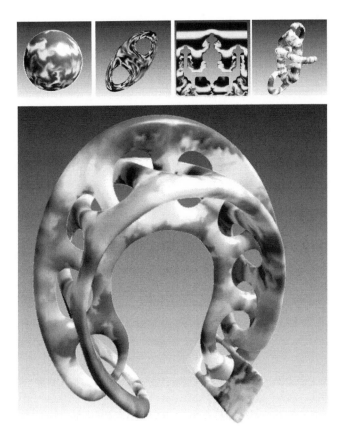

FIGURE 13.4 Images created using fluid simulations on arbitrary surfaces. They are all rendered using OpenGL.

To summarize: I combined some of my subdivision surface work and some of my fluids work. In this manner, I was able to simulate fluids on arbitrary surfaces. I left out many details, but I hope the reader gets the gist of the method. If you want to know more, check out my SIGGRAPH 2003 paper.

CHAPTER 14

Control Freaks! How to Make Fluids Do What We Want

Only you can control your future.

DR. SEUSS (AMERICAN GENIUS WRITER AND
ILLUSTRATOR, 1904–1991)

Go To Statement Considered Harmful.

TITLE OF A FAMOUS ARTICLE BY EDSGAR
DIJKSTRA (LEGENDARY DUTCH-AMERICAN
COMPUTER SCIENTIST)

Usually, we stir up fluids with a swine's hair and see what happens. That is not acceptable for animators who want to create a particular special effect involving a fluid animation. Let's say you want your fluid over time to move some density into a particular shape. In the interim, you want the fluid to look natural and nice and smooth while possibly following the laws of physics.

Let's control fluids!

Professor Zoran Popovic from the University of Washington in Seattle proposed a solution to this problem. I was hanging out at "You Dub" at the time in rainy Seattle when I was not in the Pioneer Square loft. At first I was very skeptical that this approach would work at all. Two graduate students we worked with were known as A&A: Adrien Treuille and Antoine McNamara. They implemented a solution first and made it work. They deserve all the kudos for this work.

They proved me wrong. Anytime please. I like to be proven wrong. That is progress to me. Being proven wrong means you have to work harder to be confident in your solution next time. Being wrong some of the time is the name of the game in research. Learn from it. I hope I do.

I did write my own version in that loft in Seattle once I knew it was possible. And I did not use FORTRAN like A&A. I used *f2c* a tool that translates FORTRAN code to C code. The translator called f2c creates one of the craziest and ugliest C codes on the planet. But hey it will talk to your C code without you having to buy and install a FORTRAN compiler. FORTRAN compilers are free if you live in the Linux hood of town. To use f2c, you have to include a header file called f2c.h, which starts with the following two comments:

```
/* f2c.h  --  Standard Fortran to C header file */

/** barf  [ba:rf]  2.  "He suggested using FORTRAN,
    and everybody barfed."

       - From The Shogakukan DICTIONARY OF NEW ENGLISH
         (Second edition) */
```

That is geek humor folks. Here is a snippet of code of what f2c translates some code from FORTRAN to C:

```
/* Subroutine */ int poistg_(nperod, n, mperod, m, a,
  b, c__, idimy, y, ierror, w)
integer *nperod, *n, *mperod, *m;
real *a, *b, *c__;
integer *idimy;
real *y;
integer *ierror;
real *w;
{
    /* System generated locals */
    integer y_dim1, y_offset, i__1, i__2;
```

```
/* Local variables */
static integer iwba, iwbb, iwbc, modd, mhmi, mhpi,
irev, i__, j, k;
static real a1;
static integer mskip;
extern /* Subroutine */ int postg2_();
static integer mh, mp, np, iwtcos, ipstor, iwd,
   iwp, mhm1, iwb2, iwb3, nby2, iww1, iww2, iww3;

/* more ugly nonsense and then */

/* … */

/* Parameter adjustments */
   --a;
   --b;
   --c__;
   y_dim1 = *idimy;
   y_offset = 1 + y_dim1 * 1;
   y -= y_offset;
   --w;

/* … */

L107:
    switch ((int)*nperod) {
      case 1:  goto L108;
      case 2:  goto L108;
      case 3:  goto L108;
      case 4:  goto L119;
    }



/* etc etc etc and more automatically generated ugly
  crazy C code*/
```

What is up with the double underscores by the way?

In the C language, it is considered a big *no no* to use the *goto* statement. But sometimes you have to use it to get out of a rabbit hole. But it is considered heresy. In FORTRAN, gotos are all over the place. For those of you who are not familiar with gotos or jumps, they tell your Slave to take a hike and go somewhere else, sometimes far away. Kind of like a *chutes* and *ladders* game.

I have to tell this story. I sent some of this automatically translated code to a programmer in Toronto from my loft in Seattle. He thought I was crazy to write code like that. No human C coder writes code like that. Only computers automatically write code like that. I have since then written my own Fish Solver in clean C. See earlier text.

14.1 SHOOTING CANNONBALLS IN TWO DIMENSIONS

I hate small towns because once you've seen the cannon in the park there's nothing else to do.

LENNY BRUCE (AMERICAN COMEDIAN, 1925–1966)

Here is the basic idea.

In the spirit of keeping things simple in this book, I will illustrate this idea with a simple example in two dimensions first.

Figure 14.1 shows the situation. The goal is to shoot a 2D cannonball (blue) to hit the target shown in red on the right. The curve in red illustrates the actual trajectory that the red *cannonball* takes given the initial velocity: angle plus speed. In the first two snapshots on the left of Figure 14.1, the blue cannonball misses the red target. But, yes the blue guy hits the red guy in the third snapshot.

Question: How did we get there?

Answer: Through the yellow curve depicted at the top of the four frames in Figure 14.1. This curve is the distance squared between where the blue ball ends up and the red target. The solution is where the corresponding yellow dot is at a minimum of the yellow curve (actually zero in this case). One solution is shown in the third snapshot of Figure 14.1. But there is also another solution shown in the fourth snapshot of Figure 14.1. In this case, the trajectory of the red cannonball takes less time. This is probably

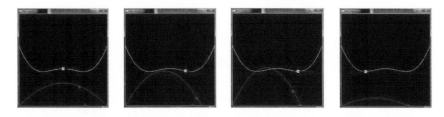

FIGURE 14.1 Optimizing the trajectory of a cannonball in two dimensions.

the preferred one: this is Occam's razor principle (mentioned earlier) all over again. From multiple solutions one usually chooses the simplest one.

There are two solutions because the distance function in yellow has two *valleys* of equal depth.

This is an important point.

We already discussed nonlinear problems earlier. For this particular nonlinear problem, the two valleys are equally valid solutions. If we add another term that is equal to the time that the blue cannonball takes, then the first valley is the right solution.

The gradient of the yellow curve is used to eventually find the solution. Remember the gradient is the direction of steepest ascent and its inverse is the direction of biggest descent. The gradient of the yellow slope is illustrated as a blue vector in Figure 14.1.

Let us analyze this situation. What we have here is

1. The *controls*: initial velocity of the blue cannonball. Two parameters: in this case angle and speed.

2. The *simulation* that creates a result from the controls.

3. The *goal* we want to achieve. In this case it is the distance squared between the red dot and the blue cannonball when it hits the floor.

4. The *optimizer*: a mechanism that updates the initial velocity (controls) given the goal function.

The key ingredient is Step (4). In our simple cannonball example, we were just interactively updating the controls by following the gradient of the goal function. Just like those reckless skiers going for the direction of steepest descent until they hit the bottom of the hill.

14.2 COMPUTER OPTIMIZERS

Premature optimization is the root of all evil.

DONALD ERWIN KNUTH
(AMERICAN COMPUTER SCIENCE LEGEND)

We can abstract the simple situation described earlier with the following nomenclature. Mathematicians like to do these kinds of things.

1. A set of controls

2. A simulator

3. A cost function (*energy function*)

4. An optimizer

This is a very general framework. You can add additional constraints to this list as required. The bottom line is that this list is an outline of a *nonlinear* optimization problem.

To find a solution, keep on refining the controls based on the result of the objective function and on using an optimizer. This is shown in Figure 14.2.

This figure illustrates what happens when you run a simulation of something that is dependent on some *controls*. The *simulated output* is entirely determined by the controls that drive the simulation. Once that output is generated by the simulation, it is compared to the *desired output* proposed by the animator. The mismatch between the output of the simulation and the desired state is then passed onto the optimizer. The optimizer takes these results and updates the controls accordingly.

The magic happens in the optimizer.

Then we go through this again and again until our fatigued *optimizer* tells us: "Enough, guys. We got a solution and I have to take a nap." Or alternatively: "Your input is garbage, get your gradients right."

The optimizer is the key to this process.

What Zoran and A&A proposed was to use an optimizer called BFGS: another geek name. It is an acronym for the four researchers who came up with the technique in the early 1970s. Their last names are **Broyden, Fletcher, Goldfarb** and **Shanno**: hence the name **BFGS**.

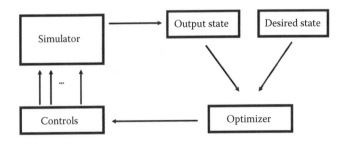

FIGURE 14.2   The basic framework of optimization.

Back then I had never heard of this optimization technique. That is why it is good idea to work with smart people. You learn from them while having fun. Geez and as a bonus, A&A also speak French.

Let us treat BFGS as a black box.* By *black box* I mean we are not going into the internals of the optimizer. This has nothing to do with orange boxes in airplanes. What it needs is the current controls, the value of the goal function and the *gradient* of the goal function and *voilà* you get a new set of controls.

The controls are explicit. The goal function is just computed by running the simulation and comparing the final state to the desired state: easy.

However, what about computing the gradient?

To explain this I will guide you through a simple example. It illustrates how you can compute the gradient of some code with respect to some controls *automatically*. For real.

Ready?

The simple code is shown in Figure 14.3.

It is a toy, not a serious example, of course. The goal is to minimize the goal function f. But what about the value of the gradient of f with respect to the controls u and v? To this end, we add a set of new variables. We actually differentiate each line of code. For each variable, we associate a cousin who is bigger. The cousin's size is relative to the number of controls: two in this case. Not that big really, but hold on.

Figure 14.4 shows the original code with their bigger cousins. Each operation is also applied to the cousins. They are different but related through calculus.

Shame on me, I promised not to mention calculus in this book. Readers who know calculus will figure out the recipe. Others please go along

```
float x, y, z;            /* variables */
float u, v;               /* controls */
float f;                  /* cost variable */

x = y + z + u*u;     /* statement #1 */
y = z*y + x*v;       /* statement #2 */

f = x*x + y*y + u*u + v*v; /* cost function */
```

FIGURE 14.3   Some simple code.

---

* Okay, if you know the lingo: it is a Quasi-Newton method, which maintains a sparse inverse of the Hessian updated using a user-provided gradient. It also involves a local line search in each step.

```
float x, y, z, dx[2], dy[2], dz[2]; /* variables */
float u, v, du[2], dv[2];           /* two controls */
float f, df[2];                     /* cost variable */

dx[0]=dx[1]=dy[0]=dy[1]=dz[0]=dz[1]=df[0]=df[1]=0;
du[0]=1; du[1]=0; dv[0]=0; dv[1]=1;

x = y + z + u*u;     /* statement #1 */
   dx[0] = dy[0] + dz[0] + 2*u*du[0];
   dx[1] = dy[1] + dz[1] + 2*u*du[1];

y = z*y + x*v;       /* statement #2 */
   dy[0] = z*dy[0] + y*dz[0] + v*dx[0] + x*dv[0];
   dy[1] = z*dy[1] + y*dz[1] + v*dx[1] + x*dv[1];

f = x*x + y*y + u*u + v*v; /* cost function */
   df[0] = 2*x*dx[0] + 2*y*dy[0] + 2*u*du[0] + 2*v*dv[0];
   df[1] = 2*x*dx[1] + 2*y*dy[1] + 2*u*du[1] + 2*v*dv[1];
```

FIGURE 14.4   The code from Figure 14.3 augmented with their big cousins.

the flow. Or skip the math and the code and move on. Maybe it is time for an Intermezzo, perhaps?

For those who are still with me, here is the method to this madness.

I am not going to dwell on this further but in C++ you can overload operators. That to me is one of the coolest features of C++. The computer language called *Java*, for example, does not have this feature that makes for uglier code but according to their *aficionados* makes it more explicit and more readable and less bug prone. I am not religious about these matters. Use whatever computer language that works for you. Some people dress like hipsters, squares, mods, punks, and so on. Who cares?

So, welcome to the world of *Automatic Differentiation*, also known in vernacular geek speak as *AD*.

By overloading the usual operators like "+," "−," "*," "/," "sin," "cos," and so on, with including your big cousins, you can just write, for example:

```
dfloat<666+1> x, y, z;
dfloat<666+1> f = x*x + y*z;
```

What is a **dfloat**? It is a float forced to hang out with his bigger fellow cousin at all times. The big cousins are told exactly what to do. In Figure 14.5, we provide a C++ class that implements automatic differentiation for *N* controls. This class can be used for pretty much any optimization problem that uses a gradient like BFGS. I have to mention that for some problems that are not smooth it might fail miserably. There might not even be a gradient defined at some places. But BFGS works surprisingly well even in these particular nonsmooth cases.

```
#include <math.h>

template <int N> class dfloat
{
public:
        float v[N+1]; // change this to your favorite "pretend real."
// and all references to floats. Use a typedef or a define or whatever.

        dfloat () { for ( int i=0 ; i<=N ; i++ ) v[i] = 0.0f; }
        dfloat ( float s ) { v[0] = s; for ( int i=1 ; i<=N ; i++ ) v[i] = 0.0f; }
          float val ( void ) { return ( v[0] ); }
        float val ( int i ) { return ( v[i] ); }
        void val ( float s ) { v[0] = s; }
        void val ( int i, float s ) { v[i] = s; }

        dfloat & operator = ( dfloat & a ) {
                      for ( int i=0 ; i<=N ; i++ ) v[i] = a.v[i];
                      return ( *this ); }

        dfloat & operator = ( float s ) {
              v[0] = s;
              for ( int i=1 ; i<=N ; i++ ) v[i] = 0.0f;
              return ( *this ); }

        dfloat & operator += ( dfloat & a ) {
              for ( int i=0 ; i<=N ; i++ ) v[i] += a.v[i];
              return ( *this ); }

        dfloat & operator -= ( dfloat & a ) {
              for ( int i=0 ; i<=N ; i++ ) v[i] -= a.v[i];
              return ( *this ); }

        dfloat & operator *= ( dfloat & a ) {
              for ( int i=1 ; i<=N ; i++ ) v[i] = v[i]*a.v[0] + v[0]*a.v[i];
              v[0] *= a.v[0];
              return ( *this ); }

        dfloat & operator /= ( dfloat & a ) {
              float g = a.v[0]*a.v[0];
              for ( int i=1 ; i<=N ; i++ ) v[i] = (v[i]*a.v[0]-v[0]*a.v[i])/g;
              v[0] /= a.v[0];
              return ( *this ); }

        dfloat & operator += ( float s ) {
              v[0] += s;
              return ( *this ); }

        dfloat & operator -= ( float s ) {
              v[0] -= s;
              return ( *this ); }

        dfloat & operator *= ( float s ) {
              for ( int i=0 ; i<=N ; i++ ) v[i] *= s;
              return ( *this ); }

        dfloat & operator /= ( float s ) {
              for ( int i=0 ; i<=N ; i++ ) v[i] /= s;
              return ( *this ); }

        dfloat operator - ( void ) {
              dfloat c;
              for ( int i=0 ; i<=N ; i++ ) c.v[i] = -v[i];
              return ( c ); }

        dfloat operator + ( dfloat & a, dfloat & b ) {
              dfloat c;
              for ( int i=0 ; i<=N ; i++ ) c.v[i] = a.v[i] + b.v[i];
              return ( c ); }

        dfloat operator - ( dfloat & a, dfloat & b ) {
              dfloat c;
```

FIGURE 14.5   Automatic differentiation implementation in C++. Operator overloading rules! Templates in this case too.   (*Continued*)

```
            for ( int i=0 ; i<=N ; i++ ) c.v[i] = a.v[i] - b.v[i];
            return ( c ); }

dfloat operator * ( dfloat & a, dfloat & b ) {
            dfloat c;
            c.v[0] = a.v[0] * b.v[0];
            for ( int i=1 ; i<=N ; i++ ) c.v[i] = a.v[i]*b.v[0] + a.v[0]*b.v[i];
            return ( c ); }

dfloat operator / ( dfloat & a, dfloat & b ) {
            dfloat c;
            c.v[0] = a.v[0] / b.v[0];
            float g = b.v[0]*b.v[0];
            for ( int i=1 ; i<=N ; i++ ) c.v[i] = (a.v[i]*b.v[0] - a.v[0]*b.v[i])/g;
            return ( c ); }

dfloat operator + ( float s, dfloat & a ) {
            dfloat c;
            c.v[0] = s + a.v[0];
            for ( int i=1 ; i<=N ; i++ ) c.v[i] = a.v[i];
            return ( c ); }

dfloat operator + ( dfloat & a, float s ) {
            dfloat c;
            c.v[0] = a.v[0] + s;
            for ( int i=1 ; i<=N ; i++ ) c.v[i] = a.v[i];
            return ( c ); }

dfloat operator - ( float s, dfloat & a ) {
            dfloat c;
            c.v[0] = s - a.v[0];
            for ( int i=1 ; i<=N ; i++ ) c.v[i] = -a.v[i];
            return ( c ); }

dfloat operator - ( dfloat & a, float s ) {
            dfloat c;
            c.v[0] = a.v[0] - s;
            for ( int i=1 ; i<=N ; i++ ) c.v[i] = a.v[i];
            return ( c ); }

dfloat operator * ( float s, dfloat & a ) {
            dfloat c;
            for ( int i=0 ; i<=N ; i++ ) c.v[i] = s*a.v[i];
            return ( c ); }

dfloat operator * ( dfloat & a, float s ) {
            dfloat c;
            for ( int i=0 ; i<=N ; i++ ) c.v[i] = a.v[i]*s;
            return ( c ); }

dfloat operator / ( float s, dfloat & a ) {
            dfloat c;
            c.v[0] = s/a.v[0];
            float g = a.v[0]*a.v[0];
            for ( int i=1 ; i<=N ; i++ ) c.v[i] = -s*a.v[i]/g;
            return ( c ); }

dfloat operator / ( dfloat & a, float s ) {
            dfloat c;
            for ( int i=0 ; i<=N ; i++ ) c.v[i] = a.v[i]/s;
            return ( c ); }

dfloat dsqrt ( dfloat & a ) {
            dfloat c;
            c.v[0] = sqrtf(a.v[0]);
            for ( int i=1 ; i<=N ; i++ ) c.v[i] = 0.5f * a.v[i] / c.v[0];
            return ( c ); }

dfloat dacos ( dfloat & a ) {
            dfloat c;
            c.v[0] = (float) acos(a.v[0]);
```

FIGURE 14.5 (*Continued*) Automatic differentiation implementation in C++. Operator overloading rules! Templates in this case too. (*Continued*)

```
float g = -1.0f/sqrtf(1-a.v[0]*a.v[0]);
for ( int i=1 ; i<=N ; i++ ) c.v[i] = a.v[i] * g;
return ( c ); }
};
```

FIGURE 14.5 (*Continued*) Automatic differentiation implementation in C++. Operator overloading rules! Templates in this case too.

You can use this code to optimize or *tame* any existing code you have. The AD of *pretend real numbers* do not have to be **dfloats** by the way: they could be **ddouble** or **ddoubledouble**, and so on. It is pretty easy to change the code provided in Figure 14.5 to accommodate other worms. Just change the one line at the top as mentioned in the red comment and replace floats by whatever worm you are using.

For example, the code shown in Figure 14.4 can be written more succinctly using the code from Figure 14.5. Let us call that file "ad.h" so we can cleanly include it in the code below. Make sure it lives in your project directory. Or change your IDE to include the directory where it lives. The latter is probably better as you can use the code for different projects that need it.

With this header file, our useless code becomes "AD&C++-sanitized" as shown in Figure 14.6.

The code is much simpler. Even better you can take any of your favorite code and simply replace your **floats** with **dfloats**. Make sure to include the "ad.h" file and use C++ not C. Your C code will not compile with "ad.h." There is no need to include fancy libraries either. All the automatic differential meat is in the header file.

For fun I applied this methodology to some *vanilla* rigid body code that was gathering dust in my drawer in that Seattle loft. The experiment

```
#include "ad.h"

dfloat<2> x, y; // variables
dfloat<2> u, v; // controls
dfloat<2> f;    // cost variable

u.val(0) = 1.0f; v.val(1) = 1.0f;

x = y + z + u*u;       // statement #1
y = z*y + x*v;         // statement #2
f = x*x + y*y + u*u + v*v; // cost function
```

FIGURE 14.6 The code of Figure 14.4 rewritten using the Automatic differentiating code.

FIGURE 14.7   Three snapshots of a control of a rigid body trying to hit the target when it turns yellow.

the code implements is the simple cannonball simulation illustrated in Figure 14.1 earlier, but it runs in 3D space. However, in this case, there are three controls modeling the initial impulse exerted on the rigid body at the start of the simulation. Just like in the 2D cannonball example, the rigid body has to hit a target when it turns yellow at a specified time. This is illustrated in Figure 14.7.

The demo is cool. The three frames shown in Figure 14.7 do not capture the optimization process. The figure only shows one simulation attempt at hitting the target when it turns yellow. In this case it failed. But lo and behold, the almighty BFGS optimizer will modify the controls and try to improve the next attempt at reaching the bullets' eye when it turns yellow.

For fluids we control the motion using an array of forces that guide an initial blob of density into a particular shape. The controls in this case are an array of 5×5 forces that are applied at different times. So if there are N frames, then the number of controls is $N \times 25$. The basic setup is depicted in Figure 14.8.

Let me explain this figure again.

The figure shows all the controls that are the force vectors for each frame arranged in an area. The fluid simulator uses these force vectors to move densities around. At frame N, the end frame, the resulting state of the density is compared to the desired state. The difference (squared) between the simulated density and the desired state is then computed and fed to the optimizer beast along with the current state of the $N \times 25$ force controls. The optimizer then updates the force controls. This is similar to the earlier simpler examples. Depending on the value of frames N and the number of forces, you can see that we get many controls.

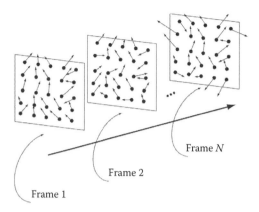

FIGURE 14.8 The force controls for a fluid simulation. In this case an array of 5 × 5 force grids separated over *N* intervals.

Figure 14.9 shows a sequence of simulations of a piece of density initially localized at the bottom: just a rectangular blob. The objective of this blob is to morph in the letter "C" using the array of control forces distributed over time. Notice how the forces shown as yellow arrows change over time. The red arrows show the drop off vector field created by the force fields. The red vectors are the ones that actually affect the evolution of the density. Of course, we also enforce incompressibility. That is what makes the fluids look cool and swirly.

Figure 14.10 shows an animation where an initial blob of density morphs into our old MAYA software logo using this technique. The cool aspect is that we go from a coherent blob of density to another coherent state. It is of course easy to go from a coherent state to a chaotic state. Just drop some milk in your morning coffee. It will swirl around and diffuse and mix your brew into a light brown state. But I bet it won't eventually turn into our MAYA logo in your coffee cup. That would be cool though but you would have to be lucky I guess. Like winning the lotto:

FIGURE 14.9 An initial blob of density is morphed in a fluidlike manner into a "C" character. The yellow force arrows drive the density to its target over time.

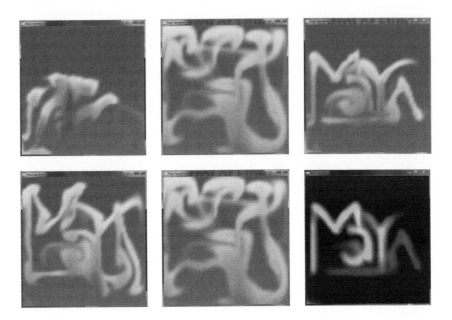

FIGURE 14.10 Five frames from an animation of a blob of density turning into our now defunct MAYA logo. The sixth one is more psychedelic just for fun.

very improbable. By the way, this is also related to the Second Law of Thermodynamics: entropy increases over time. If it wasn't for the sun, the entire world would just be covered with a homogeneous glob of stuff: probably ice.

Sometimes the optimizer beast goes crazy on a subsequent attempt but then miraculously recovers eventually. It is very entertaining to watch how the BFGS optimizer finds a solution to this problem.

What happens when there are a lot of controls? What if you have 1,002,345,402,401 controls? In this case you get differentials like:

```
dfloat<1002345402401+1>one_skinny_
        dude_with_a_huge_cousin;
```

Each differential cousin of a variable dude is getting bigger and bigger. That is lots of extra weight to carry around. "Cousin Dude you are taking up too much space and slowing me down."

What to do?

What if we replace the big *differential* cousin dude with their skinnier *adjoint* cousin dude?

Adjoint cousins are faster and light weight and they are weird. Cool!

To summarize: Most optimizers are hungry for differentials. One way to feed them big cousins from good old code is to use automatic differentiation. Take any good old code and use C++ and the header file provided earlier to feed the beast. In exchange, the beast will tell you how to update your controls to achieve whatever goal you want to achieve: Etta my boy.

14.3 THE AD, THE JOINT, AND THE PATH BACK TO THE OPTIMIZER

> And, uh, lotta strands to keep in my head, man. Lotta strands in old Duder's head. Luckily I'm adhering to a pretty strict, uh, drug regimen to keep my mind, you know, limber.
>
> THE *DUDE* IN THE BIG LEBOWSKI MOVIE PLAYED BY
> AMERICAN ACTOR JEFF BRIDGES

The title of this section sounds like a stoner trip but it is not.

The *adjoint method* is a somewhat obscure technique. At least it was obscure to me back in 2003. Its explanation is usually obfuscated with fancy mathematics. I will try to explain the adjoint method through the process of *generalization*. Sometimes it is easier to explain something in a general abstract framework. That is simple mathematics without complicated mathematics.

You get rid of all the messy details like triple integrals, partial derivatives, and other complicated mathematical exotica. I love mathematical exotica by the way. But it gets in the way.

Through generalization you get to the core of the problem and strip it bare. The benefit is that you understand the core technique, and this technique can potentially be applied to a variety of other problems as well. I hope to share with you the power of this methodology in the explanation that follows.

This is an outline of my explanation.

> Start with concrete code and show that it can be turned into linear algebra. Then explain the adjoint method in one figure using simple algebra. After that I will go to my basement and get the contents of my safe upstairs without having to move the safe upstairs.

If you want to follow the entire argument and are not too familiar with vectors and matrices, please consult the material in the first Intermezzo

```
y = z*y + x*v;
    dy[0]  =  z*dy[0] + y*dz[0] + v*dx[0] + x*dv[0];
    dy[1]  =  z*dy[1] + y*dz[1] + v*dx[1] + x*dv[1];
```

FIGURE 14.11   Concrete code and their differential cousins in red.

provided earlier. If that is too much work, just skip all the algebra and think of an analogy about a safe full of cash in my basement and an angry landlord knocking on my door. I will explain what I mean in a minute.

Figure 14.11 shows some concrete C code that we have encountered before. The original code and their cousins below can be cast into a matrix vector equation. This works for any code by the way.

The code shown in Figure 14.12 earlier can be turned into matrix algebra for the red-faced cousins. Here is how.

The cousins stored in a vector are continually being multiplied by matrices that are derived from each line of the code. So really we have the following sequence for the code in Figure 14.6, in math speak:

$$X_3 = A_3 A_2 A_1 X_0$$

This sequence starts with the initial 6×2 "vector" X_0 equal to

$$X_0 = \begin{pmatrix} 0 & 0 \\ 0 & 0 \\ 0 & 0 \\ 1 & 0 \\ 0 & 1 \\ 0 & 0 \end{pmatrix}.$$

In the final step, we care only about the two last elements of the vector, namely **df[0]** and **df[1]**. This seems like a phenomenal waste of space

$$\begin{pmatrix} dx[0] & dx[1] \\ dy[0] & dy[1] \\ dz[0] & dz[1] \\ du[0] & du[1] \\ dv[0] & dv[1] \\ df[0] & df[1] \end{pmatrix} = \begin{pmatrix} 1 & 0 & 0 & 0 & 0 & 0 \\ v & z & y & 0 & x & 0 \\ 0 & 0 & 1 & 0 & 0 & 0 \\ 0 & 0 & 0 & 1 & 0 & 0 \\ 0 & 0 & 0 & 0 & 1 & 0 \\ 0 & 0 & 0 & 0 & 0 & 1 \end{pmatrix} \times \begin{pmatrix} dx[0] & dx[1] \\ dy[0] & dy[1] \\ dz[0] & dz[1] \\ du[0] & du[1] \\ dv[0] & dv[1] \\ df[0] & df[1] \end{pmatrix}$$

$$X_2 = A_2 X_1$$

FIGURE 14.12   The differential of one line of code is turned into a matrix equation.

and effort. All the matrices are large and sparse in general and in the end we care only about the value of the last two cousins at the bottom. Another thing to notice is that these two cousins have been carried all along in their comfy limousines only to be put to work all the way at the end. This does not seem fair. None of the previous matrices woke them up and slapped them in the face. Their other cousins did all the hard work.

We can concatenate all the matrices into the following single equation:

$$X_{final} = A X_{start}.$$

This is the beauty of abstraction and generalization. We just condensed the differential of any code in a simple equation with three symbols. This not only works for our silly example. It is a generalization, remember.

The differential we have to feed to the optimizer beast can be obtained by stuffing the bottom cousins in a vector through a projection. Mathematically

$$df_{big\ cousins} = p^T X_{final} \quad \text{where } p = \begin{pmatrix} 0 \\ \vdots \\ 0 \\ 1 \end{pmatrix}.$$

This equation just says: "use a projection to grab the value of the cousins at the bottom. Those are the only dudes the beast wants to eat."

This is how the adjoint method works.

We run the simulation forward in time to get the value of the objective function. This is typically the difference between the final result and the desired state squared. From that we compute the projection vector. And then we go backward in time and update skinny cousins using the adjoint of the matrices that correspond to the adjoint of the differentials of the code. Mathematically

$$p_{initial} = A^T p_{final} \quad \text{and} \quad df_{skinny\ cousins} = p_{initial}^T X_{initial}.$$

The crucial question is why are $df_{big\ cousins} = df_{skinny\ cousins}$ using a different technique?

The proof of this fact is so simple that I will provide it here in a one-liner proof:

$$df_{big\ cousins} = p_{final}{}^T X_{final} = p_{final}{}^T A X_{initial} = (A^T p_{final})^T X_{initial}$$
$$= p_{initial}{}^T X_{initial} = df_{skinny\ cousins}$$

That is it!

This was another epiphany.

This proof was so cool to me. The simple proof shows that the adjoint method can be explained in such a simple manner with just standard linear algebra.

Figure 14.13 is a visual depiction of the sizes involved in the forward differential (top) versus the adjoint method (bottom). This figure shows that the skinny cousins do the same job as their bigger twins. That is the magic of the adjoint method in a nutshell.

It is hard to explain the adjoint method honestly without mathematics.

But let me try with an analogy.

Mathematics is basically making stories more precise and making them sometimes more amenable to computer implementations. But they are still stories in the end.

Analogies are very helpful and make it more fun to memorize math.

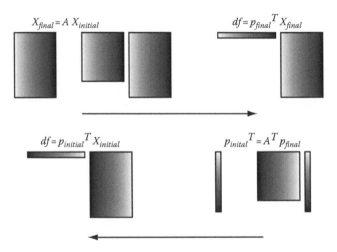

FIGURE 14.13 Pictorial comparison of big cousins being moved around versus skinny cousins.

Let's say you have a big heavy safe in your basement that contains some important stuff like loads of cash. You want to retrieve some of that cash from the safe because your landlord is knocking on your door.

Your first option is the differential method. You carry your safe upstairs and then use your key to open the safe and collect the cash. You probably also have to move the safe downstairs after that. The idle big cousins can come in handy at this point. By the way the differential technique does not require you to do that. But who wants a safe in their living room? I don't. They are usually ugly looking and are an easy target for hoodlums breaking into your house.

Your second option is the adjoint method. You take your key downstairs in your basement, open the safe, and grab the amount of cash that you owe to the landlord. Then lock the safe, if you still have any money left. The adjoint method requires you to take the key upstairs by the way. But hey a key fits in your pocket: no sweat. A safe doesn't fit in your pocket on the other hand. Not in my world at least. Besides, you do not want the key near the safe in the case those hoodlums break into your house and wander into your basement.

Figure 14.14 illustrates two strategies of unlocking a safe in the basement to pay the rent to the landlord who is knocking on your door. This is an example of how mathematics can be explained without mathematics at all. Alright, I know the figures are decorated with math symbols. But the basic argument can be explained without mathematics. At least I tried my best.

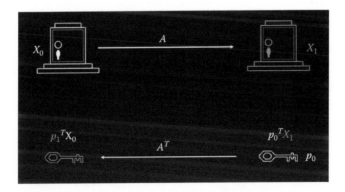

FIGURE 14.14 Figure 14.13 explained with a safe in the basement and greedy landlords.

I hope you got the gist of the adjoint technique through this analogy. You can find more information on the web of course. I also wrote a more extensive version with adjoint code in a paper I wrote for a SIGGRAPH 2004 course. It also includes an adjoint version of my simple fluid code.*

To summarize: The adjoint technique is a more efficient method to feed the optimizer beast with a gradient. However, it is less straightforward than automatic differentiation. The adjoint method is more complicated to understand and implement. Nothing comes for free after all. I have also left out the details of the adjoint method. You can find these details on the web, in my course notes or in our SIGGRAPH 2004 paper.

To summarize: A&A proved me wrong but I did not use FORTRAN. I wrote my own stuff in my loft in downtown Seattle in Pioneer Square using the IDE† called Visual Studio 6 from Microsoft. I also used automatic differentiation.

---

* You can find the paper at http://www.autodeskresearch.com/publications/adjointcontrol.

† **IDE** stands for **I**ntegrated **D**evelopment **E**nvironment. It helps you to write code more efficiently. Look it up. Hipster coders on the other hand like to use the **vi** editor and run **Makefiles** on LINUX. Well they also listen to LPs. I like to think that I was a hipster in the 1980s.

CHAPTER 15

Real Experiments, Computer Experiments, and Validation

Real knowledge is to know the extent of one's ignorance.

CONFUCIUS (CHINESE PHILOSOPHER, -551, -479)

I promise this section will be brief.

When I first started to talk about my fluid work, I would always get questions like "how accurate are your simulations?" "What is the Reynolds number?" And other stuff that experts seemed to pull out of their back packs. Then I bought Van Dyke's book. Remember from earlier that I mentioned his wonderful book called an *Album of Fluid Motion*. It has black and white pictures of famous fluid experiments. I decided to reproduce them with my fluid solver. But animated and interactive! A user could always alter the simulation because it was running in real time for reasonable grid sizes.

My simulations did not *exactly* reproduce the experiments but they did so *qualitatively*.

What does *qualitatively* mean?

This means that you get the same overall behavior, which does not necessarily match the values from an experiment. No existing fluid solver can reproduce the *exact* flow behind a large complicated structure anyway.

This is because the computer representation of the fluid is too coarse to capture all the details of the fluid. Therefore, there is a need to model the smaller scales not captured by the discrete computer representation. Remember turbulence models?

How do you validate computer code in the *serious world*? Well, you usually show that it works on simple examples and then reproduce some emergent properties. As an example, the *drag* behind a sphere.

15.1 SPHERES ARE SUCH A DRAG

> Avoid the world, it's just a lot of dust and drag and means nothing in the end.

JACK KEROUAC (AMERICAN BEAT POET, 1922–1969)

What is drag?

Well it is something that drags you down, slows you down, stops you from moving faster, and so on. That is how the word *drag* is commonly used in English. Drag queens and drag car racing stretch the meaning in interesting ways. *Drag* is a multifaceted word in the English language. But for our purposes, we'll go with the first meaning mentioned.

For a sphere, drag is a single number that varies with the Reynolds Number. Remember the Swiss dude being thrown into a gigantic pool? The drag value for spheres has been experimentally measured in a lab. That is of course tested limited by the precision of the measuring devices involved. What you get is the curve shown in Figure 15.1. The curve should be thicker, to convey the amount of uncertainty. No measurement is absolutely precise. Curves in real life have width, unlike their skinny mathematical cousins who are of measure zero. You can never be too thin. In the mathematical world you can. Math won't make you too rich on the other hand, unless you win the Clay Prize.

The curve shown in Figure 15.1 is very interesting. The first part is what you expect. Let's keep the size of the experiment fixed: say the size of an Olympic-sized pool filled with a fluid.* It is pretty obvious that swimming in a pool full of honey is more challenging than swimming in a pool filled with water. The Reynolds number of honey is lower than that of water. Therefore, according to the experimental results, drag is higher for honey than for water. This I think is pretty obvious to anyone who did some

---

* I want to jump in my bathtub again. But no one except the superrich can swim in their bathtubs and fill it up with honey. At least not that I know of.

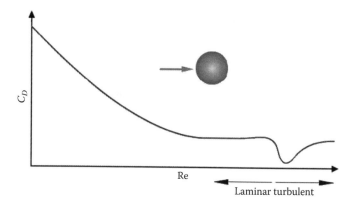

FIGURE 15.1   Plot of drag as a function of the Reynolds number.

swimming both in honey and water. I know of no one who has done both. I should get out more. (I have heard that there is a *MythBusters* episode about swimming in syrup, though). But no worries experiments confirm this observation.

The second part of the curve shown in Figure 15.1 is not really what most people expect. Most people are used to a linear world. One thing increases causing another thing to decrease and vice versa. Drag is not like that. There is a point when you decrease viscosity that the drag starts to increase again. Why? That is because of turbulence, we are told. Turbulence, that elusive phenomenon that no one really understands, creates drag.

If the goal is to reduce drag, for example in the car industry, you have to build a shape that hits the sweet spot, the valley, as in Figure 15.1. Less drag means a more fuel-efficient car.

Drag allows you to validate your simulation if it can reproduce the curve shown in Figure 15.1. You run your simulation with a pretend sphere and fix the Reynolds number. By the way, real-life spheres are also pretend spheres. Then through a magic formula that I will not mention, you compute the drag value. By varying the Reynolds number you get different drag values. And there you go: you get a curve. And if it matches the experimental curve closely enough, you can light up a cigar and claim that your solver is accurate.

That is how folks validate their solvers.

Of course this is just one example. There are other examples and many other criteria to validate a fluid simulation. It is a bit of a public relation coup to get customers to trust a piece of software. But it is also a sanity check for any piece of serious CFD code.

This is the *quantitative* approach: reproduce experimental results by comparing them to numerical values resulting from the simulation.

I am interested in the *qualitative* approach: try to create animations and compare them to pictures from experiments. That is why I love Van Dyke's book mentioned earlier. It is all pictures: no boring curves.

Remember that the book you are reading is all about whatever it takes to create animations of fluids. But to me less is more: try to find simple models that can create and control complex fluid motion. That is the gist of my research.

To summarize: Spheres actually are not a drag. They are just spheres after all. The drag they create when being blown on can be useful to validate fluid code. Even though drag is a simple measure, it reveals an interesting link to turbulence theory.

15.2 CURLY FLOWS BEHIND SPHERES, WAVY FLOWS IN TUBES, AND TURBULENT PLUMES BETWEEN PLATES

> You may have heard the world is made up of atoms and molecules, but it's really made up of stories. When you sit with an individual that's been here, you can give quantitative data a qualitative overlay.
>
> WILLIAM TURNER (ENGLISH SCIENTIST 1508–1568)

Figure 15.2 shows three experiments documented in Van Dyke's book. These are 3D experiments. I used my simple solver in two dimensions to

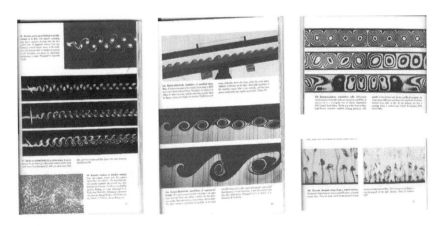

FIGURE 15.2   Three famous experiments from Van Dyke's book.

recreate the visuals of these experiments. I will go over all three of them. I just cherry-picked these three because they are cool.

First, I want to make an important point.

All the qualitatively visual phenomena are emergent. They are a result of the basic laws of fluid dynamics and the boundary conditions. You set it up and then you get these results that qualitatively match the experimental results. That's it.

There is no cheating at the equation level. There are no secret spices and sauces. The reason I created these simulations was to prove that I was indeed using the Navier–Stokes equations. Not just some hacked together computer graphics–specific model.

Let's go over the experiments.

15.2.1 Experiment Number One: Curly Flows behind Spheres

The visuals of this experiment are shown on the left-hand side of Figure 15.2.

This is the setup. A sphere, well a circle actually, is placed near the left-hand side boundary. Its size shouldn't be too large. The boundary conditions are as follows:

Left edge: an inflow

Right edge: an outflow

Top and bottom edges: a slip condition

Think of a pipe with slippery boundaries with air being blown from the left side being allowed to escape from the right side. At the front, there is a tiny marble. And that's it. That is the setup.

Since the pipe size and the viscosity are fixed, one can change the Reynolds number through the inflow velocity. The higher the velocity the higher the Reynolds number, and the lower the velocity the lower the Reynold's number.

Figure 15.3 shows a snapshot of the simulation using my simulation code.

The animation is much cooler of course. These patterns oscillate just like in the experiment. Because the solver is fast, a user can interact with it and *mess it up*.

15.2.2 Experiment Number Two: Wavy Flows in Tubes

The visuals of this experiment are shown in the middle of Figure 15.2.

FIGURE 15.3   A frame generated with my code simulating the Von Karmann experiment.

In this case, a tube is initially filled with a fluid injected with a dye in the bottom half. Then the tube is slowly tilted and wave-like patterns appear at the boundary of the density. Sometimes you can observe this phenomenon up in the sky when two layers of different densities collide. Figure 15.4 shows an example. Next time you are on a flight try to look for them. It is a truly cool emergent phenomenon: waves in the sky.

This is the setup. Fill the bottom half with a density field. The density of the fluid is still constant. The bottom density is some substance put into the fluid. Apply a slowly varying rotating gravity force field to the velocity. The boundary conditions are as follows:

Left and right edge: periodic

Top and bottom: slip

That is it. The curly waves emerge automatically. Figure 15.5 shows a snapshot of a frame from a simulation with this setup.

The results are not as crisp as the experimental result, but they are pretty close to the real-world clouds. At any rate they exhibit the qualitative behavior that is to be expected. Actually, our simulations show waves within waves. Cool!

FIGURE 15.4   Kelvin–Helmholtz in the sky. For real. (Copyright: Michael deLeon Photography.)

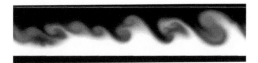

FIGURE 15.5 A frame generated with my code simulating the Kelvin–Helmholtz experiment.

15.2.3 Experiment Number Three: Turbulent Plumes between Plates

The visuals of this experiment are shown on the right-hand side of Figure 15.2.

This is another example of a *Hopf Bifurcation* discussed earlier for the lid-driven cavity problem. As a parameter is increased, the system goes through bifurcations resulting in more complex systems. In this case, the bifurcation parameter is the difference between the temperatures between two plates.

This is the setup. Fix the difference in temperature between the top and the bottom edge. This is our bifurcation dial. As we increase the dial the flow becomes more chaotic. This is clearly shown in Figure 15.2 (bottom right). If the difference in temperature is zero, nothing happens. Like a glass of water just sitting on your kitchen counter: Boring.

Figure 15.2 (top right). For certain ranges of the dial one gets what are called *Rayleigh–Benard* cells. That is probably the coolest regime. Regular cells form. They are even cooler looking in three dimensions as depicted in Figure 15.6. The image on the left is done in a controlled laboratory environment, while the one on the right is an image of clouds exhibiting this behavior. They are *Voronoi diagrams* computed by nature using

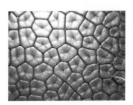 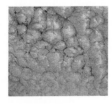

FIGURE 15.6 Two examples of real-world Rayleigh–Benard cells. (From Maroto, J.A., Perez-Munuzuri, V., and Romero-Cano, M.S., 2007, Introductory analysis of Bernard-Marangoni convection, *European Journal of Physics*, 28, 311–320, http://oiswww.eumetsat.org/WEBOPS/iotm/iotm/20010823_benard_cells/20010823_benard_cells.html. With permission.)

FIGURE 15.7   A frame generated with my code simulating the Rayleigh–Benard experiment.

fluids! How amazing is that. No space here to explain this connection. I just mention this connection to point out that some mathematical concepts do occur in nature. Look it up if you're interested.

When you increase the temperature difference dial you get into a cool fiery regime as depicted in Figure 15.2 (bottom right). No need for fancy turbulence or fancy computer graphics noise functions. This behavior emerges from the equations of fluids and the boundary conditions.

The boundary conditions are as follows:

Left and right edge: periodic

Top and bottom: slip

Figure 15.7 shows a snapshot of our simulation of this case when the temperature difference is cranked way up. You get into the interesting chaotic zone. Again it is a bit chalky compared to the pictures in Figure 15.2. But qualitatively they show the same behavior.

The point again is that this behavior completely emerged from just an initial state and the boundary conditions.

It is time for another analogy.

Grab a pencil or anything that has a sharp end. Try to make it stand still on its sharp end on a flat surface. Not easy. At least I cannot do it. Mathematically it is possible. In practice, however, it is hard to achieve. Why am I mentioning this? Because it happens that the zero velocity solution is a valid solution for any of the values of the temperature difference dial. When I launch my program, nothing happens until I apply a tiny disturbance. Then the show is in full swing.

The point I am making here is the following.

Depending on how you stir the fluid, you will get a different result. No matter how hard you try to place your pencil straight, you will get a different final state when it falls down and hits the plane. The qualitative conclusion is: *the pencil will fall down and come to a rest state on the plane but we cannot predict exactly where it will end up.*

To summarize: I pointed out the difference between *qualitative* results and *quantitative* results. In these experiments, it is hopeless to predict all the exact values of the fluid. Emergent values like drag, for example, can be simulated *quantitatively*. But these emergent values obfuscate all the visual details of the fluid. And visual details are what we want in animation. I have presented three of our simulations that *qualitatively* agree with the visuals of three experiments. *Qualitative* agreement is easier than *quantitative* agreement. That is why I chose the former. But still it is a challenge.

CHAPTER 16

Epilogue

Let's Call It Quits

You have your way. I have my way. As for the right way, the correct way, and the only way, it does not exist.

FRIEDRICH NIETZSCHE
(GERMAN PHILOSOPHER, 1844–1900)

I have a lot more material that I want to share with you, my dear reader who got this far, but I have to call it quits. My editor is knocking on my door and my safe is empty and I already paid off my landlord.

I sincerely hope that you enjoyed this book and that you learned some about the art of fluid animation. I tried to convey to the reader some of the basic magic and science behind fluid effects in movies, games, web apps, etc.

I also provided concrete code. I hope it compiles in your hood. No arguing. It either runs or it doesn't. Coders have a straightforward religion. You are not coding for a supernatural being but for a dumb speedy piece of hardware.

There is not going to be a grand *finale*!

No fireworks.

I always joke that we will always be employed in this business of ours. As soon as you create better data structures or improve the speed of your software, animators will increase the size of their simulations.* And then we are back in business. As far as I can tell, it is an endless process. This makes Fluid Animation distinct from parts of Mathematics, where when a result is proven it is proven once and for all.

More is more.

But I strive to create more from less.

Thanks for listening.

---

* There is an upper limit however. The number of atoms in the universe is estimated to be roughly 10^{80} atoms.

Index

Printed and bound by CPI Group (UK) Ltd, Croydon, CR0 4YY

22/10/2024

01777624-0010